"The author's conclusions that the 1990's are going to be a decade of American resurgence are refreshing after years of hearing Japan had the only key to the future."
—*Orange County Register*

"IMPORTANT . . . The authors compile an impressive array of corporate experiments as hints of what lies ahead for the future workplace."
—*Futurist*

"PROVOCATIVE . . . an intriguing assessment of organizational trends."
—*Kirkus Reviews*

"UNIQUE . . . provides a clear view of the workplace of the future."
—*Oklahoman*

JOSEPH H. BOYETT and HENRY P. CONN are consultants with the international management consulting firm of A. T. Kearney, Inc., whose clients include Sara Lee, Coca-Cola, AT&T, Ford, and General Electric. They live in Atlanta, Georgia.

WORKPLACE 2000

The Revolution Reshaping American Business

JOSEPH H. BOYETT
&
HENRY P. CONN

A PLUME BOOK

PLUME
Published by the Penguin Group
Penguin Books USA Inc., 375 Hudson Street, New York, New York 10014, U.S.A.
Penguin Books Ltd, 27 Wrights Lane, London W8 5TZ, England
Penguin Books Australia Ltd, Ringwood, Victoria, Australia
Penguin Books Canada Ltd, 10 Alcorn Avenue, Toronto, Ontario, Canada M4V 3B2
Penguin Books (N.Z.) Ltd, 182-190 Wairau Road, Auckland 10, New Zealand

Penguin Books Ltd, Registered Offices: Harmondsworth, Middlesex, England

Published by Plume, an imprint of New American Library, a division of
Penguin Books USA Inc. Previously published in a Dutton edition.

First Plume Printing, May, 1992
20 19 18 17 16 15 14 13 12 11

Ⓟ REGISTERED TRADEMARK—MARCA REGISTRADA

LIBRARY OF CONGRESS CATALOGING-IN-PUBLICATION DATA
Boyett, Joseph H.
    Workplace 2000 : the revolution reshaping American business /
Joseph H. Boyett & Henry P. Conn.
        p.   cm.
    Originally published: New York: Dutton, 1991.
    Includes bibliographical references and index.
    ISBN 0-452-26804-4
    1. Personal management—United States—Forecasting.   2. Corporate
culture—United States—Forecasting.   I. Conn. Henry P.   II. Title.
[HF5549.2.U5B69   1992]
658.3'00973'0112—dc20   91-45675
                                                     CIP

Printed in the United States of America
Original hardcover designed by Leonard Telesca

BOOKS ARE AVAILABLE AT QUANTITY DISCOUNTS WHEN USED TO PROMOTE PRODUCTS OR
SERVICES. FOR INFORMATION PLEASE WRITE TO PREMIUM MARKETING DIVISION, PENGUIN
BOOKS USA INC., 375 HUDSON STREET, NEW YORK, NEW YORK 10014.

Contents

Acknowledgments

In conducting the research for *Workplace 2000*, we relied upon the popular press, academic research, case studies of best practices in U.S. industry, and the advice and assistance of numerous individuals at various national productivity and quality associations. We are particularly indebted to Carl Thor, Jack Grayson, and the staff of the American Productivity and Quality Center; Bill Ginnodo, Leon Skan, and the staff of the Quality and Productivity Management Association; the staff and membership of the Association for Quality and Participation; and Bob Meyer and the staff of the Work in Northeast Ohio Council.

In addition to the above associations, we would like to express our gratitude to the following individuals whose advice, counsel, and willingness to share experiences was invaluable. In particular, we are grateful to Jim Edwards, President and CEO, Spencer Industries of Dale, Indiana. Jim is a true visionary who has done much to shape our thinking about the future of American business. In his own company, he has experimented with and demonstrated the validity of many of the new management and compensation practices we describe in this book. We would also like to thank Bill Werther, Samuel N. Friedland Professor of Executive Management, University of Miami; Richard Whisenant, Executive Vice President of Burke Mills of Valdese, North Carolina; and Paul Fulton, Chuck Chambers, Bruce Jenkins, Jerry Warren, Bill Flinchum, Jim Burch, and hundreds of other managers and executives at Sara Lee Corporation. All of these individuals taught us much about the revolution occurring in American business.

We would also like to thank our current and former colleagues at Tarkenton Conn & Company for giving us the benefit of their experiences. In particular, we are indebted to Jane Porter, Shirl Handly, Dot Mohr, Vicki Silvers, Edith Onderick-Harvey, Michele Williams, and Mark Dillard. These individuals spend countless hours each year implementing the changes we describe in this book and see the impact on American workers firsthand. They were a valuable source of real-life information on the effect of changes in the American workplace on the lives of American workers and managers. We also express our gratitude to Beth Dale, David Johnston, John Leffert, and particularly Bill Reeves—four management students at the University of Georgia who shared with us considerable research they had conducted on Wal-Mart which we used in preparing the final chapter of this book. Finally, we would like to thank Don Shilling, a former Tarkenton Conn & Company consultant now working with Weyerhaeuser Paper Company. Don's extensive notes and documentation on change efforts at TRW and Sara Lee Corporation were a valuable source of inside information on the application of *Workplace 2000* concepts in major U.S. companies.

For administrative support as we worked on this book, we would like to express our gratitude to Leigh Ann Conn and Theresa Bowker. Leigh Ann in particular deserves credit for making this book a reality. For the second time in as many years she has almost singlehandedly shouldered the burden of typing, copying, mailing, editing, and a thousand other details associated with preparing a manuscript for publication. We are also extremely grateful to Maria Carvainis, our literary agent, who first suggested that we write this book. Her interest in the subject matter of this book has been a continuing source of inspiration. Finally, we would like to thank our wives—

Jimmie and Becky—and children—Lisa, Christa, Phillip, and Leigh Ann—for their continued faith and support for our endeavors.

All of the above deserve credit for what is right about this book. Any errors or omissions are ours alone.

... the huge middle class of America was matriculating in a school for the blind. Their eyes had failed them, or they had failed their eyes, and so they were having their fingers pressed forcibly down on the fiery braille alphabet of a dissolving economy.

TENNESSEE WILLIAMS, *The Glass Menagerie*

The sort of life I had ... was one that required endurance ... a life of clawing and scratching along a sheer surface and holding tight with raw fingers to every inch of rock higher than the one caught hold of before, but it was a good life because it was the sort of life for which the human organism is created.

TENNESSEE WILLIAMS, "Essay on the Catastrophe of Success"

CHAPTER 1

The Future American Workplace

Picture a 130 employee Kansas plant where worker output has increased 80 percent in just six years. Absenteeism is a mere 2 percent. Employee turnover is one percent.

There are no time clocks. No supervisors. No job classifications. No definite work assignments.

If something has to be moved with a fork-lift truck, no one yells to the fork-lift truck driver—because there isn't such a driver. Instead, anyone at hand hops onto the truck and gets the job done.

There are no hourly workers. Everyone is salaried. In six years, the plant work force has grown by only 12 percent. Yet the workers produce as much as a plant with 33 percent more people.

Everyone is involved in major decisions affecting the plant.

The workers also participate in such matters as production scheduling, solving quality problems, evaluating performance and recommending new equipment. They undertake disciplinary actions. They even hire and train other workers.

In fact, the plant's entire operation, top to bottom, is in the hands of "worker teams." What there is of old-style management, in the form of a general manager and his staff, now exists merely in a support role. They are there to assist the workers who, quite literally, run the plant.

Productivity, September 1982

That description of a Kansas plant was written in 1982. It is a reality—a description of TRW's Oil Well Division at Lawrence, Kansas. It could be a description of the typical American workplace in the not too distant future.

The world of work is changing. Where Americans work, how they work, the relationship they have with their boss and peers, how they are paid—all of these things and much more will change in the organization of the future. These changes are drastic—even revolutionary—and they will affect every American. If Americans are to survive in the workplace of tomorrow, they need to know what to expect so that they can prepare themselves.

Workplace 2000

The company that employs the average American in the future will be flatter, leaner, and more aggressive than the company he or she works for today. It will have to be that way in order to have the flexibility to respond to rapidly changing customer demands. Downsizing has made this flatter workplace a reality in most companies even today, and this trend toward flattening the organization will continue. The layers of management, supervision, and support that were eliminated during the 1980s will not return. In fact, the search for ways to simplify and tighten the organization will continue, at least for the next decade.

In part, the downsizing that occurred in the 1980s was made possible by a new generation of technology that is less expensive, more flexible, and enables employees at the lowest level of an organization to make critical decisions. Continued rapid advancement in technology will make further belt-tightening possible. In short, Americans who process information, analyze information, and/or make routine decisions are likely to find their positions in danger within the next decade. The processing, analysis, and decision making they currently perform will be moved to lower levels who will be aided in the performance of these tasks by new, sophisticated, and more "intelligent" software.

With the flatter and leaner organization, there will be fewer opportunities for advancement for most Americans. As a result, even Americans who survive their company's downsizing and restructuring may be forced out or may opt out of corporate America to start their own business. The real job growth and opportunity for professional and financial advancement for the next decade will come from these new, smaller, entrepreneurial concerns. Additional avenues will open up for Americans who continue to work in major companies through the creation of "small business units" within these major concerns. Thus, instead of going out on their own, they may have an opportunity to start their own business within the larger company.

In the next decade, no job will be entirely secure, whether inside or outside of a large company. Because of their high failure rate, small entrepreneurial companies will continue to be volatile places to work. Large companies will offer, at most, "employment security"—a limited guarantee of long-term employment, but not necessarily in the same job or same workplace. It is very unlikely that most Americans will be able to join one company and stay with it throughout their working life. In fact, the average American will most likely work in ten or more different types of jobs and at least five different companies before he or she retires.

This instability in the workplace and enormous competitive demands on businesses—large and small—will result in extraordinary pressure for maximum performance. A "cult of performance excellence" will engulf most businesses. Americans will be expected to buy in, join up, become a part of the company values and culture, or be forced out. Such a workplace is in part frightening since strong demands will be placed upon employees for performance and for enmeshing themselves in the business as full partners in the "team" or members of the company "family." Yet in a positive sense, the new structure and culture will provide membership, purposefulness, belonging, and meaning. For many Americans, these were probably many of the things they missed in their current job and were seeking.

Success in the flatter, leaner *Workplace 2000* will depend upon several factors that are significantly different from those that contributed to success in traditional American organizations. Traditionally, Americans were more likely to be successful in a company if they started work with that company when they were young and stayed with the same organization throughout their career or for a significant portion of their career. Advancement was a function of longevity as much as performance. Endurance, loyalty, and the development of significant relationships with upper-level managers (mentoring) were the keys to promotional opportunity. Seniority rules and the organization's commitment to promotion from within reinforced long-term associations. Often, advancement to at least the initial levels of management and supervision was dependent upon a worker's superior performance in a technical speciality, since such individuals were the first to be tapped to fill vacancies in supervisory positions.

In *Workplace 2000*, flexibility and creativity will be more important for success than endurance and loyalty. Since the new organization will be flatter and leaner, there will be fewer opportunities for promotion to management or supervisory ranks. Within business units of large organizations and within small companies, the most valued employees will be those who are flexible and can perform a wide range of functions. Breadth of knowledge concerning business operations and customer needs is likely to be more highly valued than depth of knowledge in a narrowly defined specialty. Broad knowledge and experience in performing a wide variety of tasks will not only increase an employee's value to the new organization but will also increase his or her chance for identifying a market need and developing a spin-off business within or outside the organization. The real opportunities for professional and financial gains will lie in the ability to creatively identify these small business opportunities that can be exploited either within the organization (via a new "business unit") or outside (as an entrepreneurial business start-up).

In the new organization, the flow of information will change drastically. The sharing of information will be of critical importance to sustain performance, and new technology will make the sharing possible. Feedback on performance will become critical to the success of every business and will have both positive and negative effects (each deserved). "Scorekeeping" will be much easier and more immediate. American workers may receive almost instantaneous feedback on their performance, particularly if they perform their work using a computer or other automated device. Even if they still perform a relatively manual task, they will receive specific, objective, data-based feedback daily, weekly, bi-weekly, or monthly. Annual performance reviews will become either unnecessary or merely formal reviews of data already known to the employee and his or her supervisor. At last, every American worker will have a readily available, objective answer to the question "How am I doing?" High performers will thrive on this information. Their contribution will be recognized. Average performers will feel heightened pressure to perform at levels they have not previously attained. Low performers will find their peers and management alike demanding, at the least, their "best effort" as a minimum condition for retention of their jobs.

Since *Workplace 2000* will be characterized by a tremendous increase in the availability of information, success in the organization will flow to those who can effectively use the data presented to them to modify their own behavior or to identify new opportunities for the organization. Americans who want to succeed will need the ability to analyze data, draw conclusions, and present recommendations. Computer literacy and at least a rudimentary knowledge of statistics for business will be critical for advancement or even to survive!

In *Workplace 2000*, prerogatives of status—such as executive dining rooms and private parking spaces—will vanish, not to be replaced with equality so much as with recognition based upon performance. There will no longer be relatively automatic entitlement to "perks." The company car, the company plane, the special privileges will have to be justified. Praise, symbolism, and token rewards will be used to reinforce results and behavior of value to the company. American workers will be disciplined and punished for poor performance not only by their managers and supervisors but also by their peers.

Peer pressure will become a powerful force compelling each to exert his or her best effort or risk being banished from the group. In part, the growth of peer pressure will result from revolutionary changes in pay practices.

In most cases, rewards, recognition, and reinforcement provided in *Workplace 2000* will be for team rather than individual performance. Teamwork and cooperation will be the basis for creating value in the new organization. The most valued individuals will be those who can work effectively with other employees in a team effort. Team leadership roles will flow to those who have the skills to assist teams in surfacing ideas, being creative, and reaching consensus. Since peer pressure will be such a powerful force in the new organization, a premium will be placed upon building strong and positive peer relationships. In fact, in the new organization, leadership and acceptance within one's own peer group may be more important than building relationships with higher-level managers.

Methods of compensation will change drastically in the new organization. Most companies will slow or even stop the growth in base compensation—Americans will receive less frequent or perhaps no annual increases. Certainly, annual increases will no longer be automatic or something to which a worker is entitled by virtue of another year of seniority. Instead, most companies will offer incentive pay where a substantial portion of a worker's total compensation will be tied to his or her group's or company's performance and thus will vary from year to year. On the positive side, American workers will have the potential to make sizably more money than before. In some cases, their bonus potential may reach 150 percent of their base salary. Yet this bonus—which will constitute a significant portion of their total income—will always be at risk and subject to the company's or work group's performance. In addition to installing incentive pay as a substantial portion of total compensation, many companies will adopt a "pay-for-knowledge" system. In these companies, workers will have the opportunity to increase their base pay by learning and maintaining skills to perform multiple jobs within the organization. With pay-for-knowledge, these companies will encourage and reward flexibility in addition to performance. Highly motivated and highly skilled individuals will prosper in this environment.

Since in the new organization a substantial portion of total income will be variable—incentive—compensation, the average American worker's long-term financial security will depend upon having a well thought out personal financial plan. The value of one's retirement and fringe benefits will be tied much more closely to company performance than ever before. Base compensation may represent as little as 60 percent of a worker's total compensation. But it will be the only portion of the total compensation that is in any way secure. Bonus or incentive pay will fluctuate based upon company, division, or group performance. Because total compensation may vary significantly from year to year (or even month to month), the typical American will have to build and maintain larger savings (be more liquid) and keep long-term debt to a minimum.

Finally, *Workplace 2000* will move away from managerial control to employee self-control. Significant research in the 1970s and 1980s has already demonstrated the value of involving employees in running the business. Widespread employee involvement will be typical of *Workplace 2000*. With the change to employees becoming self-directed and self-controlling, traditional supervisors will no longer be required. They will be replaced by "enablers"—facilitators who help employee teams manage interpersonal relationships—and "technical support managers"—who help teams with implementing new technology and solving unusual technical problems. With these changes, tremendous responsibilities will be shifted to workers and their peers for planning, scheduling, organizing, directing, and controlling their own work process.

This new and expanded role for employees will exert enormous pressures on employees and companies alike to invest in education and retraining. Continuous learning will become commonplace to create a more flexible work force, provide employees with the skills necessary to take advantage of rapidly changing technology, and prepare employees for new jobs inside or outside the company when their old jobs are replaced by technology or eliminated due to changes in customer demands. To be successful, Americans will have to seek out training opportunities to supplement their existing skills and to learn new skills. It is likely that the training sponsored and funded by companies will be much greater than at present. But it will not be enough to ensure an employee's success. Many Americans will need to supplement the training their company provides with training they take on their own time at their own cost. Since continuous learning will be required to just maintain a position and will be even more critical for advancement, a solid basic education will be mandatory for any American to have a hope of succeeding. Obviously, basic literacy—reading, writing, arithmetic—will be essential. Much more than basic literacy will be required for success in the new organization, Americans will need to know how to solve problems, think creatively, and work effectively in a group.

Why *Workplace 2000* Is Emerging

Why are these changes occurring? Because they have to occur. The 1980s taught some bitter lessons to American business leaders. Faced with accelerated global competition, it became evident that, with a few exceptions such as Nucor Steel, Lincoln Electric, and Wal-Mart for example, America wasn't good enough. Among other things, our quality wasn't good enough, our service to customers was poor, and we were too slow in bringing new products and services to the marketplace. Worse, our expectations about what we could do were too low. We were forced to admit—finally—that the Japanese and some of our other foreign competitors weren't beating us because they had some unfair advantage. They were beating us because they tried harder and expected more—better quality, better service, and faster innovation.

The lessons of the 1980s reshaped the thinking of American business leaders about how companies had to be run to compete in a global marketplace. The changes that occurred as a result of this rethinking set the stage for *Workplace 2000*.

Lesson One: American Expectations Were Too Low

The experience of David Kearns, chairman and CEO of Xerox, is typical of the lesson American business leaders learned about the need to raise expectations. In the mid-1980s Kearns had visited Japan, where he had met with a number of Japanese businessmen. As he got on the plane for the return trip, he began to write down the differences between the Japanese businessmen he had just met and the American businessmen he knew well. Kearns says he wrote down a lot of things, but finally two words jumped out to him as the main difference—"expectation level." What it all seemed to boil down to for Kearns was that the Japanese expectation for success just was much higher than he had ever encountered among his peers in America and, Kearns admitted, much higher than he had for Xerox. Kearns's realization changed his thinking about what he should expect from his managers, supervisors, employees, and perhaps most important, himself. Just "okay," even "pretty good," wasn't good enough. If Xerox was going to compete with the Japanese, it had to get a lot better—fast.

In 1989, Kearns spoke at a conference on "World Class Quality and Productivity" in Minneapolis, Minnesota. At that conference, he described Xerox's efforts over the previous five years to get better and the company's success in key areas. The results Kearns reported were impressive. The company had made significant progress. But the results weren't the most important story. More important was Kearns' assessment of those results. Here is how Kearns described what his company had accomplished:

In the early 1980s about 92 percent of the parts coming into our Webster, New York plant were defect-free. From a competitive standpoint that is *absolutely abominable*. We're now at 99.95 percent, which is *absolutely unsatisfactory*. . . . We believe 100 percent defect-free is possible, and that is our expectation now. . . . We cut our inventory from about six months of in-process inventory to one month's, and that's just *absolutely awful*. . . . We have reduced unit manufacturing costs by about 50 percent, but that is *not nearly good enough*. We have reduced our product development cycles by 25 percent to 50 percent. That's terrific, but it is *still not nearly good enough*. Our revenue per employee is up 20 percent, but that is *not nearly good enough*. Still, we have made a lot of progress and I have very good feelings about the Xerox people who have done this[1] [emphasis added].

The Kearns speaking to the quality and productivity conference in 1989 wasn't the same Kearns who boarded the plane to Japan in the mid-1980s. He expected more. He expected continuous improvement in all areas, but particularly in quality, service, and fast-paced innovation. He had to. Kearns wasn't alone. Practically every other American business leader came to the same conclusion in the 1980s. America had to get better—fast—if it wanted to compete. And there was plenty of research to show that we had a lot of room for improvement in quality, service, and innovation.

Lesson Two: Just "Okay" Quality Isn't Good Enough

In the 1980s, no one should have been surprised to learn that America wasn't particularly noted for high-quality products. After all, long before the 1980s, when we wanted to praise a product we said, "It runs like a Swiss watch" or "It has the precision of a German machine." No one ever said, "It runs like an American watch" or "It has the precision of an American machine"—unless, of course, the purpose was to offer an insult rather than a compliment. We accepted the fact that our quality might not be quite as good. But our reputation for quality wasn't that bad, was it? Yes, it was. In 1987, the Roper organization surveyed consumers in the United States, Italy, France, the United Kingdom, and West Germany to gauge their perception of a product carrying the label "Made in the USA." The findings came as a shock. Only 34 percent of Italians, 25 percent of the French, 9 percent of the English, and 6 percent of the West Germans associated "Made in the USA" with good quality. Worse, fewer than 70 percent of Americans associated U.S. products with good quality. And note here we are not talking about "best" quality, or "superior" quality, or "excellent" quality. We are just talking about "good" quality. In his book *Thriving on Chaos*, Tom Peters summed up the attitude of foreign and many domestic consumers concerning the quality of goods and services made in America. As far as they were concerned, American-made products were "questionable"—"perhaps 'stinks,' " said Peters, "is a more accurate word."

Well, what difference did it make if American companies weren't perceived as making the best quality? Plenty. It became evident in the 1980s that consumers' perception of the quality of a company's products or services had a direct relationship to a company's performance. An analysis of confidential data on product lines of three thousand business units of companies (the PIMS data base maintained by the Strategic Planning Institute) revealed that a reputation for product or service quality was the most important determiner of a company's performance. Companies with high relative quality outperformed companies with low perceived quality by a margin of two to one. Similar results were obtained by John Groocock, the former vice president for quality at TRW. When Groocock compared TRW's business units on quality and earnings in 1985, he found that those units with the highest reputation for quality outperformed those with average quality by a margin of three to one. One of the reasons companies with high quality performed so well was that poor quality drove up costs. In the late 1980s, the cost of poor quality from increased warranty cost, scrap, rework, inspection, and testing was estimated to be 10 to 20 percent of sales dollars in the average American company or two to four times its profit. A leading quality expert went further. He estimated that the average U.S. manufacturing company spent 25 percent of its sales dollars fixing quality problems and that in the service industry up to as much as 40 percent of operating costs were spent on nonconformance. Poor quality also held down the price companies could charge for their goods and services. Research showed that American consumers wanted better quality and were very willing to pay for it. How much more would they pay? Americans said they would be willing to pay 20 percent more for a better car, 40 percent more for a better dishwasher, and as much as 60 percent more for a better pair of shoes. It was much the same with other products and services.

Lesson Three: Superior Customer Service Was Critical

If the quality of American products and services was bad in the 1980s, the reputation of American businesses for customer service wasn't much better. Practically every American consumer could cite horror stories of poor service. As the decade drew to a close, it was evident that consumers were fed up. They were complaining more about poor service and refusing to do business with companies that offered poor service. The Technical Assistance Research Programs Institute in Washington, D.C., reported that in the late 1980s, service operations of many companies were receiving nearly twice as many complaints from customers as they did in the 1970s. If such a doubling of complaints weren't bad enough, American business leaders had to ponder the significance of research evidence on how customer satisfaction (or rather customer dissatisfaction) hurt their businesses. For example, they were told:

1. Poor service was the major reason American companies lost customers. Sixty-eight percent of the customers who stopped doing business with them did so because of poor service. In fact, consumers were five times more likely to stop doing business with a company for poor service than for poor product quality or high cost.[2]
2. Most (96 percent) of a company's dissatisfied customers never complained. Most of them (90 percent) just stopped doing business with the company.
3. Dissatisfied customers were very vocal about the service problems they experienced. The average "unhappy" customer told nine other people about the poor service he or she received. Thirteen percent of "unhappy" customers told twenty or more people about the poor service.
4. The cost of losing a customer was equal to five times the annual value of that customer's account.[3]

What was the value to a company of providing good service, or at least resolving customer complaints quickly? Here is what the research findings suggested:

1. Americans would pay more for good service. In fact, an undifferentiated product accompanied by outstanding service could command up to a 10 percent price premium.[4]
2. A happy and satisfied customer would tell five other people about the company. Many of these would become customers of the business.[5]
3. Even when a customer was unhappy, he or she could be "saved" if the problem was resolved quickly. Fifty to 75 percent of the customers who complain and have their problem resolved would do business with the company again. If their complaint was resolved quickly, 95 percent would return to doing business with the company.[6]
4. It was much more cost effective to invest in improving customer service and making provisions to resolve customer complaints rapidly in order to keep a customer than to invest in marketing and sales efforts to attract new customers. It cost five times as much to obtain a customer than to keep one.[7]
5. Good customer service could even help offset not-so-good product quality. It turned out that customer service—how the customer was treated and how rapidly customer complaints were resolved—was one of the most powerful tools shaping consumers' perceptions of overall quality.[8]

Lesson Four: Learn to Innovate Fast

On the innovation front, the 1980s demonstrated that America had squandered what should have been an insurmountable lead in research and development. America invented the phonograph, color television, audio and video tape recording, the telephone, integrated circuits, and thousands of other products. In the late 1980s, America had 15 million companies, more than any other country. It had 5.5 million scientists and engineers—twice the number in Japan. And Americans had won more Nobel prizes than the rest of the world combined. America should have been the "innovation center of the world." In a way, we were. We had a lot of ideas and a lot of talent. Our problem was that it took too long for us to develop our ideas into marketable products and when we did we couldn't efficiently manufacture a high-quality product from what we had created.

In respect to speed of development, America in the 1980s was being solidly beaten by the Japanese. American automakers found themselves competing against Japanese companies such as Honda and Toyota, who had found ways to take cars from concept to market in just three years versus the five years it had traditionally taken companies like GM and Ford. In copiers, companies like Xerox found themselves losing market share to Japanese competitors who could develop new copiers incorporating the latest technology twice as fast as their American counterparts and at half the cost. It was the same in numerous other industries. By reducing development time, the Japanese gained some significant advantages. First, they were able to design products much closer to what the customer wanted. They didn't have to try to project consumer preferences those extra two or three years into the future. Second, with shorter development times, the Japanese could develop more products and make more incremental improvements to products. As a result, they had more chances to find a product or make a product enhancement that caught the consumer's fancy. Finally, and perhaps most importantly, Japanese designers, engineers, and others on product development teams got more exprience. In the course of ten years, Japanese design teams would go through the product development life cycle three or more times compared to just two for American designers. Each time the Japanese designers went through the experience they got better. American designers simply had less opportunity to learn because they had fewer experiences. Using their speed in developing new products and incorporating the latest technology in older products, the Japanese (and others) were leaving the Americans far behind. They produced the new, the innovative, and the exciting. We were left with the boring and obsolete.

It wasn't only the disadvantage in speed of development

that was killing us. The Japanese were also able to manufacture their new products more efficiently than we could manufacture ours. Worse, they could take our products or product enhancements and then dominate the market for these products. We invented the product and then all too often we let someone else, frequently the Japanese, make it and market it. We got the credit for the invention. They got the customers and the profit. The list of products we invented but somehow couldn't compete in manufacturing and marketing was long and sad. For example, in 1987 there was a $630 million domestic market for phonographs. Yet even though it was our invention, American companies controlled only one percent of the market, down from 90 percent in 1970. Between 1970 and 1987, our share of the $14 billion domestic market for color TVs dropped from 90 percent to 10 percent. During the same period, our share of the nearly $3 billion market for video recorders dropped from 10 percent to one percent. The same was true for many other products. By 1989, according to *Business Week*, we had relinquished significant market share in audio recorders (40 percent in 1970; 0 percent in 1987), telephones (99 percent in 1970; 25 percent in 1987), semiconductors (89 percent in 1970; 64 percent in 1987), and computers (97 percent in 1975; 74 percent in 1987)—all products we had invented.

Why couldn't we manufacture and market what we had invented? In part, our failure had to do with our traditional approach to new product development. We followed a sequential process. Marketing handed off an idea to designers. Designers fleshed out the concept and passed it on to engineers. The engineers took the design and built expensive prototypes. Finally, manufacturers were given the prototypes and specifications and asked to make what everyone else had designed, without manufacturing input. Our sequential, step-by-step process (often it was more of step, step, repeat step) not only lengthened development time but also meant that final designs couldn't be manufactured efficiently. No one considered until the design process was complete whether, or how, we could produce what we had designed. Yet the design process, once completed, locked in by some estimates 70 percent to 95 percent of the total manufacturing costs. Stephen

Sharf, a former head of manufacturing at Chrysler, tells a story that perfectly illustrates the kind of "design for non-manufacturability" that was common in U.S. industry. The *Wall Street Journal* reported that according to Sharf, in 1960 a Chrysler design team ordered a fin for the trunk lid of a new Plymouth model. What was the problem? It seems that no one had bothered to check with manufacturing concerning how such a fin could be fabricated or installed. As it turned out, there was no stamping machine that could press such a fin. Factory workers would have had to build and weld the fins on each car by hand. Fortunately, Chrysler dropped the idea for such a fin at the last minute. But the "fin fiasco" illustrates how lack of communication could significantly drive up manufacturing costs.

By the late 1980s, most American businesses had begun to take steps to fix quality, service, and innovation problems. No one was yet willing to boast that they had the solution to these problems, but a lot of experimentation was underway. Also, a number of companies had made substantial progress. Product quality was getting better. Service quality was still a problem, but gradually improving. And a number of companies had revamped their approach to research and development with promising results. As the 1980s ended, America was on its way to finding solutions to its competitiveness problems. While incomplete, the steps that were taken laid the foundation for *Workplace 2000*. They weren't intended to, but they did. When American business began to work on its quality, service, and innovation problems, no one envisioned revamping our approach to business. Initially, our efforts were directed toward addressing specific issues or specific problems. How could we improve quality? How could we upgrade customer service? How could we speed up the process of research and development? In tackling these problems, we experimented. And it was from these experiments that *Workplace 2000* emerged as the response to a compelling need for change.

At a labor management forum in Cleveland in March of 1987, Joseph Gorman, president and chief operating officer of TRW, described the problems facing American businesses and its need to change:

The simplest and most accurate way to describe the crisis we are facing is *competitive failure*: failure on the part of government, management, labor and society as a whole. . . . We need an on-going labor/management miracle. This cannot and will not be accomplished without major changes in how we conduct our businesses. Business as usual must be totally unacceptable. The changes must be fundamental and pervasive. . . . What is required is a new sense of collaboration and teamwork that is designed to serve not only management and labor but also the balanced best interest of all our constituents—our customers, our suppliers, our plant communities, shareholders, and the public at large. Most importantly, this collaborative effort is absolutely necessary if we are to preserve hundreds of thousands of jobs and the quality of life we have been so fortunate to create in this country. What is it then that we must do together? We must have a work force that cares more, knows more, and does more. In other words, a work force that is more involved with the success or failure of the enterprise; a work force that cares about and takes pride in the product shipped to the customer.[9]

Revolutionary change is occurring in American business simply because American business has to change to survive. There is little doubt about what businesses require for success today: flexibility, responsiveness, a strong customer orientation, the ability to explore and claim niche markets, a vastly shorter development to production life cycle, "built in" not just "tacked on" quality, and so on. And these are not just competitive requirements for the 1980s or 1990s, but requirements for all of the foreseeable future. They are not likely to go away any time soon. Every business owner and every CEO knows that. Now is the time for Americans to prepare themselves for the future.

CHAPTER 2

Future Structure and Culture

Nucor Steel of Charlotte, North Carolina, is an $850 million company. It has a corporate staff of seventeen (including stenographic and typing help) and only four levels of management. That's it. The remainder of Nucor's thirty-seven hundred employees are workers. Nucor may not be the archetypical company of the future, but it comes close. The *Workplace 2000* company will look much like Nucor—flat and lean. The implications of this future structure for American workers are enormous. This flatter and leaner "pancake" organization will radically alter the culture of the workplace for most Americans and the rules an American worker must follow for advancement.

Why Flatter Is Better—The Middle Must Disappear

The flattening of organizations that will be typical of *Workplace 2000* actually began around the middle of the 1980s. Up until that time, the stock market had rewarded companies for growth—even growth that sometimes didn't make much sense. "Big" was in. Big companies wanted to stay big and even get bigger. Conglomerates proliferated. Small companies wanted to grow and become big. Then, around 1985, the rules changed. Suddenly, the stock market—and just about everyone else—discovered that the traditionally structured big companies were having a hard time competing with a lot of their smaller and more focused rivals. Honda was creating problems for GM. Nucor and other "mini" steel mills were performing a lot better than U.S. Steel. Federal Express was taking profitable business away from the U.S. Postal Service. And in retail, upstarts like K-Mart and Wal-Mart were causing significant problems for Sears. It was the same in a lot of other industries. By the mid-1980s, large companies were in trouble. Well-known management writers such as Tom Peters and Peter Drucker—to name just two—were questioning whether big companies could survive. In 1987, Peter Drucker wrote: "The flagships of the last 40 years, the large institutions like General Motors, ITT, and du Pont basically have outlived their usefulness." Why? Because in spite of the advantages large companies had—access to resources, economies of scale, stability, and so on—size also brought with it severe disadvantages. Big companies just weren't as flexible or agile as their smaller competitors. The larger a company became, the more it built up layers of management and bureaucracy. It wasn't size so much as the lack of focus. Too often, the big conglomerates had too many dissimilar businesses. To keep track of all the various product lines, companies structured according to specialized functions. Employees and their managers lost touch with their customers and fiefdoms arose. America's traditionally structured big companies became bloated and sluggish. That didn't matter very much when big companies had few competitors, particularly when those competitors were also big, bloated, and sluggish themselves. But it mattered very much when new competitors—foreign and domestic—arose who didn't have the disadvantages of being big. Sears and GM are examples of just two large U.S. companies that were in trouble and struggling as the decade of the 1980s came to an end.

Sears, long the dominant retailer in the United States, saw

K-Mart take the lead in 1985. By 1988, K-Mart and Wal-Mart were both well on their way to surpassing Sears in the worldwide merchandising business. What were Sears' problems? Its costs were too high and it couldn't innovate. Selling and administrative expenses (as a percentage of sales) at Sears were nearly twice what they were at Wal-Mart and nearly a third higher than at K-Mart. Sears' distribution costs (as a percentage of sales) were more than double what they were at its two major rivals. When Sears tried to reduce costs or find a creative way to lure back customers, bureaucratic infighting and inertia got in the way. For example, a proposal to reduce inventories at Sears stores from a twenty-two-week supply to an eight-week supply—a move that could have significantly reduced inventory carrying costs—was stymied by indecision. A fourteen-week supply of goods was packed up, but never returned to suppliers because no one could agree upon what to keep and what to return. Five months later, the goods were unpacked, ironed, and returned to the store shelves. A similar case of bureaucratic inertia and infighting prevented Sears from going ahead with a concept for "neighborhood stores" that *Fortune* magazine called "exciting." The idea was to create small Sears stores that would specialize in highly profitable items such as apparel and home furnishings. But Sears executives in charge of sales of appliances, home improvement, automotive, and other products objected to being left out of the new stores. Because the confrontation between the executives in charge of "hard lines" and "soft lines" could never be resolved, the "neighborhood stores" were never opened and Sears lost the opportunity to experiment with this new concept. In a 1988 story, *Fortune* magazine said that compared to its fleet-footed rivals, K-Mart and Wal-Mart, Sears was like "a 2,000 pound centipede. The antennae work poorly, so the creature is directionless. When some of the 101 legs try to move ahead, others interfere and even move backward."[1]

Like Sears, GM also became a "2,000 pound centipede." As a result, its share of the U.S. auto market dropped from over 50 percent in the 1960s to 36 percent (and still declining) in 1989. To understand what happened to GM, we have to go back to the late 1960s. At that time, GM's five divisions—Chevrolet, Pontiac, Oldsmobile, Buick, and Cadillac—designed, engineered, and manufactured their own distinctive cars to meet the needs of their own target customers. Buicks looked like and drove like Buicks. Chevrolets looked like and drove like Chevrolets. Each make had the performance, appearance, and handling characteristics suited to the lifestyle and needs of its target market. GM's idea in the 1960s was to move the buyer from Chevrolets to Pontiacs to Buicks and finally to Cadillacs as he or she grew older and more affluent. The focus was to provide "a car for every age and pocketbook." But in the late 1960s, that all changed. In an economy move, GM took manufacturing responsibility away from the divisions and gave it to a new centralized General Motors Assembly Division. In the 1970s, the automotive divisions lost further control over their cars when engineering was centralized. By the 1980s, the separate car divisions had little control over design, engineering, or manufacture. They were essentially just marketing divisions. Since GM's cars were all designed, engineered, and manufactured by the same "super" division, they all began to look very much alike and drive very much alike. No longer was there much difference between a Chevrolet and a Buick. Worse, when quality or design problems occurred, instead of fixing the problems, the divisions constantly fought with each other to fix blame. Quality, performance, and profitability all began to slip. Finally, in 1984, GM partially backed away from its centralization. The General Motors Assembly Division and Fisher Body Division (the centralized division that produced body parts) were dissolved. In their place, GM created two supergroups: Buick-Oldsmobile-Cadillac and Chevrolet-Pontiac-Canada. Each supergroup was supposed to be responsible for the design, engineering, and manufacture of their own cars. But the reorganization into the supergroups (including the reassignment of two hundred thousand employees) was poorly explained to employees (if at all), resulting in months of confusion among employees about reporting relationships. In addition, GM found it difficult to divide production between plants in the two supergroups, so plants in both supergroups ended up producing cars for all five divisions. Within the supergroups, divisions still fought with each other and the cars of the various divisions still looked and drove very much alike.

As the 1980s ended, GM was still struggling with how to reorganize and facing the reality that it probably would never regain the market share it had lost.

Sears and GM are just two examples of large U.S. corporations whose size prevented them from adjusting quickly to rapidly changing markets. Practically every other large U.S. corporation experienced the same problem. Most responded by aggressively pursuing a policy of getting and acting smaller. Between 1985 and 1988, for example, IBM restructured into six smaller, independent "business units." During the same period, Eastman Kodak reorganized into seventeen small, autonomous units. This trend will continue. The 1990s will be an age of niche markets, intense competition, and extremely short product life cycles. Success in such an age demands low cost, continuous innovation, flexibility, and responsiveness—the qualities small companies possess. And that's what every large U.S. company will want to look like and act like by the year 2000—a small company.

In the 1990s, large U.S. companies will go further in restructuring. Just as GM's reorganization into two supergroups wasn't enough, much more focusing will be needed to make "big" companies act like small companies. In the 1990s, restructured divisions from the 1980s will be broken down further into small "business units" centered around the provision of products and/or services to meet the needs of a target market or customer group. Alternatively, these business units will be structured around a line of products and/or services and have responsibility for expanding the customer base for these products and/or services or retaining existing customers by continually adding value (that is, giving the customer just a little more all the time). For all practical purposes, these business units will be operated as independent small companies under a corporate umbrella. Instead of two supergroups as in the case of GM, or six business units as in the case of IBM, or seventeen autonomous units as in the case of Eastman Kodak, we will see large corporations restructuring into hundreds of small business units that can be operated like small independent companies. Present-day models for the *Workplace 2000* large corporation (although they do not yet go to the ultimate of *Workplace 2000*) are such companies as

Matsushita Electric Industrial with 161 independent business units, Hitachi Ltd. with 600 companies (27 publicly traded), Johnson & Johnson with 106 autonomous companies, and Hewlett-Packard with 50 independent units. Some *Workplace 2000* companies will even go so far as to limit the size of an independent business unit to perhaps no more than a few hundred or, at most, few thousand employees. In this respect, they will be similar to Worthington Industries, which limits the size of its plants to 250 employees.

Why Flatter Is Possible—What Technology Has to Do With It

The ability of large American companies to reconfigure themselves to look and act like small businesses can, at least in part, be attributed to the development of new technology that makes whole layers of managers and their staffs unnecessary. Those layers (such as group executives, corporate directors, and assistant vice presidents) whose primary function is to either filter information and, in some cases, manipulate data being passed up from lower levels or make routine decisions will be particularly vulnerable to technology. Why? Because filtering will no longer be needed and new software will make it possible for line employees to make many routine decisions that previously had to be referred to managers or corporate support staff.

In *Workplace 2000*, upper management in practically every company will have the technological tools not only to review company-wide performance on a personal computer but to tap directly into performance at the lowest level. Instead of waiting for some intermediate levels to compile, tabulate, analyze, and summarize information about performance on the factory floor or in the office—a process that could take days, weeks, or even months before—the senior executive will just tap into his or her data base to view summary or detailed data on yesterday's, today's, or even this hour's performance both for the company as a whole and any given location in the company. Typical of the *Workplace 2000* CEO with ready access to information is Charles Lazarus, founder of Toys "Я" Us who can already monitor each of his 350 stores simply by tapping into computers installed in his home, office, and even his beach house. Lazarus doesn't need a lower-level manager or analyst to tell him what is selling and not selling, because that type of information is available to him instantly. Another present-day example of a CEO with direct access to the information he needs is Robert Kidder, CEO of Duracell. Kidder doesn't need hoards of analysts, support staff, and intermediate managers to help him get to the heart of, for example, a profit problem. From the work station in his office, he can browse through his company's mainframe, isolating and comparing the performance of Duracell hourly and salaried employees worldwide. Not only can the colorful graphs and charts displayed on his work station tell him, for example, that German sales per employee are less than U.S. sales per employee, but by asking the computer to probe a little deeper, Kidder can find out why—German salespeople are spending too much time calling on small stores. With the information at his disposal, and relying on his own analysis, Kidder can make a decision in a few minutes or hours that might have taken months before (assuming the problem was ever detected and brought to his attention). What does Kidder do? He cuts the German sales staff and signs up distributors to handle small accounts.

Kidder and Lazarus are examples of CEOs whose "executive software" gives them access to a broad range of information about their businesses. The emergence of such software was the result of several developments in information technology that came together in the 1980s. Chief among these were

- More powerful personal computers and work stations
- Enhanced graphic capabilities that allowed masses of data to be presented in simple, colorful, easy to understand tables and charts
- Touch screens and the "mouse" that made software easier to use
- Interconnections that made it possible for software to access data from a company's wide range of hardware and data bases

At least two major suppliers were selling and supporting "executive support systems" in the late 1980s. Others will follow in the 1990s.[2] The impact of executive support systems is far-reaching. On the one hand, such systems make middle managers and support personnel who spend most of their time compiling, tabulating, and analyzing data unnecessary. On the other hand, with the security of knowing that they can easily and quickly access summary and detailed information on far-flung business units and thereby reassure themselves that all is well, top corporate executives are more willing to push decision making further down the flattened hierarchy. For example, top managers at Phillips 66 were much more willing to turn over control of pricing to motor fuel terminal managers once the executives were assured they could easily and quickly monitor pricing trends via their desktop terminals.

In addition to making middle-level managers "relayers" and interpreters of information unnecessary, technology will also eliminate the need for "routine" decision makers, thanks to wider application of artificial intelligence (AI). Routine decisions will be preprogrammed in software so that line employees no longer have to go to managers or specialists when a question arises. Already, airline clerks can make decisions about pricing, special meals, seating, special fares, and so on by selecting from menu options on their computer screens without ever having to ask a manager or supervisor for assistance. In some high tech firms today, sales people can prepare proposals, conduct margin analyses, do credit checks, enter orders, establish delivery schedules, initiate billing, and even accomplish some product customization directly from the customer's site using portable computers connected by telephone to their company's information system. In many *Workplace 2000* companies, it will be a common practice for sales people to transmit orders for customized products directly from the customer's site to the manufacturing facility where teams of employees will use robots and artificial intelligence to produce the product to customer specification for shipment to the customer within a matter of days. In the apparel industry, this is already happening. The Limited tracks consumer preferences daily using point-of-sale computers. Orders with facsimile illustrations are then sent by satellite to suppliers around the world. Within days, the ordered clothing begins pouring into The Limited's distribution center in Ohio, where it is priced and shipped to stores within forty-eight hours. Using its technology, The Limited bypasses numerous order processing steps and cuts its total time from order to manufacturing to restocking from the traditional six months to sixty days or less.

The Limited's automation of order processing is an example of the use of technology that was becoming commonplace as the 1980s came to an end. Technology will have an even greater impact on *Workplace 2000* as artificial intelligence, also called expert system, becomes popular. Throughout the 1980s, researchers and company executives struggled with how to put AI to use. Most felt they should be using AI, but at times the technology seemed like a solution in search of a problem. By the late 1980s, however, a number of innovative uses for it had been found. For example, companies were using it for such things as truck routing (to design more efficient delivery routes) and for matching computer systems to customer needs (for example, proper configuration of computer and peripherals). Additionally, companies such as Westinghouse, Digital Equipment Corporation, General Electric, AT&T, and Boeing were spending tens of millions of dollars in research and development to develop AI.[3] A typical application of AI was the mortgage loan analyzer (MLA) that could expedite the processing of mortgage loans for a major bank. Loan approval was a good candidate for AI since it was rule-based and rule-intensive. The decision process for loan approval was well documented and of limited complexity. Working with Fannie Mae and Freddie Mac guidelines, written bank policies, and rules of thumb provided by an expert underwriter, programmers could design computer software that would prompt users for the right information, apply the "rules," and recommend a course of action—approve, disapprove, or obtain more information. The advantages of such a system for a bank were that it could make sure all regulatory standards were met so that loans approved with the system could be sold on the secondary loan market. More importantly, nonexpert underwriters could use the system to process twice the number of loan applications in a day.

In the 1990s, we will see wider application of AI software. We will also see the application of more advanced, "intelligent" software that will further reduce the need for routine decision makers. Particularly promising are what are called neural networks. Neural net technology goes beyond traditional AI software in that it enables computers to learn from experience and make decisions closer to the way humans do. Unlike less sophisticated AI, neural nets do not require that elaborate rule structures be specified in advance. Neural nets can learn rule structures and patterns on their own from historical data or through experience. As the 1980s ended, we were already seeing applications of neural nets. A February 1989 *Fortune* article reported that Ford, for example, was using neural nets to spot faulty paint finishes. American Express was using neural nets to evaluate credit risks. And GTE was using neural nets to determine optimum manufacturing conditions for making fluorescent bulbs. In all three instances, neural nets were being used to make routine decisions that otherwise would have required human intervention.

What It Means to American Workers When "Big" Companies Look and Act Like Small Companies

The decline of the traditional "big" company with its bureaucracy and hierarchy has enormous implications for the American worker. Here are just a few of the changes that will occur in *Workplace 2000*:

Corporate Jobs Will Disappear

Some types of jobs are becoming what Robert Tomasko, author of *Downsizing*, calls "an endangered species." Who is endangered? Planners, economists, corporate marketing and public relations staffs, analysts of all types—anyone who sits around "thinking" and "advising" others who do the work. Gone, too, will be the gleaming corporate "mansion" that used to house all of the "thinkers" and "advisors." The country club atmosphere of corporate headquarters largesse will be a thing of the past. Responsibility and accountability for decisions once made at the corporate level will be shifted to the division level or even lower in *Workplace 2000*. Division and lower-level managers will run their own businesses, decide what services they need, and decide whether to get those services from corporate headquarters, from outside consultants and suppliers, or from their own staffs. Typical of the *Workplace 2000* approach to corporate staff will be that of Nucor Steel, which was mentioned at the beginning of this chapter. Nucor is decentralized into fourteen divisions. Each division is operated like an autonomous company. Nucor's headquarters restricts itself to monitoring cash flow, budgets, and overall operations. Other decisions are left up to the division managers, who are responsible for deciding what they need and what they are willing to fund. The emerging trends for corporate headquarters staff are clear. Desirable ("nice to do") but unessential corporate/headquarters activities will be eliminated. Duplicate and overlapping activities will be eliminated with preference given to relocating them to the division level or lower where they can generate the greatest value. Many such services will be provided at the division ("business unit") level or even lower by small—sometimes part-time—staffs or will be provided by outside contractors. Those retained at headquarters will be expected to fund themselves by charging divisions for their services (without the requirement that the divisions purchase such services from them) and/or by selling their services outside the corporation.

Many Managerial and Supervisory Jobs Will Disappear

Entire layers of management and supervision will be erased from the organization chart. Traditional ideas about a "span of control" where a manager or supervisor was needed for every four, five, or six employees are being discarded. Instead of a narrow span of control, companies are now beginning to look at a much broader span of communication or span of information as the basis for establishing the number and levels of management. No longer are the number of employees per manager constrained by how many he or she can "control."

Rather, the constraining factor is "how many he or she can communicate with effectively." And thanks to information technology, that number is becoming quite large. Lower-level supervision for control purposes will no longer be needed or desired in *Workplace 2000*, since the key results for *Workplace 2000* companies—world-class quality, superior customer service, continuous innovation, flexibility—cannot be obtained through control. Instead of being controlled, employees in *Workplace 2000* will be expected to be self-controlling. Management's job will be to communicate a vision of the company's future and the key results each work group or business unit must obtain for that vision to become a reality. Business units will then have wide discretion concerning how they structure themselves and operate to obtain the desired results. And they will be held accountable for doing so. Top-level monitoring of performance will be accomplished through the use of technology that allows senior management, perhaps thousands of miles away, to instantaneously examine both macro measures of "business unit" performance and the details of that performance.

Traditional Paths for Career Advancement Will Be Closed

In *Workplace 2000*, traditional paths of career advancement will be closed for most people. They won't be promoted because there simply won't be a job to promote them into. Carl Thor, president of the American Productivity and Quality Center, has noted that in the traditional organization of ten or even fifteen levels, an enterprising employee could expect to be promoted six or seven times throughout his or her career. A very talented employee might be promoted ten times or more before the pyramid narrows to a point where further promotion would be possible only for the highly select few. No more. With fewer levels, there will just be no room for rapid or even semi-rapid promotion in *Workplace 2000*. At best, the typical employee can expect a few promotions and a number of lateral moves. And physically, these moves will not be from one nice office to an even bigger and nicer office with more square footage of thicker carpet. Rather, each new office is likely to look much like the rest, with few status symbols attached. In *Workplace 2000* we can expect the traditional career path (a steady, predictable, long rise up the hierarchy or short-cut "fast track") to become an anachronism. Instead, most Americans can and must expect a degree of uncertainty in any job and will have to rely on themselves rather than betting their future on a specific organization. Rosabeth Moss Kanter, Harvard Business School professor and author of *The Change Masters*, has equated the "new career path" to that of a Hollywood film producer. Rather than a career "under contract" to a major studio, film producers have careers based upon "projects," often completed for a variety of studios. Under such conditions, says Kanter, "firm specific knowledge"—who and what I know about a specific company—becomes less valuable than general expertise, the problems I can solve and value I can create. Equally important skills for the new professional wishing to be on the "fast track" are flexibility and the ability to learn. Kanter says that a reputation for results will be more important in *Workplace 2000* than "what my superior thinks of me."[4]

Companies Will "Disintegrate"

During the 1990s, whole groups of American workers will lose their jobs or find their association with a particular company terminated as major companies "disintegrate" and refocus on a "core business" where they can be really good. In *Workplace 2000*, traditional notions about the value of vertical integration, where companies seek competitive advantage by bringing all parts of the business under their control, will be rejected. Thus, a car builder will not try to make its own steel as Ford once did. A bus company will not attempt to make its own buses as Greyhound once did. Instead, the new corporate model will be more like a "solar system" than a pyramid. Instead of acquiring companies outside their core business, *Workplace 2000* companies will seek instead close relationships with a network of smaller, independent companies as key suppliers. Parts of companies outside the core business will be sold off or closed.

The rejection of vertical integration by American business

represents a significant departure from prevailing notions about how businesses should seek competitive advantage. "Backward integration"—a manufacturer acquiring ownership of raw materials or a distributor developing its own manufacturing capability—was smart, according to conventional wisdom, because such integration would assure a business an uninterrupted supply of products and services. "Forward integration"—a manufacturer acquiring a distributor, for example—was equally smart since it assured an outlet for goods and services. Both types of integration in theory would position a company to take advantage of whatever line in the economic chain that was most profitable at a given time— raw materials to manufacture, manufacture to distribution, or distribution to retail sales. Since a vertically integrated company could have a presence throughout the chain, it could maximize profits by taking advantage of opportunities at any point in the chain. Vertical integration also brought with it the possibility of enhancing profits throughout the chain by applying cost reduction, quality improvement, and other techniques developed in one segment to all other segments. Such sharing of knowledge would be feasible because all parts would benefit and there would be no danger of revealing critical information and/or techniques to a competitor. Finally, a vertically integrated company would supposedly react faster to the market since it would control all resources from marketing to production to sales and could marshal those resources toward one common goal. That was the theory of integration. In reality, integration failed to deliver the promised advantages and had severe disadvantages.

Too often, vertical integration brought with it standardization. In an effort to maintain consistency across a wide variety of businesses, vertically integrated companies imposed the same policies and practices from one segment of the business to another. But personnel, management, financial, compensation, and other policies and practices that worked well in one segment often failed to work well in others, and sometimes created major problems. All segments of the economic chain could not be managed and administered in the same way.

A second, and more damaging, disadvantage of vertical integration was the difficulty companies had in being very good in all aspects of the business. Managers who were very good in one area frequently were less successful—and sometimes incompetent—when it came to running a business that was foreign to them. In his book *Downsizing*, Robert Tomasko tells of a large supermarket company that discovered the disadvantages of trying to do too many things. Over time, this supermarket company had become highly diversified. It owned full-service supermarkets, discount food warehouses, drugstores, food-packing and -manufacturing plants, trucking and warehouse operations. At headquarters, the company had built up a large staff to design stores, manage construction, and select and price products. Control and decision making were exercised primarily at headquarters. It wasn't until senior managers became concerned about the company's poor showing in return on equity that they objectively evaluated the performance of their various enterprises. When they did, they learned that they were good at buying food and merchandising it in their stores. But they were terrible in most other parts of the business. It was costing them more to manufacture their own private label merchandise than it would have to purchase private label goods from outside manufacturers. They weren't good at running independent pharmacies. They were tying up vast amounts of capital in their trucking and warehousing operations. And the services provided by their large headquarters staff could have perhaps been performed by store managers or contracted out at less cost. Eventually, the company sold off its drugstores and manufacturing arms. It also convinced managers of the trucking and warehouse operations to buy them out and operate as independent companies. Finally, headquarters staff functions were streamlined by delegating some to store managers and contracting others to outside vendors. The restructured company eventually improved its performance by focusing on what it did well—running supermarkets.

Workplace 2000's movement away from vertical integration and toward "solar system" or partnering with suppliers is a direct response to overcoming the disadvantages of vertical integration while retaining some of the advantages. "Partnering" involves the creation of close, mutually beneficial relationships with suppliers. This relationship can be as simple as a supplier guaranteeing availability and delivery of products or services at a fixed price, or as complex as supplier participation as a full partner in research and development efforts or joint ventures. The advantages of "partnering" seem to match those of vertical integration without the inherent risks of integration. For example, Ford improves its overall quality and gains a competitive advantage by turning over the manufacture of paint to a very competent supplier like du Pont, while retaining the same benefits that it would enjoy through vertical integration—single sourcing, just-in-time inventories, vendor certification of quality, and co-development; du Pont gets the advantage of a predictable stream of business, plus the ability to work on the joint development of new products that it may be able to sell to other customers after the exclusivity period expires. Both parties to such an arrangement retain the flexibility to reach partnership agreements with other customers or suppliers and to terminate the partnership if competitive conditions change.

Specialty and Staff Functions Will Become Small Businesses

In *Workplace 2000*, large companies will look for ways to offset the cost of centralized staff and specialized functions by transforming them into small businesses that can market their expertise to other companies. Control Data, for example, already sells personnel services to other companies. Xerox sells distribution services to its customers, and Parson Brinckerhoff's public relations office has become an accredited advertising agency able to offer its services to other companies for a fee. Similar efforts have been made by Polaroid, Security Pacific National Bank, Union Carbide, and others. This trend toward making support functions look and operate like small, entrepreneurial professional service firms is a direct response to dissatisfaction with the performance of support functions in the traditional large organization. In-house service and support in most large companies had a de facto monopoly. Operating divisions had little choice but to use in-house support services. As a result, there was little incentive for these support groups to reduce cost, improve quality, or improve service to customers. In fact, there were disincentives for improvement since rewards to support function managers came for increased size and complexity. Size meant larger budgets and increased personnel with a corresponding increase in salaries and prestige for staff function managers. As the reputation of these support groups deteriorated, they became a dumping ground for employees who were unwanted or unneeded in other parts of the business. It was easier to transfer them to some nebulous staff function such as the "long-range planning staff" than it was to fire them. Faced with a further deterioration of the reputation of staff groups and the recognition that few people ever got promoted to a top-level position (CEO, COO) out of such groups, excellent performers did not want to stay in a staff role.

The new movement to transform staff functions into intrepreneurial profit centers is an attempt to revitalize them. The objectives are threefold:

- To reduce overhead costs by recouping part or all of their operating costs from fees charged for services to outside companies, as well as internal divisions
- To make such functions more responsive to internal and external customers by forcing them to compete for business
- To upgrade the image of these functions by making them highly competitive "professional service groups" that can attract and retain high performers

But Where Do the People Go?—"Let's Start Our Own Business"

As we have seen, *Workplace 2000* will result in the elimination of whole layers of managerial and support functions. Additionally, entire segments of some companies will be eliminated as companies identify and refocus on their core business. While good jobs will remain in big corporations for multiskilled people who want operational responsibility, traditional middle-manager and support roles will disappear. What, then, will happen to the people who once filled these positions? And in the newer and flatter organization where there is little opportunity for promotion, how does an enterprising employee advance? The answer to both of these questions is the same as it has been for the last decade. The real job growth and opportunities for rapid advancement will be found in three types of small, entrepreneurial companies.

The "Micro-Business"

In *Workplace 2000*, we will see the continued growth of truly entrepreneurial "micro-businesses"—those started up with less than four employees. Many of these will be started by executives or middle managers of large companies who are forced out as a result of cutbacks or downsizing. Being unable or unwilling to relocate to another large company, these displaced executives and managers will create their own small businesses using their own money or money borrowed from friends or relatives. These executives and managers will be following the same path chosen by an estimated one out of six middle managers and executives who lost their jobs due to corporate downsizing and restructuring during the late 1980s.[5]

Another source of micro-business start-ups will be from employees in large companies who have not been hit by downsizing and restructuring, but who no longer feel their jobs are secure. Rather than wait for the next wave of displacement to reach them, many of these employees will decide to start their own business. Some will resign from big business and devote themselves to turning an idea or hobby into a business of their own. Others, less willing to forego a regular paycheck, will continue to work full time or part time for a large company while they start a separate business on the side. Initially, the separate business may be only a way to supplement their income or to provide a fall-back position should they lose their regular job. Eventually, if the "after five" business is successful, they may may resign to devote full time to their start-up business.[6]

The "Venture-Backed" Start-Up

A second type of small business start-up will have the advantage of venture backing from a larger company. Such arrangements increased dramatically in the 1980s (from only 32 in 1980 to 477 in 1987) and are likely to become even more popular in the 1990s. Typical of such an arrangement is the funding provided by Compaq Computers to a start-up in 1986. In this case, Compaq Computer Corporation was looking for a supplier of advanced disk drives for a new line of portable computers. Finis Conner, who had co-founded Seagate Technology, had a idea for developing a new disk drive that would be light, reliable, and provide high performance. But Conner needed venture capital to fund the development. Compaq stepped in to provide Conner with $12 million in start-up funding in return for 49 percent of the stock in the new company—Conner Peripherals, Inc. As a result of the deal, Compaq got a jump on its competition by having reliable access to an advanced drive, which it later offered in all of its machines. Conner got the start-up funding he needed and an instant customer for his drives. Other companies that have engaged in such strategic partnerships with start-up ventures include such giants as IBM, 3M, Corning Glass, and Digital Equipment. Often, the advantage of such an arrangement for the start-up company goes far beyond just a source of funding and a ready customer. Because of the relationship, the investing "partner" company will often work closely with the smaller start-up company in product design, manufacture, and testing. In short, the start-up company receives not only funding, but valuable advice to help it avoid pitfalls. John Squires, executive vice president of research and development for Conner Peripherals, said of the Conner Peripherals/Compaq arrangement: "Usually, you just keep walking down a road until you fall into a ditch. . . . The Compaq people told us where the ditches were and helped us avoid them. It wasn't just a matter of building a good drive, but of building one that would work in the real world for a real customer."[7]

The "Intrepreneurial" Venture

Finally, some small entrepreneurial companies will be started as "intrepreneurial" ventures within large corporations. In the 1980s, a number of major corporations created special units or provided special funding to encourage employees with innovative ideas to start their own businesses. For example, in the late 1980s, Colgate-Palmolive Company created Colgate Venture Company, a small, entrepreneurial "oasis" where people with a flair for risk-taking could pursue the development of specialized, innovative, and nontraditional products as various as a deodorizing pad for cat litter boxes and a cleaning solution for teenagers' retainers. General Foods Corporation has a similar group called Culinova Group that was experimenting with the development and marketing of refrigerated take-out food. S. C. Johnson & Sons, Inc., makers of Johnson Wax and Raid, took a different route. Rather than setting up a separate entrepreneurial (or intrepreneurial) unit, it created a $250,000 seed fund available to any employee with a good idea.[8]

Working in the Small Company Environment

As a result of the restructuring of large corporations into small entrepreneurial business units and the continued growth of new start-up companies with or without the assistance of major corporations, most Americans will find themselves working in a small company environment by the year 2000. For those Americans who have always worked in a small company, the day-to-day environment of *Workplace 2000* will just be a continuation of the intense pressure for performance they already experience. For Americans accustomed to working in a traditional large American corporation, the change to *Workplace 2000* will be dramatic. Here is what to expect.

Less Job Security

Throughout history, small companies have been notorious for offering poor job security. The conventional wisdom has held that four out of five new companies fail in the first five years. That may not be totally true. In 1988, Bruce Kirchoff, a professor at Babson College, and Bruce Phillips, an economist with the Small Business Administration's Office of Advocacy, examined a large SBA data base derived from Dun & Bradstreet's marketing data base of 8.5 million companies. They found that 39.8 percent of new companies survive six years (that is, only six out of ten fail). That finding is slightly more encouraging than conventional wisdom, but not much. The odds of working for a small company doomed to failure are still pretty high. Many small start-up companies will fail in the 1990s just as they have always failed. Entrepreneurial business units within restructured large corporations will likely have a better chance of success simply because of the support they will receive from the parent corporation, but they too will be insecure. Large corporations will look for these businesses to create value by providing a return exceeding the cost of capital invested in them. If a business unit isn't creating value, then the parent corporation will move quickly to sell or otherwise dispose of the business unit. In the high-pressure environment of the 1990s, no part of a large corporation will be allowed to "devalue" the other parts of the business for very long. This pressure to compete will likely jeopardize long-term projects that don't offer the prospect of an early return on investment. Long-term research projects within companies will most likely be abandoned altogether or sharply reduced. Instead of pursuing such projects internally and absorbing their high cost, large corporations will look to consortiums (alliances with other large companies and the U.S. government), partnerships with universities, joint ventures with suppliers and customers, and collaborative international efforts to meet long-term development needs.

Pressure for Performance Will Be Intense

Given the tenuous nature of most small start-up businesses and the insistence that each large corporate entrepreneurial business unit create value, the pressure on employees for performance will be much higher than it was in traditional large organizations. The reason is simple. In a small business, there is just very little room for failure and fewer people to carry those who aren't pulling their own weight. This pressure for performance will be typical of *Workplace 2000* companies whether they are small start-up companies or business units within a large corporation. Charles Lazarus, founder of Toys "Я" Us, makes each Toys "Я" Us store the key business unit within his company. Here's what he says about expectations he holds for store managers: "We want our store managers to take the business home in their stomach. We want them to think that their store is the only store in the world."[9] In *Workplace 2000*, many people will be taking the business "home in their stomach." And it won't just be store managers.

In a *Wall Street Journal* article Peter Drucker pointed out that the new American business will be disciplined with strong leadership much like an orchestra with a first-rate conductor. And, says Drucker, "first rate orchestra conductors are without exception unspeakably demanding perfectionists. What makes a first rate conductor is, however, the ability to make even the most junior instruments at the last desk way back play as if the performance of the whole depended on how each one of those instruments renders its small supporting part."[10] In *Workplace 2000*, even the "smallest supporting player" will be expected to contribute to the success of the business in a major way.

Everyone Will Be Expected to Be "Part of the Team"

"BUY IN, JOIN UP, OR LEAVE—YOU DON'T JUST "WORK HERE" ANYMORE"—that's probably the kind of slogan that will be posted in *Workplace 2000*. A central thrust of management will be to create excitement about the future of the company and about belonging to the company. This will go far beyond pep talks and motivational speeches. Every employee's compensation will be very closely tied to performance, not just those at the very top of the company. Consequently, there will be heightened peer pressure for everyone to contribute and be "part of the team." Performance evaluations will be more rigorous. Problem performance will be dealt with more swiftly and directly. There will be a greater focus on training and developing flexible people—those who truly understand the company's needs and are capable of playing a multitude of roles to help the company meet its needs. Specialists and special assistants will be rare. Those that exist will be shared. Ad hoc task forces will be put together to solve tough problems. A key way employees will find to increase their value to the company will be through service on these task forces. By serving, they will gain greater knowledge of the company and demonstrate their ability to work effectively in a team effort to find innovative solutions to problems.

Even social gatherings in *Workplace 2000* will take on special meanings. Here's how journalist Robert Howard, author of *Brave New Workplace*, described the kind of company-sponsored social occasion we will see more of in the future:

> [E]ven the archetypal beer bust . . . is not some trivial social occasion (or, as one manager says, "not just everyone sitting around drinking beer"). It is a ritual of corporate loyalty and belonging. . . . The purpose of such rituals, says our manager, "is to have everyone know where things are going, from the top level people all the way to little Suzy down there stuffing the printed circuit board. She gets information on what the product is for. She has an idea of the whole board."
>
> It is a striking image. Suzy may be "down there" on the assembly line. Nevertheless, she gets some of the same information as the people at the top. She is able to transcend the concrete limits of her particular job and become linked to the purpose of the corporation as a whole. Through this broad-based structure of motivation, she is "locked in mentally" to the future of the company. It is a kind of parallel production process whose purpose is to manufacture not products, but attitudes and expectations.[11]

In a *Harvard Business Review* article, two other writers, David Kirp and Douglas Rice, describe the expectations of these new hard-driving companies this way: "What these 'work hard, play hard' companies want is nothing less than total responsibility and over-the-edge loyalty. . . . Employees are constantly on view and the line between work and play, the line between public and private becomes fuzzy."[12]

The Positive Side—I Belong

The migration of the American workplace from large company to small company environment is, in one sense, frightening. *Workplace 2000* will undoubtedly place greater demands on workers for performance. Additionally, the new American workplace is likely to demand a much stronger commitment and dedication to the organization than most companies (particularly large companies) have asked from their employees in the past. Yet there are many positive aspects to *Workplace 2000*, just as there are for working for a small company.

In 1987, *Inc.* magazine and the Hay Group of Philadelphia surveyed 2,800 workers in sample companies with 10 to 500 employees and asked them what they liked about working for a small company. The findings from these surveys reflect many of the advantages of working for a small company environment most Americans will experience in *Workplace 2000*. In the *Inc.* survey, workers in small companies were more satisfied with their companies and their jobs than workers in larger companies. Why? Because they felt they had more challenging and interesting work, had a better chance to see their ideas adopted, and felt a higher sense of accomplishment than they would in a larger company. Additionally, when comparing their company to American business as a whole, employees of small companies felt that their company was more concerned about quality and did a better job of listening to customers. Interestingly, the smaller the company, the more likely employees were to perceive these benefits.

Beyond a sense of personal satisfaction and pride in contribution, a number of authors have noted something else about hard-driving, small companies. Often, these companies have a certain "spirit" that is frequently missing in larger organizations. Perhaps Robert Howard expressed this "feeling" of working in this new environment best. He said in such businesses, the organization is not perceived as "an impersonal bureaucracy, but as a caring community; the workplace as a realm of self-fulfillment; business enterprise as the fundamental source of identity in modern society. . . . They promise a world where traditional dissatisfactions dissolve in an atmosphere of unity and good feeling, where conflict and division are abolished, and where the ambivalences of modern industrial life disappear."[13] In short, rather than being disconnected from the enterprise—the "I just work here" syndrome of the traditional large corporation—employees in *Workplace 2000* will feel (and will be expected to feel) that they are an integral part of the organization. Joining a *Workplace 2000* company will be more than contracting for a "fair day's work." Rather, it will be more like joining a "family" or "team" with all of the consequent benefits, responsibilities, and obligations.

Surviving in Workplace 2000

As we enter the 1990s, the transition to *Workplace 2000* is well underway. Throughout the next ten years, most companies will complete this transition. In order to succeed in this new workplace, American workers need to start now to prepare. What should they do? Here are some of the critical steps Americans should take.

Ensure That They Work in a "Value-Added" Piece of the Business

Earlier we noted that certain types of jobs are "endangered species" and will likely be eliminated in *Workplace 2000*. Now is the time for every American to begin examining his or her own job and the value it brings to the company. If the job doesn't generate revenues (directly or indirectly), or if it is a corporate staff function or any staff function that is primarily advisory, it is endangered. The same is true for jobs in non-core segments of a business. Here it is critical that every American know how his or her company defines its core business. Is the company market/customer driven or product/service driven? What are the markets/customers? What are the core products/services? Americans who want to stay with a company long-term should seek value-added jobs firmly within the confines of the company's primary mission.

Every American Worker Should Become "Flexible"

As American companies restructure into small business units, and small companies grow, employees in greatest demand will be those who are "flexible" and can perform a wide variety of jobs. Small companies can afford few specialists. Everyone in a small company must be willing and able to do everything, or at least a wide variety of things.

Americans Who Are Locked into a Specialty Because of Professional Training or Personal Preference Should Plan to Go into Consulting or Professional Services

In *Workplace 2000*, companies will still need professional services (such as legal, public relations, and personnel), but they will contract for those services on the outside rather than maintain internal staff specialists. As a result, internal staff support groups, departments, or divisions will be eliminated. At the same time, there will be a growing need for outside speciality firms to provide services on a contract basis that can no longer be provided internally. Specialists who are very good in their profession will find increased opportunities to create or join highly successful professional service firms.

Americans Should Avoid Jobs That Involve Routine Decision Making

Rapid developments in artificial intelligence throughout the 1990s will make it unnecessary for companies to employ managers, supervisors, or professionals to make routine decisions. Any decision that can be made by following some predefined set of rules (if this, then that) will be automated in the near future. Such jobs will be eliminated just as manual, repetitive jobs were replaced by automation in the 1980s.

The Most Successful Employees in *Workplace 2000* Will Be Those Who Can Identify a New Business Opportunity

Throughout the 1990s, companies will be looking for new business opportunities. Many companies will provide financial backing for innovative employees who are willing to take a risk and develop an idea for a new product or service. Where will these ideas come from? Where they have always come from—work and professional experience in an industry. Those Americans with the greatest chance of developing an idea that can turn into a growth business will be those who, because of their flexibility, get wide exposure to a particular business or industry. Such exposure will greatly increase the chance that they will identify an emerging trend or a market niche that can be filled with a start-up business. Additionally, their experience and wide exposure will increase their chances of developing a relationship with both potential customers and financial backers for the new enterprise. In a sense, the flattening of businesses in *Workplace 2000* is a two-edged sword. On one side, the elimination of layers of management drastically reduces opportunities for promotion. On the other hand, the expansion of small businesses and the creation of entrepreneurial business units within large organizations greatly expands opportunities for enterprising Americans to run a business. In the past, there was only one CEO in a large company and most employees could never expect to rise to that rank. In the *Workplace 2000* large corporation, there will be fifty, one hundred, or more CEOs each leading an autonomous, small business unit.

All Americans Should Expect (and Prepare for) Periods of Unemployment

With *Workplace 2000*, the days of job stability are at an end. No more will an American worker expect to join a company and stay with that company until retirement. Most Americans will experience repeated job changes throughout their careers and perhaps months of unemployment as they move from one failed large company business unit or small company to a new business with, hopefully, a better chance for success. Since every American can expect periods of unemployment, having four to six months of salary readily available in cash or assets that can be quickly converted to cash will be critical.

To Avoid Unpleasant Surprises, All Americans Will Need to Keep a Close Watch on the Financial Performance of the Small Company or Business Unit That Employs Them

Because as many as four out of every six small businesses or business units of major corporations may fail within any five- to six-year period, Americans will need to pay attention to the performance of the company that employs them to avoid being caught unprepared should the business fail. What are the warning signs? Obviously, new start-ups or new business units that are not moving toward profitability in a few years are in danger of failing. Also, businesses that start small (five or fewer employees) and don't grow should be a matter of concern even if they are profitable. Only 26 percent of such businesses survive six years or more. In contrast, over 77 percent of such companies make it if they add ten or more employees in the first six years. Adding just one employee during the first six years more than doubles a company's chances of survival (26 percent to 65 percent).[14]

All Americans Should Expect to Work Harder and Longer Hours, Particularly if They Want to Play a Leadership Role in the New Smaller Business Units or Start-Up Companies

Small companies have always demanded a lot from every employee, but particularly from those at the top. *Workplace 2000* companies will be equally, if not more, demanding of their leadership. For top managers and those aspiring to be top managers in *Workplace 2000*, sixty-hour weeks (and perhaps even seventy-, eighty-, or ninety-hour weeks) will not be uncommon.

Finding the Right "Fit" with a Company
Will Be Critical

In *Workplace 2000*, employees won't just work for a company, they will be expected to "join the team" and "become a part of the family." Additionally, as we have seen, the line between work and play, public and private life will become fuzzy. Employees who are able to find the right match between their personal values, beliefs, aspirations, and lifestyle and that of the *Workplace 2000* company that employs them will enjoy the experience. For them, the mixing of work and play won't be an invasion of privacy but a natural extension into private life of a relationship with people who have common beliefs and goals that just happened to begin in the work setting.

American Workers Shouldn't Assume That They
Are "Lucky" if Their Company Is Slow in Making
the Transition to *Workplace 2000*

The new American workplace is emerging because it has to emerge. To remain competitive, the leaders of most American companies recognize that fundamental changes are required. In the next ten years, these leaders will shepherd their companies through the changes we have described in this chapter. Still, some companies will resist these changes. These few will desperately cling to traditional structures and culture. They will try to operate like companies of the 1950s, '60s, and '70s. For a time they may even succeed. But not for long. Before the decade of the 1990s is out, they too will change or . . . *they will fail*.

CHAPTER 3

Future Information Sharing

In *Workplace 2000*, the newest and lowest-level employee will be expected to know more about the company that employs him or her than many middle managers and most supervisors knew about the company they worked for in the 1970s and 1980s. If we visited a *Workplace 2000* company and approached any employee at random, here are just a few examples of the types of questions our randomly selected employee would be able to answer:

1. What makes your company unique? How does it differentiate itself from its competitors?
2. Who are your company's major competitors?
3. What are your company's strengths and weaknesses versus its major competitors?
4. How do your company's costs for producing goods and services compare to those of your company's major competitors?
5. How is your company performing in respect to sales and profits?
6. Who are your company's major or target customers?

What types of needs or expectations do these customers have that your company is trying to satisfy? How satisfied are these customers with your company's performance in meeting their needs or expectations?

7. What is your company's business strategy? What are the key objectives for your company over the next one to five years?

8. What is the role of your work group in helping your company to implement its business strategy?

9. What are the key goals/objectives for your work group over the next one to five years? How do these goals/objectives support your company's business strategy?

10. What are the key measures of performance for your work group?

11. What is the current performance of your work group on these key measures?

12. What projects does your work group have underway to improve performance on these measures?

In the traditional American company, few, if any, lower-level employees would have been able to answer these questions. In fact, most were not allowed to know the answers to such questions. Traditionally, key information about the business—particularly information related to competitive strategy and financial performance—was considered confidential. It was only shared with those few who had a "need to know." In *Workplace 2000*, every employee will have a need to know this type of information. In fact, every employee will not only have a need to know, but will be expected to know the answers to questions such as those we listed as a condition of employment. This change in American business from secrecy to openness in respect to information has important ramifications for American workers. Not only will Americans be expected to know more about the company that employs them—its problems, successes, and objectives for the future—than ever before but, more importantly, American workers will be called upon to act on that knowledge to continually improve their own performance, the performance of their work group, and the performance of the company as a whole.

The Importance of Information in the New Organization

The increased information sharing we are predicting for *Workplace 2000* is the result of a consensus that emerged in the late 1980s that the danger of sharing information with employees was minimal compared to the advantage of having an informed work force. Traditionally, most information about company performance was kept from employees for fear they might improperly disclose the information to a competitor. In reality, such fears were unfounded. There was very little evidence to suggest that employees and line supervisors were any more likely to leak sensitive information to a competitor than were executive vice presidents. Companies who had always been open with information (companies such as Tandem Computers and Herman Miller to name two) had not experienced any damage as a result of employee leaks. Besides, a determined competitor could probably ferret out even the best-kept secrets. Consequently, there was just very little reason to keep secrets.

If there was little reason to keep secrets, there was considerable reason for sharing information. When employees had access to the same information as their managers, they were much more likely to understand decisions about needed workplace changes and to work cooperatively to implement these changes. Too often in the past, relationships between managers and employees had become adversarial when information was withheld from employees. Distrust and suspicion grew as employees misunderstood and misinterpreted management's actions. Take, for example, a decision by management in a manufacturing company to shift from long production runs to short runs and frequent changeovers—a decision many manufacturing companies made in the 1980s. For managers with access to information about the cost of maintaining excess inventory and expectations of customers for shorter lead times and greater flexibility, the need for such a change was obvious. Shorter runs would result in less inventory and also allow the company to be more responsive to changing customer demands. In the typical American company of the 1980s, managers would make a rational decision to make such a change and announce it to employees. In some cases, managers might explain in general why such a change was necessary. Few, however, would provide employees with any detailed information supporting their decisions. Inevitably, employees would resist the change. For them, the change would make no sense. Traditionally in manufacturing, long runs were easier, more efficient, and resulted in less waste. Short runs just placed a greater burden on employees. Without access to the information that supported the need for change, employees saw the change as just further evidence of managers acting irrationally with little regard for how such decisions impacted workers. Such misunderstanding and miscommunication created significant problems for labor/management relations, particularly during the 1980s when most American companies were having to make major changes to adjust to new market conditions. Gradually, American managers began to recognize that labor/management relations could be greatly improved if managers shared information with employees and explained the rationale for their decisions. When management shared such information, employees could understand the need to change. While neither managers nor employees might like the change, at least they shared a common understanding of why it was occurring. With access to the same information, managers and employees were more likely to operate as partners than adversaries.

A second, and more important, advantage of sharing information that most American business leaders recognized was that providing information to employees could be highly motivating. The more employees knew about their own and their work group's performance, the better they performed. Numerous studies had been conducted throughout the 1970s and 1980s on the effects of providing employees with information about their performance. The results of these studies were consistent. Feedback (data-based information provided to employees about performance) almost always resulted in performance improvement. And the amount of improvement was usually substantial. For example, a *National Productivity Review* survey of twenty-seven such studies on the use of objective feedback reported performance improvements of 6 percent to 125 percent, with half of the studies reporting improvements of 53 percent or better. Feedback had several effects, all of which led to improved performance.

1. Feedback corrected misconceptions employees had about their performance. In the absence of feedback, employees often assumed they were performing well when they weren't. A study conducted in 1976 illustrated an early example of how feedback can correct misconceptions. Telephone reservation clerks were provided with feedback on their verbal behaviors obtained from unobtrusive monitoring of their telephone calls. Many of the clerks were surprised to find that they were failing to follow procedures the company had defined and trained them to use in handling customer calls. For example, after reviewing the results on her calls, one clerk said: "When asked previously whether I used the customer's name I would have said—and believed—'Of course, we were trained to do that.' I was really surprised when I saw objective evidence on how little I was actually doing it."

2. Feedback created internal consequences for employees. It became obvious from a number of research studies that employees enjoyed keeping score. They wanted to know how they were doing. When provided with feedback—particularly if they had received little feedback previously—employees almost inevitably improved their performance. For example, when cash management clerks at a major U.S. bank were provided feedback on the average level of cash balances, they responded by improving cash flow by 72 percent. A supervisor explained the clerks' response to the feedback as follows: "The areas are completely aware of cash flow now (as a result of the feedback); everyone gives 100 percent to the program. There seems to be that extra effort on the part of people to get more involved in cash flows. . . . People are now trying to solve problems before they occur. People are looking to help out other individuals rather than saying 'that's not my job.' I can say as a supervisor that it [the feedback] has a big impact on my own feelings toward the people who work for me. I feel a sense of accomplishment."[1]

3. Feedback also had positive social consequences. Numerous studies conducted during the 1970s and 1980s found that management/employee relations improved when managers and supervisors were provided with feedback on performance. Interestingly, the feedback did not have to be positive for improvement to occur. The fact was that employees—even high performers—wanted information about their performance and responded positively when it was provided. In the absence of feedback, their feelings about the relationship was much more likely to be negative. In his book *How to Motivate People*, our friend and business associate Fran Tarkenton, the former NFL star quarterback and Football Hall of Fame member, tells the following story about his days playing for the Minnesota Vikings and his own need for feedback on his performance. The year was 1974 and Fran had just returned to the Vikings team after a stint with the New York Giants. Here is how he described what happened:

> With an 0–3 record behind us, we were facing the St. Louis Cardinals out in Bloomington, and getting nowhere. I knew we had to pull out a surprise play to save the game, and there is nothing more likely to surprise a defense than a play where the quarterback blocks.
>
> The play in question was a reverse where I handed off to Ed Marinaro. Ed handed off to John Gilliam, and I took out a tackler who was trying to get to John. The way I took him out was a little unconventional: I fell down on the ground in front of him, and he tumbled over me. But what the hell, it worked. John went in for the touchdown, and we won the game.
>
> The next day, watching the films, I was all hyped up for Coach Bud Grant's readout. When it came around to "my" play—the one where I had sacrificed my body for the team— I was all ready to sit back and bask in the glory. It never came. Bud praised everybody involved in the play: Marinaro, Gilliam, the entire line, but not me. After the meeting, I asked him why. "You saw my block didn't you, coach? How come you didn't say anything about it?"
>
> . . . [Bud said] "Yeah, I saw the block . . . It was great. But you're always working hard out there, Francis, you're al-

ways giving 100 percent. I figured I didn't have to tell you."

"Well," I told him, "if you want me to block again you do."

4. *The process of measuring performance and providing feedback to people created a heightened sense of concern on the part of employees for performing well on whatever area of performance was being measured.* Employees recognized that measurement required effort and that if management was willing to devote the time and effort to measuring an area of performance, then performance on what was measured must be important. The implications of measurement to employees was that performance on something being measured would be rewarded if good and punished if bad. As a result, "what got measured, got done."

5. *Finally, the research on feedback suggested that it had a positive impact on performance because it was instructional.* Feedback provided direction (insight into what needed to be done) and confirmation (information about current performance and any required changes). In his excellent work, *Human Competence*, Thomas F. Gilbert equates feedback on performance to a road sign. "Suppose," he says, "that you are driving a car, in a hurry to get to Mountainville, and you see a road sign for it.... This sign does two things simultaneously: It gives direction; it also confirms that you are on course and are making good time and need not speed up." Like the road sign, says Gilbert, feedback tells employees what to do next, or it confirms that they have been acting correctly, or it does both.

The motivational impact of feedback, and the importance of information sharing to improve employee understanding of management's rationale for undertaking major changes, presented two good reasons for *Workplace 2000* companies to be more open with information about company performance. There was also another reason for sharing information. Throughout the 1980s, American managers gradually began to accept the idea that significant improvements in quality, customer service, cost reduction, and more would not be possible without employee involvement. The problems facing

American business could not be solved by managers alone. We needed employee ideas. Not only were employees closer to the problems—after all, they experienced them day in and day out—but often employees had the best ideas. In addition, when employees participated in the problem-solving process, they were much more willing to implement solutions to the problems. However, employees could not participate in a meaningful way in problem-solving efforts without access to information about company performance. Providing employees access to such information meant changing the flow of information in organizations. Traditionally, data had been collected and aggregated to provide middle- and upper-level managers with data for control and appraisal. Such information was used occasionally for rewards, but most frequently for punishment. The flow of information was from the bottom to the middle or top. Information about such areas as cost, quality, and customer satisfaction was rarely shared with workers and even when it was shared wasn't specific enough for workers to use it to identify, prevent, and solve problems in their own work areas. That flow of information had to change if employees were to become involved in the problem-solving process. Instead of just aggregating up, companies would have to push information down to the work group level. Priority would have to be placed on getting information into the hands of those who could use it most efficiently to change performance results—the workers themselves.

Changes in Employee Communication and Performance Appraisals

By the end of the 1980s, there was widespread agreement among American business leaders that American companies had to do a better job of communicating with employees and providing them with feedback on performance. However, the question of how to accomplish that remained. Ultimately, the answer involved significant changes in measurement systems and the linkage of measures throughout the organization. Later in this chapter, we will describe how measurement systems changed and what they will look like in *Workplace 2000*.

Before doing so, we need to describe changes in two very traditional vehicles for communication and performance feedback—employee publications (such as newsletters and company magazines) and performance appraisals.

Traditionally in most U.S. companies, employees received general information about their company through company newsletters or company magazines or by reading notices posted on bulletin boards. For specific feedback on their performance, employees (and their bosses) were forced to endure annual performance appraisals. Neither of these vehicles were very effective. Consequently, both will change drastically in *Workplace 2000*.

Changes to Expect in Employee Communications

In *Workplace 2000*, we will see a shift in the content of company newsletters, magazines, and material posted on employee bulletin boards. In the past, these publications and posted notices have dealt only superficially with company performance. Instead of serving as a vehicle for communicating with employees, these publications have more often resembled family scrapbooks or hometown newspapers. Most have been filled with announcements of promotions, bowling team scores, recipes, social news (who had a birthday or who just got married), and, occasionally, suggestions for how to work safer on the job. No more. In *Workplace 2000*, we will see these publications redesigned to focus on providing employees with information they can use to gauge their own and the company's performance. Instead of birthday lists and pictures of the company's softball team (or perhaps more precisely, in addition to such items), we will see items such as the following:

- Articles discussing national and local business trends and how the state of the economy may impact company performance
- Charts and tables analyzing company performance in critical areas
- Reports on the status of incentive programs (payouts or

expected payouts under profit sharing, gain sharing, and other group incentive programs)

- Articles discussing employee benefits and changes in these benefits (such as life insurance and health insurance)
- Reports on company profits and sales year-to-date compared to previous years and the company's business plan, stock performance, and so on
- Information or news on the company's products and services with particular attention given to information that will help employees to serve customers better
- Information about new products or services soon to be announced by the company to the general public
- Information regarding ongoing research and development efforts and plans for new product development
- Educational articles aimed at improving employee skills in areas such as quality improvement, customer service, problem solving, teamwork, and communication

Changes We Will See in Performance Appraisals

As practiced in most American companies in the 1980s, performance appraisals were once-a-year paperwork exercises dreaded by employees and managers alike. Under the typical appraisal system, employees were evaluated on traits such as "dependability," "punctuality," and "loyalty," not on their accomplishments. There was, at the most, only a vague connection between the appraisal content and the work results that were needed by the company to be successful. By the late 1980s, a number of companies such as AT&T, Cyanamid, Ford, GTE, Honeywell, Kodak, 3M, Westinghouse, and Xerox were totally revising their approach to employee performance appraisal. The changes adopted by these companies suggest the approach that will be adopted by most *Workplace 2000* companies. Here is what we are likely to see:

1. Personality trait ratings will be replaced with more objective measures of performance focusing on job-related outcomes and behaviors. Instead of a rating form, most companies will use nothing more than a blank sheet of

paper on which employees and their bosses list specific objectives to be accomplished during the appraisal period. These objectives will encompass areas including learning and development goals (such as training the employee will participate in, skills to be developed and used); teamwork goals (such as personal contributions the employee agrees to make to help his or her team improve feedback; communication or problem solving such as participating on a problem-solving task force; taking on leadership responsibility in meetings); and plans for personal contribution to team goals such as quality improvement, cost reduction, or improvements in customer service. Each of these goals will relate to personal accomplishments consistent with the goals of the employee's team or work group.

2. Appraisals will be changed from once-a-year events to ongoing processes with short formal reviews every quarter or six months. Formal reviews will focus on a discussion of progress in meeting personal goals and plans for the next appraisal period.

3. Employee development (setting specific goals for training and education) will become an important part of the appraisal process. Each employee can expect to have one or more objectives for improving an existing skill or developing a new skill of value to the work group.

4. In many *Workplace 2000* companies, employees will receive appraisals from their peers. Peer review—which may involve feedback in a group session—will be used either as the sole method of appraisal or as an adjunct to an appraisal from a manager or supervisor.

5. *Workplace 2000* companies will change the process from a paperwork exercise into an ongoing communication system where there could be no once-a-year surprises.

6. With fewer opportunities for promotion and significant changes in compensation systems (as we describe in Chapter 5), appraisals will have a less direct connection with raises or promotions. The performance-appraisal process will focus more on increasing an employee's value to the team and personal satisfaction with his or her current job.

The Development of *Workplace 2000* Measurement Systems

Changes in employee publications and revisions to performance appraisal systems will move American companies toward *Workplace 2000* information sharing. But by themselves, they are inadequate. Real employee partnership, involvement in problem solving, and motivation won't come from what employees read in newsletters or on bulletin boards or from change in appraisal systems. Real change will occur because measurement systems will change. As strange as it might seem, the two most significant factors that will lead to *Workplace 2000* team measurement systems are the development of "new math" cost accounting and the development of measurement systems for white-collar workers.

"New Math" Cost Accounting

In the 1980s, many American companies provided each of their managers with a monthly report comparing the actual costs in his or her plant, division, and so on to planned or standard costs. The manager was required to review this "cost accounting" report and explain any unfavorable variances (that is, items where actual costs exceeded planned or standard costs). In many businesses, so much emphasis was placed on this monthly cost accounting report that managers were said to "live and die by their ability to manage variances." The problems with cost accounting reports were that they frequently encouraged the wrong kind of behavior and they were often misleading.

In the late 1980s, executives in most U.S. companies agreed that American business had to change the way it operated in order to compete. No longer could a manufacturer, for example, hope to be successful by competing on cost alone. To be competitive, American manufacturers had to cut inventories in order to reduce inventory carrying cost; shorten lead times for product development so they could bring new and enhanced products to market faster; improve product quality to meet world-class standards; lower total operating costs (not just the production costs of individual units); shorten manufacturing throughput time; cut delivery time (order to shipment) in order to meet customer demands for fast turnaround; and develop the flexibility to produce exactly what the customer wanted when he or she wanted it. The problem with cost accounting systems was that they focused attention on managing costs while ignoring needs for flexibility, quality, and responsiveness.

A second problem with traditional cost accounting systems was that they misled managers about the true cost of products and services. Under most cost accounting systems, overhead costs (for such non-production activities as design, engineering, marketing, distribution, and administration, etc.) were allocated on the basis of direct labor hours. As a result, products with higher direct labor costs were allocated proportionately more of the overhead cost. The problem was that direct labor as a percentage of total costs declined throughout the 1980s and the assumed relationship between direct labor and overhead costs was no longer valid. As a result, overhead allocations distorted the true cost of products, making some products seem more (or less) profitable than they actually were.

Responding to the problems with traditional cost accounting systems, a nonprofit consortium of industrial organizations called Computer Aided Manufacturing-International (CAM-I) assembled a group composed of CAM-I members, representatives of professional accounting firms, and representatives of government agencies in 1988 to discuss new approaches to cost accounting. The result of CAM-I's efforts was a "new math" approach to cost management.[2] It differed from traditional cost accounting in several ways.

1. The new approach attempts to account for non-value-added costs separate from value-added costs. Under traditional cost accounting systems, the cost of certain activities that could be eliminated without adversely affecting the performance, function, quality, or perceived value of a product or service ("non-value-added costs") were included in standard costs as an assumed cost of doing business. As a result, it was often difficult or impossible to isolate these costs and hold managers and employees responsible for reducing them. Under the new math cost accounting system, all non-value-added costs (or at least the most significant) will be accounted for and reported. In a manufacturing environment, non-value-added costs are those associated with product movement, inspection (other than during processing), storage, and so on. The only value-added costs are those associated with actually producing the product. Under the new cost accounting, *Workplace 2000* teams will have access to information about non-value-added costs and will be held responsible for monitoring, controlling, and eliminating to the extent possible these costs in addition to reducing value-added costs.

2. *Under the new approach, overhead costs are tied directly to products or services and costs are reported for specific business activities.* Traditional cost reports in most U.S. businesses broke down costs according to financial statement lines (cost of goods sold, sales expense, sales); expense category (salaries, supplies, utilities); department; or product. Rarely, if ever, were costs reported by major activity, and without such activity level reporting, it was difficult, if not impossible, to identify and track value-added as opposed to non-value-added costs. Compounding the problem, traditional accounting systems allocated overhead costs (all non-value-added) based upon direct labor costs. As we noted previously, throughout the 1980s direct labor costs declined as a percentage of total costs, and the assumed relationship between direct labor and overhead costs was no longer valid. New math accounting supports the tracking of value-added versus non-value-added costs by reporting costs according to specific activities (or at least the most significant activities) and by tying overhead costs directly to each product or service. With activity accounting and the direct assignment of overhead costs, data will be available not just at the product or service level but broken down so that the benefits of activities can be weighed against their costs. *Workplace 2000* measurement systems will thus track costs at a level of detail and accuracy not possible before.

The focus of new math accounting is to tie cost systems more closely to company strategies by identifying and reporting value-added and non-value-added costs to the level of specific activities. Cost data under the accounting systems we are likely to see in *Workplace 2000* will break data down to the point that not only individual business units but also small work-group teams can be held responsible for their contribution to corporate cost containment goals. Additionally, new math accounting explicitly supports the development and utilization of nonfinancial as well as financial measures as a basis for business decisions. In respect to the latter, the ability to create a "family of measures" at the work-group level that are linked back to a company's business strategy will be critical. Companies will have that ability in *Workplace 2000* largely as a result of successful efforts in developing white-collar/ "knowledge worker" measures during the 1980s.

White-Collar Measurement

By the early 1980s, there was growing concern for finding ways to improve the productivity of white-collar employees—executives and managers; professionals; and sales, administrative, and support personnel. Such employees constituted over 50 percent of the U.S. work force by the mid-1980s and were increasing in number. By some estimates, white-collar workers would represent nearly 90 percent of the U.S. work force by 1990. Given the preponderance of white-collar workers and expectations concerning growth in white-collar and service jobs, the lack of improvement in white-collar productivity was a major concern. In the mid-1980s, labor productivity in the white-collar sector was hardly growing at all. In fact, in some industries such as insurance and finance, labor productivity was actually declining from year to year. A key factor that most authorities assumed was inhibiting productivity growth in the white-collar sector was the lack of measurement. As a result, a number of surveys and research projects were undertaken during the 1980s to find ways to measure the performance of white-collar workers, particularly professional, technical, managerial, sales, and service workers—the so called knowledge workers.

Up until the late 1980s, American business had little success in measuring the performance of white-collar "knowledge workers." Early attempts to apply measurement techniques that had worked for blue-collar manufacturing jobs had not been successful, primarily because they depended upon counting some identifiable unit of production. In white-collar "knowledge worker" jobs, there were either no countable units of production or those that could be identified, such as lines of code for programmers, were meaningless. Measuring and increasing the number of lines of code from a programmer, or engineering drawings from an engineer didn't necessarily increase the value of what the programmer or engineer was producing for the company. After a number of failed attempts at using traditional measurement techniques (which were usually met with bitter resistance from the white-collar workers being measured), a number of U.S. companies began to look for totally new ways of developing measurement systems. These experiments in white-collar measurement, particularly those conducted by the American Productivity and Quality Center, led to new approaches to measurement that will be applied throughout companies (not just in white-collar areas) in *Workplace 2000*. The primary differences between these new approaches to measurement and traditional approaches to measurement are summarized in Table 3-1.

Traditionally in manufacturing, one or two "efficiency" measures were developed by managers or outside "measurement experts" for the purpose of monitoring and controlling the performance of individual employees. Typical of these measures were labor efficiency measures and production quotas set for individual operators based upon, in some cases, highly sophisticated "engineered" time studies. Attempts at applying these traditional measurement techniques in white-collar areas, particularly with "knowledge workers," failed for several reasons. First, white-collar professionals resisted being measured by outsiders or management, particularly if the purpose of measurement was to monitor or control the professionals' work performance. Such resistance to measurement wasn't new. Blue-collar workers had resisted measurement also. What was new was the ability of white-collar professionals to make their resistance stick. Many of these profes-

Table 3-1

New Measurement Versus Traditional Measurement Systems

	Traditional	New
Basis of measurement	Activity or behavior	Results or accomplishment
Number of measures	One or two	Five to ten
Focus of measurement	Efficiency	Effectiveness
Development of measures	By management; internal staff specialist; or outside consultant	By employees within work group
Level of Measurement	Individual	Work group or team
Purpose of measurement	Control	Monitor and provide feedback; reinforcement; support problem solving

NOTE: For a more complete explanation of the American Productivity & Quality Center approach and other approaches, see American Productivity Center, White-Collar Productivity: The National Challenge, APQC, Houston, Texas, 1982; U.S. Department of Labor, Bureau of Labor-Management Relations and Cooperative Programs, Participative Approaches to White-Collar Productivity Improvement, BLMR 116, 1987; American Productivity & Quality Center, White Collar Productivity Improvement: Results of the American Productivity & Quality Center's Two-Year Action Research Project, APQC, Houston, Texas, 1986; and American Productivity and Quality Center, Measuring White Collar Work, APQC, Houston, Texas, August, 1988. For an explanation of an alternative approach, see Joseph H. Boyett and Henry P. Conn, "Developing White-Collar Performance Measures," *National Productivity Review*, Summer 1988, pp. 209–219, and Ford Motor Company, Total Quality Excellence, Casting Division, Goals and Measurements.)

sionals were highly paid, mobile (could easily relocate with a competitor), and could not be easily replaced. It was one thing to tell a machine operator he or she had no choice about being measured. It was something else to tell that to a highly prized research scientist, engineer, or computer programmer. Eventually, it became clear that no measures could be developed and implemented for white-collar professionals unless they were involved in designing their own measures. Involvement increased their commitment to and acceptance of measures and legitimized the measures.

A second problem with applying traditional approaches of measurement to white-collar "knowledge workers" was that it was difficult, if not impossible, to measure the performance of these professionals at the individual employee level. In manufacturing, measurement usually started at the level of individual employees. Individual scores were then aggregated to derive shift, department, division, and plant totals. Such individual measurement was possible because a single employee often performed a discrete operation, produced a countable product, or completed an identifiable phase in the manufacturing process, relatively independently of other workers. There was something of value to the company that could be counted and tied back to an individual operator. Such was not the case in the work performed by white-collar professionals. They worked in teams and were much more dependent on their co-workers for support and assistance. Individual white-collar professionals, in most cases, did not produce something of value to the company by themselves. Results valuable to the company came from group or team efforts. Consequently, white-collar measures had to be developed at the team rather than the individual level if the measures were to be meaningful, and considerable effort had to be devoted to defining just what "results" of the team effort were valuable. In manufacturing, key results of work behavior were assumed—a product produced to certain quality standards at certain costs. Desired "results" of white-collar professional groups were less clear. In many cases, the mission statement and written objectives for such white-collar groups were vague—"provide a high level of consistent and professional support for . . ." It became clear that meaningful measures for these white-collar groups could not be developed until fundamental questions about the results desired from these groups and their role in supporting the company's business strategy could be answered. Thus, the new white-collar measurement methodologies all incorporated an extensive analysis designed to clarify the role of the work group and the key results it should be obtaining. Usually, this analysis involved having the work group members identify their "customers"— both internal and external—and assess their customers' expectations.

A final problem with applying traditional measurement techniques to white-collar professional groups was that traditional measurement focused primarily on efficiency. Yet, when white-collar groups undertook the kind of analysis of their role and customer expectations as described above, it became quite clear that efficiency was less important than effectiveness—that is, quality, timeliness, customer satisfaction, cost. White-collar work was complex and had a variety of dimensions, all of which had to be met for the results of the activities to be of value to the company. For example, projects completed on time but with poor quality (acceptance to users) and excessive cost were not successful projects. Effective measurement of white-collar performance would require more than just measurement of efficiency. What was needed was a balance between timeliness, cost, quality, and perhaps a number of other factors. Since no single measure or even a couple of measures could capture all of these factors, white-collar workers would require a variety of measures or "family of indicators" as the American Productivity and Quality Center called them. Each measure in the "family" would tell part of the story, but not the whole story. Rather, scores on a balanced range of measures (perhaps as many as five or ten) taken together would reveal success or failure.

Workplace 2000 Measurement

Workplace 2000 measurement systems will differ considerably from the measurement systems most U.S. companies had in the 1980s. Traditionally in American businesses, measurement has been used to monitor and control employee behavior. Rarely has it been used to provide employees with feedback on performance, to reinforce good performance, or as a tool for helping employees to solve problems. That will change in *Workplace 2000*. Measurement will become the primary vehicle for communicating business strategy to employees, for triggering recognition of good performance, and for supporting employee problem-solving efforts. In *Workplace 2000*, every employee will be part of a work group or team that will have a "family of measures"—five to ten key measures of performance that the team is responsible for monitoring, controlling, and improving. Not only will employee teams have measures, but the measures of each team will be "linked" to measures of a higher-level team. Level by level, team measures will be linked back to the company's overall business strategies. In *Workplace 2000*, measures will be revised annually in conjunction with the revision of a company's strategic plan. Key measures will be set for the company as a whole so that progress on implementing the business strategy can be monitored. Once these top-level measures are set, each subsequent level of the organization will develop new measures or revise existing measures consistent with the company-wide measures and business strategy. The actual process of revision will be a group or team effort and involve everyone. The result? Every team, by working to maximize performance on its measures, will be simultaneously working to implement the company's business strategies.

Obviously, the specific measures that work group teams will monitor on a regular basis will vary from team to team and company to company. However, several types of measures will likely be found within the "family of measures" of most teams.

1. Quality measures. In *Workplace 2000*, most U.S. companies will focus on quality as a key competitive strategy. That quality emphasis will be reflected in the measures tracked at the team level. We are likely to see two types of quality measures—internal and external. Internal measures of quality will include measures of scrap, rework, rejects, and waste. Most companies will also calculate, and teams will monitor, their "cost of quality," or perhaps more precisely, the "cost of nonconformance" as an internal quality measure. "Cost of quality" is defined by John Groocock in *The Chain of Quality* as the sum of appraisal costs (inspection and testing) + failure costs (rework, scrap, and warranty costs) +

prevention (all those costs required to reduce appraisal and failure costs. In the past, such costs were difficult to track with any degree of accuracy because they were frequently buried in overhead costs. With new accounting systems that provide activity-level accounting and no longer allocate overhead, these overhead costs will be easier to identify. External measures of quality will focus on customer satisfaction with the delivered product or service as reflected in customer surveys, customer complaints, and returned items. Then the "internal" measures will be "calibrated" to ensure they are making the "external" measures improve.

2. *Financial measures*. These will be particularly those related to unit costs and contribution to profitability. Many of the changes in cost accounting we discussed earlier will make it possible for companies to track costs with a level of accuracy and precision not previously attainable.

3. *Timeliness measures*. In addition to cost and quality data, most teams will also monitor one or more measures of timeliness—on-time delivery, schedule compliance, cycle or throughput time, waiting time.

4. *Productivity/efficiency*. Finally, many work groups will monitor productivity or efficiency measures. These will include traditional input/output ratios such as labor hours per physical unit of production or materials usage per physical unit of production. In white-collar and service organizations, we are likely to see utilization measures rather than traditional productivity measures. Utilization measures resources used compared to resources available or planned. For example, in data processing a utilization measure might be the ratio of staff hours on maintenance of old programs versus total hours available in the department. Other utilization measures may look at physical resources such as equipment that represents a large capital investment. For example, service teams that use a fleet of vehicles may monitor vehicle utilization. Teams that have substantial capital tied up in computers or telecommunications networks may monitor computer usage or network usage. A related type of utilization measure many teams will use is downtime.

Regardless of the specific measures a *Workplace 2000* team may have, the important point is that the team will monitor a balanced "family of measures" on a regular basis that it has developed, and those measures will be linked back to the overall company business strategies. The following description of the measurement development process and results of that process for an advertising department of a large U.S. direct marketing firm illustrates how measures for work group teams will be developed in *Workplace 2000* companies and how they will be linked to overall company strategy.[3] In this case a measurement development team composed of the department manager, supervisors, and four representative employees developed the department's measures. The first activity of the team was to review the corporate mission and key objectives, and the department's mission. They were as follows:

Company mission: To achieve aggressive earnings growth as a diversified direct marketer of consumer products by becoming legendary for customer service and for offering unique and meaningful products to meet a wide variety of market segments.

Company's key objectives:

1. Increase operating profit
2. Increase inventory turns
3. Increase net sales
4. Increase customer list size
5. Increase average order size (in dollars)
6. Decrease distribution or promotional costs per order

Advertising department mission: Design and produce customer catalogues, brochures, package inserts, and other direct mail and media advertising materials to support corporate strategies for earnings growth and consumer satisfaction.

The next step of the measurement development team was to identify the department's key internal and external customers. Examples of external customers were current or potential corporate customers who would use the department's catalogs and brochures to make purchasing decisions and place orders and outside vendors who were relied upon for printing and distributing the catalogs. Internal customers were corporate management, marketing, and order processors.

After interviewing internal customers and surveying external customers, the measurement development team then identified "key result areas" for the department. One key result area was quality. Customers placing orders and employees processing orders required accurate and informative product descriptions, price quotes, and ordering information. Outside vendors required error-free production copy and artwork to minimize unnecessary revisions. Upper management wanted accurate and creative advertising copy and layout to improve customer satisfaction, increase net sales, and increase average order size.

A second key result area identified by the measurement team was "timeliness." Marketing needed compliance with production and distribution schedules so that it could implement its plans for seasonal product offerings and promotions. Customers needed to receive catalogs in sufficient time to take advantage of these offers.

Finally, the measurement team determined that cost containment in a number of specific areas was critical to meet management's objective of reducing distribution and promotional costs per order and improving operating profit.

Based upon its analysis, the department measurement team then developed seven measures that became the "family of measures" for the department.

1. *Average order size (in dollars)*. This measure corresponded exactly to a stated corporate goal. While the advertising department did not have total control over this measure, it could impact order size by creative use of advertising copy and the placement of items within the catalog.
2. *Response rate*. This was a standard direct mail advertising measure the department had used for some time that was considered to be a useful indicator of quality and customer satisfaction.
3. *Unit costs for brochures, catalogs, and other direct mail pieces*. The measurement team selected this measure

because it related directly to the corporate goal of decreasing cost per order.

4. *Cost as a percentage of sales.* Another cost-reduction measure that the measurement team felt the department could improve by enhancing the impact of advertising on the customer, thus increasing the likelihood of an order, and by reducing internal creative and production costs.

5. *Revision costs.* Revision costs were those caused by alterations to copy and artwork during production. Revision costs impacted both unit cost and cost as a percentage of sales. The measurement team decided that revision costs could be reduced through better proofing of copy, better preparation of artwork, and improved communication with vendors.

6. *Customer order error rate.* The measurement group felt the department could reduce the chances of customers making errors in filling out order forms by improving the design of the order form and making instructions simple and easy to follow.

7. *Percentage of due dates met.* Due dates tracked by this measure were dates for direct mail drops in accordance with the marketing schedule. This group did not control the schedule but was responsible for meeting it. Performance on this measure was considered critical, since some catalog items were seasonal and catalog sales had to be coordinated with other advertising efforts.

It is important to note that several things about the measures and the measurement development process followed by the advertising department are different from what we saw in the 1980s. First, the measures were developed by a team composed of managers, supervisors, and employees from the department. They were not dictated by management or developed by outside consultants. Second, the measures all reflect the company's overall business strategy and key objectives. Top-level strategy was set first, then the measurement team developed department-level measures consistent with company strategy. The measurement development process proceeded from the top down. Third, in developing measures, the measurement team first identified the department's customers, both internal and external to the company, and developed measures to meet the needs of these customers. The measures were very much customer-driven. Finally, in addition to traditional cost and timeliness measures, the team included measures that reflected the impact the department's activities had on company-wide measures such as average order size and customer order error rate. These latter two measures, in particular, were only partially controllable by the department, but were included in the group's family of measures since the department could impact performance on these measures to some degree. Obviously, these two measures were shared with several other departments.

My Goals, Your Goals—The Legacy of Goal Setting

In *Workplace 2000*, each work group will have a family of measures similar to those used by the advertising department. Each family of measures will be developed by managers and employees in the work group and will be consistent with company strategy and customer needs. Associated with each measure will be three goals—a long-term goal (dictated by world competition); a short-term goal; and a minimum or standard for performance. The short-term goal and minimum or standard will prescribe a range within which performance might be expected to vary from day to day, week to week, or month to month as a result of random fluctuation in performance or imprecision in measurement. The short-term goal will represent a cut-off point that will trigger reinforcement or recognition for performance improvement. The minimum or standard will represent a similar cut-off or "trigger point" that will signal the need for problem solving or action planning. The setting of multiple goals for each measure of performance that will be characteristic of *Workplace 2000* is a response to an inconsistency between corporate needs for continuous improvement and world-class performance versus the need to establish goals that will be motivational and "makable."

In *Workplace 2000*, every company will need world-class

performance and continuous improvement to be successful. Quality cannot be just 10 percent, 20 percent, or 50 percent better than last year. It has to be perfect or closer to perfect than any competitor can achieve. In our opening chapter, we said that American managers learned in the 1980s that their expectations for performance were too low. The Japanese and others had expectations for performance far beyond those of American managers. That had to change, and it will change in *Workplace 2000.* Perhaps the best illustration of the change in philosophy concerning acceptable levels of goals for company performance is the change in philosophy we are likely to see concerning how product and service unit cost goals are established.

In the traditional American company in the 1980s, "standard costs" were established for product and service lines. These standard costs were usually based upon historical experience in producing or providing the same or a similar product or service, with perhaps small incremental decreases they became the "cost goals" American managers were expected to meet. Rather than using standard costs, *Workplace 2000* companies will use a "target cost" determined by the marketplace. To establish the target cost, management will determine the sales price necessary for a product or service that is most likely to help the company achieve a desired market share and profit margin. Once the desired sales price is determined, a desired amount will be deducted from the sales price for profit. The remainder will be the target cost for that product or service. Managers, designers, engineers, and employees will then be held responsible for finding a way to develop and produce the product or service to meet or beat the target cost.[4] Cost goals in *Workplace 2000* will be determined by market demands, not by what was achieved by a company in the past. The same will be true of quality, customer service, delivery, flexibility, responsiveness, and other goals. Since the goals will be market- and customer-driven, they are likely to be much more demanding than traditional goals that were established with reference to a company's historical performance. Managers and employees will be asked to attain levels of performance previously considered impossible. Whereas in the past a 2 percent defect rate may have been considered acceptable, in *Workplace 2000* the only acceptable long-range goal will likely be "zero defects." In the past, a 10 percent year-to-year reduction in unit costs might have been admirable, but in *Workplace 2000* we may be looking for cost reductions of 50 percent or more to retain market share against a foreign competitor. The problem with these "stretch" market-driven goals is that they are inconsistent with research conducted from the late 1960s throughout the '70s and '80s on the effect of goal setting on management and employee performance.

Goal-setting theory in the United States is traceable to work by Edwin Locke as first reported in 1968.[5] Locke's theory was that goal setting in organizations had an important influence on employee motivation. The research of Locke and others demonstrated that specific and difficult goals led to higher employee performance—provided the goals were accepted by those who had to attain them. The degree of employees' acceptance of goals was a function of their level of participation in setting goals and the extent to which they perceived that the final goals were attainable. These findings present some difficulties for the kind of goals needed in *Workplace 2000*. There is no doubt that *Workplace 2000* goals will be challenging. It is extremely difficult for any organization to attain and sustain world-class performance. However, goals in *Workplace 2000* will be dictated by competitive requirements and corporate strategy. Employees and even managers will have little control over the level of ultimate goals. Market conditions and customer demands will dictate performance requirements. How, then, can *Workplace 2000* provide an opportunity for employee participation in goal setting and ensure that goals will be seen as attainable? The answer is to have more than one goal. Long-term, the goal required for quality, customer service, and flexibility, will be dictated by the company's strategy. Once the strategy is set and the competition is identified, it will be necessary to identify the best in the world to develop a target or long-term goal. In the short term, however, an intermediate target can be set and employees can be involved in setting the short-term goal. It will be better than current performance, but not necessarily as challenging as the long-term goal of world-class performance. Not only will setting a short-term goal be consistent with goal setting theory (by providing for participation in establishing a goal that would be seen as challenging but attainable), but a short-term goal will be consistent with other research on motivation, in particular, research in behavior modification on the importance of "shaping" as a tool for teaching employees new behavior. (In a later chapter, we will discuss research on behavior modification in more detail, since the results of that research in the 1970s and 1980s will have a profound impact on the use of praise and punishment in the *Workplace 2000* organization.) For now, we will only note that the fundamental principle of behavior modification is that employee behavior is strongly influenced by the consequences of that behavior. Behavior that is reinforced is more likely to reoccur. The relationship of reinforcement to goal setting in the workplace is that the motivational impact of goals comes from *employees'* anticipation that they will be reinforced for attaining a goal. (In fact, there is evidence that goal attainment itself is reinforcing since it enhances a person's sense of accomplishment and self-worth.) The problem of goal setting is that if the goal is too difficult employees won't try to attain the goal (and therefore the reinforcement) or they will become frustrated with trying to attain the goal (and resulting reinforcement) and stop trying. Shaping provides a way to reinforce approximations of the final desired behavior or result of behavior. In other words, the motivational impact of a difficult long-term goal can be retained if employees are reinforced for successive improvements toward the long-term goal. A short-term goal provides a trigger point for such intermediate reinforcement. Also, consistent with research on the application of shaping, the short-term goal can be made gradually more difficult over time, thus establishing a pattern of continuous improvement toward the long-term goal, which itself will probably become more difficult over time.

With the short-term goal, *Workplace 2000* companies will have a trigger point to signal the need for reinforcement and a method for shaping employee behavior toward the long-term goal of world-class performance. The third of the multiple goals for each measure in *Workplace 2000* will be the minimum or standard, which will be a trigger point for problem solving. Since practically every company in *Workplace 2000* will be looking for continuous improvement in performance, the minimum or standard of performance will most likely be set at or close to the current level of performance. The reason for this is that any deterioration in performance will represent a significant problem. As the short-term goal is adjusted to bring it closer to the long-term goal, we can expect to see similar upward adjustments in the minimum or standard. Also, we can expect the difference between the minimum or standard and short-term goal to narrow. In effect, the range of performance between the minimum and short-term goal will represent the range of fluctuation in scores on a measure that might be expected due to random variation.

The concept of random variation in data is a carryover from statistical techniques used in quality control (like statistical quality control, or SQC) by most manufacturing companies in the 1980s. The idea behind SQC was that no matter how well a product was designed or manufactured, a certain amount of variation would occur in the characteristics of individual units of the final product that were produced. A certain amount of this variation was inevitable and due to random causes that could never be defined. Other variation resulted from specific causes that could be defined and eliminated. The trick in improving quality was to distinguish between variation due to random causes and that due to specific or assignable causes. The central question was: When was a variation in a product characteristic so extreme that there was little likelihood it could have resulted from chance? To answer that question, most manufacturing companies in the United States started using something called statistical process control charts. Actual control charts weren't new. They were first suggested by W. A. Shewhart, a statistician at Bell Laboratories, in 1931.[6] Shewhart demonstrated how manufacturing managers could collect data on the characteristics of a product being produced over time and from this data calculate upper and lower limits of variation on these characteristics. Once these limits were established, charts could be maintained to monitor the characteristics of new units of the product. Any variation in the product characteristics that fell within the preestablished "control limits" could be considered to have occurred by chance. No action was required. In fact, management would be wasting time looking for a cause of the variation. However, if the variation was outside the preestablished "control limits," it was very likely that something had changed, a specific cause or specific causes of the change could be identified, and the cause of the variation could be corrected. Control charts and statistical quality control generally became popular during World War II and peaked in the late 1940s. Interest in control charts waned in the 1950s as American manufacturers became more concerned about production to meet postwar consumer demand than about quality. Control charts were then rediscovered in the late 1970s as Americans began to recognize they had a quality problem. In fact, control charts became the centerpiece of many companies' quality-improvement effort and actually were misused in the mid and late 1980s. Experience in establishing control limits for product characteristics in manufacturing to detect actionable changes in product quality will carry over to general practices for measurement and goal setting in *Workplace 2000*. The short-term goals and minimum/standards established for measures in *Workplace 2000* will be treated much like control limits. Their purpose will be to trigger action—reinforcement in the case of attaining the short-term goal, or corrective action when performance drops below the minimum or standard. American experience with statistical quality control will also influence how *Workplace 2000* employees receive feedback on their performance.

Feedback, Feedback, Feedback—The Legacy of Behavioralism

The primary reason *Workplace 2000* companies will invest the time and energy in developing measures of performance and setting goals will be to provide employees with feedback on performance in order to motivate them to improve their performance. At the beginning of this chapter, we said that feedback was motivational because it corrected misconceptions employees might have about their performance; provided employees with important internal and social consequences; and was instructional. The power of feedback to motivate improved performance is well established. In fact, knowledge of the impact of feedback on human behavior in organizations can be traced back to the 1960s and in the field of psychology generally all the way back to the 1930s. As a result of the long history of research and application of feedback, much is known about how it can be used most effectively. *Workplace 2000* will make maximum use of that accumulated knowledge. Consequently, we can describe with some confidence the type of feedback systems most *Workplace 2000* companies will use.

First, feedback systems in *Workplace 2000* will be highly visual. There will be little doubt that feedback is being provided. Large, colorful graphs and charts will adorn the walls of most offices and factories of the workplace of the future. Three types of graphs will dominate the workplace: baseline graphs, trend graphs, and statistical control charts (the legacy from statistical quality control). Examples of these charts are shown in Figures 3.1, 3.2, and 3.3. Many of these *Workplace 2000* graphs will use color to highlight critical states—for example, red to show a problem, orange or yellow as a warning, green to indicate goal attainment or improvement. (See Figure 3.4.)

A second characteristic of *Workplace 2000* feedback will be its frequency. Every effort will be made to provide employees with immediate feedback. In the 1980s, most employees got very little feedback, either on their own or their team's performance. In *Workplace 2000*, feedback will be monthly, weekly, daily, and in some cases hourly or even instantaneously. It will be as frequent as data can be made available. And with the increased use of technology in *Workplace 2000*, the time delay between performance and the availability of data to provide feedback on performance will be continually shortened. For example, managers, supervisors, and employees in many highly automated factories can already access data on this day's, this hour's, or even this minute's performance for the plant as a whole, individual product lines, or individual pieces of equipment as a result of monitoring of performance by computers. We will see more of this type of automated and instantaneous feedback in *Workplace 2000*. And it will not

Figure 3.1
BASELINE GRAPH
% On-Time Delivery

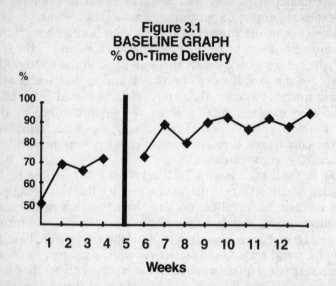

Baseline graphs provide information on performance before and after an "intervention." An intervention is any change in method, processes, procedures, or technology. The point or date of the intervention is represented on the graph by a solid vertical line. A baseline graph actually consists of two graphs placed side by side. To the left of the intervention line is a graph of performance prior to the intervention, or change. The results after the change are shown to the right of the intervention line. Baseline graphs may also contain horizontal lines extending to the left and right of the intervention line, representing performance before the change and goal or desired performance after the change.

be limited to manufacturing. As more white-collar employees use computer terminals to perform their work, instantaneous feedback on performance will become commonplace. It is already in existence in a number of white-collar jobs. For example, airline reservation computers measure and continually update such information as how long reservation agents take to handle calls, how many calls are handled, how long calls take, how much idle time occurs between calls, and even the time an agent takes for a break or lunch. Optical scanners in retail stores not only ring up sales but also keep track of sales and the number of items handled.

Finally, feedback systems in *Workplace 2000* will compare current performance to goals and will emphasize trends in

Figure 3.2
TREND GRAPH
% On-Time Delivery

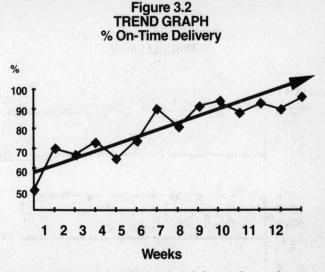

Trend graphs show actual performance and the trend in performance over time. They provide a visual representation of how performance is changing over time. Trends may be calculated in a variety of ways (moving average, linear/straight line, seasonal variation, etc.). Methods of calculating trends and plotting trend lines are available in most basic texts on statistics.

performance over time. All companies in *Workplace 2000* will seek continuous improvement against goals that have been established. Part of the attractiveness of graphs and charts (such as the baseline graphs, trend graphs, and control charts mentioned earlier) is that they provide an easy and informative way to show current performance compared to both the goal and past performance. Instantaneous feedback via computer terminals will also emphasize graphic depictions of performance over time and against goals. The message will be "here is where you were before, here is where you are now, and here is how far you have to go."

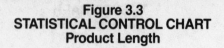

Figure 3.3
STATISTICAL CONTROL CHART
Product Length

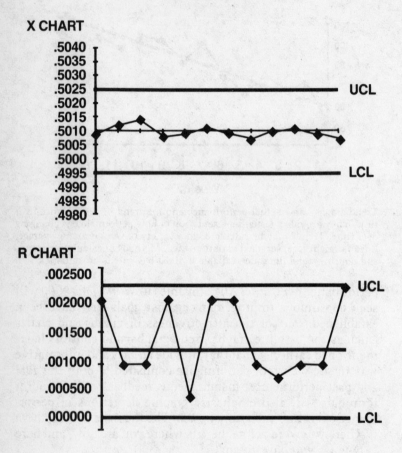

Statistical control charts provide employees with visual feedback on changes in product characteristics over time and were a key tool used in statistical process control in the 1980s. (See Chapter 10 for a more complete discussion of statistical process control.) There are actually two types of control charts—the X̄ Chart and R Chart. The X̄ Chart provides a visual record of the average (mean) of a product measure (in the case of the above chart, length of product) of periodic samples of the product taken through the day (for example in this case, every hour). The R Chart shows the range for each sample (highest value minus lowest value). Upper control limits (UCL) and lower control limits (LCL) displayed on both the X̄ and R Charts show the amount of variation in product characteristic (in this case, length) that could be expected to occur by chance. If a measure for any sample falls outside the allowed control limits on either the X̄ Chart or R Chart, the operator must stop production and identify and correct the cause of the variation. As long as the measures for each sample stay within the control limits, the process is considered to be "in control" (only random variation is occurring) and production can continue.

Figure 3.4
USE OF COLOR
Variation in Product Characteristics

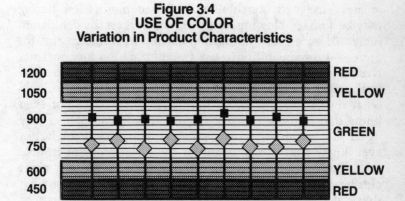

Color is sometimes used on charts to provide a visual signal to an employee concerning action that should be taken. In the above example, the employee takes measurements on two consecutive units produced at various times throughout the day and plots the resulting scores on the chart. If on any two consecutive units the employee gets two greens or one green and one yellow, the production can continue. If he or she gets two yellows or one red, production must be stopped until the problem is identified and corrected.

The Positives and Negatives of Information Sharing

In the workplace of the future, the average American worker will know more about his own, his work group's, and his company's performance than ever before. And he will be expected to use that information to improve performance and to help his company attain its strategic goals. From the American worker's viewpoint, the new openness of information sharing will have both positive and negative consequences. On the positive side, whole groups of Americans will no longer live in limbo not knowing whether what they do from day to day makes a difference. In *Workplace 2000*, the results of work efforts will be tracked, measured, graphed, and exposed for everyone to see. There will be no doubt about who (at least at the work group level) is contributing and who isn't. Also, the free exchange of information in organizations should lead to increased trust between employees and management and a greater sense of partnership. But increased information sharing may be a mixed blessing for American workers. By definition, increased access to information carries with it demands for increased responsibility to use the information for constructive purposes, along with increased accountability for results. In the past, many American workers could come to work, do what they were told to do, and leave. They might not even know that costs were up or quality was down because they never saw information on costs and quality. They might not even know that the company or their plant was in trouble until, suddenly, management announced layoffs or a plant closing. Workers had no responsibility for the results of what they did. The responsibility was management's. Management controlled the information and made decisions based upon that information. Managers were responsible for those decisions. The manager who failed to control costs or who let quality deteriorate was eventually replaced. Workers might also indirectly suffer the consequences of poor decisions by managers (layoffs, wage freezes), but workers weren't responsible for those decisions. They blamed management. No more. In *Workplace 2000*, increased information sharing will push responsibility for results lower in the organization. When things go awry, American workers will have no one to blame but themselves.

CHAPTER 4

Motivating Workers in *Workplace 2000*

Workplace 2000 will fundamentally and permanently alter the relationship between American managers and workers. The line of demarcation between manager and worker will blur. American labor and American management—traditional adversaries—will become partners. Managerial control will give way to employee self-control. Nearly a century of tradition that dictated the proper roles and relationship of labor and management will be abandoned as outdated and unworkable. In 1974, Peter Drucker, the noted business writer, signalled the end of traditional American management. He wrote, "The basic fact—unpalatable but inescapable—is that the traditional . . . approach to managing, that is, the carrot-and-stick way, no longer works. In developed countries, it does not work for manual workers, and nowhere can it work for knowledge workers. The stick is no longer available to the manager, and the carrot is today becoming less and less of an incentive."[1] It took American management over fifteen years finally to accept the truth of Drucker's words. *Workplace 2000* will operationalize that truth. Authoritative, directive, and controlling management is dead or dying. No longer will

American managers seek "reliable" performance from workers through forced obedience. Instead, *Workplace 2000* managers will seek to empower employees to achieve maximum performance. Every employee will be treated as a partner with all of the rights and responsibilities of partnership. Workers/partners will have personal responsibility for the quality of the products and services they produce. They will perform their own inspections, identify defects and causes of poor quality, and make adjustments that they deem necessary to correct quality problems they detect. Workers/partners will monitor their relations with customers and exercise initiative to respond immediately to customer needs, most of which they will anticipate in advance. Workers/partners will work cooperatively with others to identify existing and emerging customer needs and rapidly create products and services to meet these needs. Most importantly, workers/partners will be flexible—willing to take on any assignment or perform any task necessary to help their company succeed. Workers/partners will do what needs to be done when and where it needs to be done. They will adapt to and learn to love change. Workers/partners will willingly do all of these things because of the way they will be motivated and managed to align their personal needs and satisfaction with those of the company as a whole.

The American Management Tradition

The American management tradition was clean and simple. In 1979, William G. Scott and David K. Hart, authors of *Organizational America*, categorized three major groups within every American organization: a small group of "significant" people, a larger group of "professionals," and a much larger group of people who were, as far as the organization was concerned, individually "insignificant." "Significant" people in American organizations were the managerial elite—those at the top of the organizational pyramid or close to the top. "Professionals" were the technical and middle-management core—the sales managers, engineers, factory superintendents, cost accountants, scientists, computer programmers. Professionals had one purpose in common. They were responsible for maintaining the organization. They made sure that the organization ran in accordance with the desires and wishes of the significant managerial elite. At the bottom of the pyramid were the mass of "insignificant" workers. The insignificant operated the machines, waited on customers, packed boxes, assembled products, and provided services. They were insignificant not just because their jobs were generally boring and routine, but, more importantly, because individual occupants of these insignificant jobs were eminently interchangeable and replaceable. The jobs of "insignificant" people were designed to be that way.

The idea of designing jobs with the intent of making individual occupants of jobs insignificant can be traced to the early 1900s and the work of Frederick Taylor, Henry Gantt, Frank Gilbreth, and Lillian Gilbreth. While none of these advocates of what came to be called scientific management (and certainly none of the managers of American corporations implementing the principles of scientific management) would have used the term *insignificant* when referring to workers, the fact was that adoption of scientific management made the individual worker on a particular job insignificant. More importantly, the adoption of these practices made the individual worker feel insignificant. Therein lies the problem.

The premise behind scientifically designed jobs was that managers, with the help of professionals, could carefully and systematically analyze each task to be performed in the workplace and determine the quickest and best methods for performing the task. It would even be possible to calculate the precise time the average worker, or better, the ideal worker who would be precisely matched with the task to be performed, should take to perform the work. In the course of designing work, the tasks to be performed would be broken down to their most fundamental level. Workers could then focus on performing one or a few discrete, predefined, and carefully measured acts in the workplace. All associated functions required for designing and coordinating the efforts of the mass of workers would be performed by managers, supervisors, or specialists. Thus, the worker would have no responsibility or input into quality standards. These would be established by managers and engineers and monitored and enforced by inspectors. The same or different "bosses" would engineer work methods specifying the quickest motions each worker was to use in performing his or her prescribed task and then monitor workers as they performed their tasks to ensure that the prescribed methods were used. The set-up and care of machines; tracking of output; coordination of the flow of raw materials and finished products; and even discipline in performing the work would be externally imposed on workers. We now know that scientific management had a predictable result. For the average American, work became boring, depersonalized, monotonous, dehumanizing, and demotivating. Yet scientific management survived. It survived in America long past the point where incontrovertible evidence demonstrated that it was a failure. It survived through the '20s, '30s, '40s, '50s, '60s, and even into the '70s. As the years passed, it wasn't openly called scientific management by those who practiced it, since the term was rejected, but it still was scientific management, and American workers recognized it as such, rejected it, and rebelled against it. Sometimes the rejection and rebellion was expressed in a major way through strikes, work stoppages, and slowdowns. Mostly, however, the rebellion and resistance was more subtle. It was expressed by things being done half right or not at all. The price we paid as a nation for shoddy work and labor/management conflict was enormous. We should have known better, if not initially, certainly by the 1930s or '40s. And definitely we should have known better by the 1950s and '60s. The lessons were there starting in the late 1920s.

What We Should Have Learned From the Hawthorne Experiments

The national wholesale rejection of scientific management should have occurred as a result of a series of experiments conducted at the Hawthorne Works of Western Electric between 1924 and 1933.[2] The Hawthorne experiments began with the simple intention of assessing the impact of lighting on worker productivity. They ended by challenging many of the assumptions of scientific management and establishing that work had both social and psychological dimensions. The Hawthorne experiments actually occurred in four overlapping phases: the Illumination experiments conducted between 1924 and 1927; the Relay Assembly Test Room experiments conducted from 1927 to 1932; the Interviewing Program from 1928 to 1930; and the Bank Wiring Room experiments conducted from 1931 to 1932. Each phase yielded surprising and, at that time, confusing (even contradictory) results. Yet if the findings had been fully understood and applied, America might have reached *Workplace 2000* half a century earlier.

The Illumination Experiments (1924–1927)

The Illumination experiments were the original studies conducted at the Hawthorne Works and the only experiments originally planned. The remaining phases of experimentation at Hawthorne were initiated because of the strange findings from these initial experiments. As originally designed by Western Electric in conjunction with the National Research Council of the National Academy of Sciences, the study was an effort to determine what effect, if any, the level of lighting in a workplace had on employee output. Three illumination experiments were conducted with various groups of workers. Each experiment involved increasing or decreasing lighting and measuring worker productivity. The results of these experiments were, to say the least, puzzling to the researchers. Sometimes output went up when lighting was increased. Sometimes it went down. In some groups, output went up when lighting was first increased. Then, it went up again when lighting was decreased. Then it went up again when lighting was once again increased. Even stranger, the production of a control group (where the level of lighting had been held constant) increased. Initially, researchers attributed these strange results to inadequate control of the lighting levels in the various test groups. To remedy the problem, they set up two tightly controlled test groups under conditions where they could ensure that lighting levels were maintained at precise levels. In one group, they held the lighting level at exactly ten foot candles. In the other group, they gradually decreased the lighting level one foot candle at the time. The output of both groups increased! Something was obviously happening that went far beyond the effects of lighting.

Frustrated, the researchers decided to set up an experiment where they would vary the lighting level and ask the workers how they felt about the changes. The researchers increased the lighting level and asked the workers how they liked it. The workers said they liked the lighting better. Then the researchers just pretended to increase the lighting. The actual lighting level wasn't changed. How did the workers like it? They said they liked it better. Throughout these changes (and pretend changes), workers said the lighting was better and they could work better with the new lighting. But the workers' production hardly changed at all.

Relay Assembly Test Room (1927–1932)

It was obvious that the results of the Illumination experiments were confusing and contradictory. Obviously much more than changes in lighting was affecting worker productivity. By now, researchers suspected that their inability to totally isolate the various possible factors that might impact productivity plus the test subjects' *attitude* about the experiments and changes in their working conditions were affecting the results. Therefore, the researchers decided to conduct another experiment. This time, extraneous variables that might affect worker productivity would be tightly controlled. Also, test conditions and the selection of worker "test subjects" would be designed so that "employee attitudes would remain constant and unaffected." Thus began the Relay Assembly Test Room experiments.

Relay assembly was a highly repetitive, manual job. For purposes of the experiment, researchers constructed a small, isolated test room and staffed it with five experienced assemblers and one layout operator who would assign work and obtain parts. Initially, two assemblers who were good friends were chosen by the research team. These two then chose the remaining assemblers for the test group. Simple mechanical devices were placed in the test room to maintain an accurate record of output. To ensure that there was an accurate and complete record of what happened in the test room, an observer was stationed in the room throughout the experiment. In addition to monitoring the experiment, the observer was responsible for maintaining a friendly atmosphere and for performing some limited supervisory functions. Eventually, the Relay Assembly experiment lasted two and one half years during which a number of changes were made in working conditions. Most of these involved varying the length of the work day, varying the number and length of rest periods, and changing the level and type of supervision. As an additional measure to rule out any physical causes for changes in productivity, test subjects were given a physical examination prior to the study and at six-week intervals during the course of the experiment.

During the first few weeks of the Relay Assembly experiment, the productivity of the test subjects was measured under normal conditions as they worked in their regular departments to establish a baseline of performance against which future performance levels could be compared. After the base was established, the workers selected for the experiment were moved to the test room and given a period of five weeks to adjust to their new surroundings. An additional change made prior to the start of the experiment was the designation of the workers in the Relay Assembly Test Room as a separate incentive-pay work group. While the workers participating in the experiment had been on incentive pay before, the creation of a separate and smaller pay group meant that each person's earnings would be more directly affected by the total group's production.

The first change introduced by the researchers was the implementation of two five-minute rest periods or breaks each day. The researchers sought to determine if rest periods would reduce worker fatigue and therefore contribute to increased output across the day. Rather than simply announce the change, workers in the test group were called into the superintendent's office and consulted on when to schedule the rest periods. The workers voted to have the breaks at 10:00 A.M. and 2:00 P.M. Over the next five weeks with the two five-minute breaks in effect, production increased slightly. More importantly, the workers became more open and relaxed with their observers, freely discussing the benefits of the breaks and suggesting that longer breaks would be better, since they still got tired in the afternoon.

Since the five-minute breaks appeared to have had a positive effect on output, the researchers decided to extend the breaks to ten minutes each. Again, the workers were consulted and agreed to the change. When the longer breaks were implemented, the change was met with an enthusiastic response from both workers and observers. And output jumped dramatically.

Additionally, workers became even more open about expressing their approval or disapproval about proposed changes. For example, during this period workers objected strenuously to a proposal offered by researchers to change the timing of distributing bonus payments to make them more dramatic. The workers accused the researchers of trying to confuse them and possibly cheat them out of their bonuses. Consequently, the proposal was dropped.

After several weeks of operating with two ten-minute rest periods, researchers approached the workers about making another change. This time, the researchers wanted to go to six five-minute breaks instead of the two ten-minute. The workers objected but eventually agreed to the change, although they began to make critical remarks, engage in excessive laughing and talking, and return late from their more frequent, but shorter, breaks.

Eventually, after subsequent changes in rest periods, two of the original five workers became uncooperative and hostile and were transferred back to their original departments. Two new workers with similar performance records were brought in to replace them.

Approximately twenty-five weeks into the experiment, the researchers began changing the length of the work day. First, workers were given the choice of starting half an hour later or ending half an hour earlier. They chose stopping half an hour earlier. In spite of the shorter work day, total production increased and hourly production increased dramatically. Later, the work day was further shortened by an additional half hour; while hourly production increased, total production for the day dropped due to the drastically shortened work period.

Eventually, the researchers decided to return the workers to their standard working hours.

The researchers were surprised by the results. They had assumed that the increased production during previous periods had resulted from a reduction in worker fatigue due to the breaks and shorter working hours. Therefore, they weren't surprised when workers complained of being tired and when hourly production decreased slightly after the standard (and longer) work day was restored. They *were* surprised to find that weekly production reached an all-time high. In spite of a longer work day, employees were producing more than ever before. They didn't appear to feel the results of fatigue. But why? Perhaps, the researchers reasoned, the workers were in better physical condition due to the regular physical checkups and a heightened concern about their health. To test that theory and several others, the researchers developed and administered a questionnaire to the workers. The answers the workers gave were totally unexpected.

No, the workers said, the increased production didn't result from their improved physical condition or from work conditions in the test room. It came, they said, from the way they were managed and the way they felt about each other. They had "greater freedom," an "absence of bosses," "the opportunity to set their own pace," the test room was "friendlier," workers socialized more on and off the job, and people were more willing to help each other.

Throughout the remainder of the experiment, the test group's production varied according to worker reaction to various changes in working hours and breaks. When the workers were consulted and liked and agreed to the changes, output went up. When they didn't, output went down and/or the change was met with subtle resistance. At one point, toward the end of the experiment, workers were placed on a normal forty-eight-hour work week without breaks. They complained constantly of being tired and hungry, and they talked excessively. Also, production dropped. Eventually, the test room observer remarked to the workers that he felt they were restricting their output in order to get the breaks reinstated. Then he told them the breaks would be reinstated eventually, regardless of their output. Almost immediately, the complaints and excessive talking stopped. When the breaks were eventually provided, production exceeded all previous levels. During the last seven months of the experiment, morale reached a peak level, workers helped each other, and everyone seemed genuinely to try to beat all previous records of production. In fact, over the two and a half years of the experiment output, morale and attendance improved steadily.

The Interviewing Program (1928–1930)

Researchers attempted various explanations for the improvements in the Relay Assembly experiment. Perhaps the performance, morale, and other gains were the result of either the reduction in fatigue or the monotony of the work. Perhaps the change was a result of the informal relationship workers had with the test room supervisors or the change in incentive pay. None of the explanations appeared adequate. What seemed to have been most important was the way the workers reacted to the changes—their attitude. To find out more about employee attitudes, the researchers launched the next phase of their study, the Interview Program.

Hawthorne researchers began their interviews in 1928. Eventually, they interviewed twenty-one thousand employees. The results were in part predictable, in part astounding. The predictable part yielded numerous suggestions from employees for improving working conditions. The astounding part was what they learned about the social dynamics of the workplace and how it affected employee morale and productivity.

At first, interviews were highly structured. Employees were asked about their likes and dislikes, about general working conditions, and about their feelings toward supervisors. But, fortunately, interviewers had difficulty restricting employees to the confines of the standard interview questions. Employees would drift off into areas that seemed to have no relation to the purpose of the interview but seemed very important to them. Eventually, the interviewers just sat back, listened, and took notes. Later, these notes were converted as nearly as possible into verbatim accounts of each interview, which were then analyzed by a special team of researchers to identify and classify the employee complaints. The problem was that the special analysis often couldn't classify the complaints out of the context of the complete interview. In the interview, Joe would complain about working conditions in the shop—the smoke and fumes. But was it really the shop smoke and fumes Joe was concerned about? Later in the interview, his comments would turn to issues of health, disease, and how you never knew . . . Then he would begin to talk about his brother dying of pneumonia and how healthy his brother had looked, "but he still died." Another employee would talk about his boss, how much of a bully his boss was. Then gradually, he would start talking about his own father's domineering and overbearing nature. It soon became obvious that employee complaints, as revealed in the interviews, could not be understood in isolation from their personal experience. Employees didn't check their personal life at the plant door. They brought it with them together with all of their fears, emotions, concerns, and obsessions. The way they reacted to the workplace was strongly influenced by their own personal situation. And the workplace wasn't neutral. It created its own social order, which strongly affected each employee's morale and productivity. Work and working were much more complex than the scientific managers had imagined.

The social context of the workplace was particularly evident from interviews the Hawthorne researchers conducted with supervisors. The supervisors commented frequently about social rank and status. Often, the rank and status had little to do with the formal organization. Social status in the organization went far beyond formal distinctions such as position title and office amenities.

Rank and status were also affected by seniority, gender, and whether one's job carried social prestige with other workers. There were both formal and informal social relations on the job. And these relations affected how hard people worked and their general satisfaction with what they did. To learn more about these relationships, the Hawthorne researchers launched their fourth and final project—the Bank Wiring Room study.

Bank Wiring Room (1931–1932)

In the two previous experiments Hawthorne researchers had intervened in the workplace, making changes to the work environment in order to see what impact those changes had on productivity and employee morale. The Bank Wiring Room differed from the previous experiments in that there was no outside intervention. No changes in the work environment were imposed on the group. This time, the researchers intended just to make observations in the most unobtrusive way possible. The only change for the group of nine wiremen, three solderers, and two inspectors chosen as subjects of the study was that they would be isolated in a separate room. The group would carry out its normal function of wiring, assembling, and testing banks of equipment used in telephone central offices. For purposes of the experiment, a research observer would be stationed in the Bank Wiring Room at all times. His job would be to record production and make notes of the group's activities while staying uninvolved with what was happening. In addition, an interviewer would talk to the Bank Wiring Room employees off the job to collect information on their attitudes, thoughts, and feelings.

The Bank Wiring Room study lasted for six months and resulted in the following key findings:

1. It was obvious that the workers in the Bank Wiring Room restricted their output. In fact, the group had reached informal agreement on a range of output that was acceptable. Even at the upper ranges, the informally established "acceptable" level of production was less than the company standard and much less than the men were capable of producing. There was also a lower level of production the group tried to stay above. Over time, the group's production stayed well within the range of "acceptable" production and, in fact, was relatively level.

2. It became evident that the group restricted its output because of several widely accepted fears and assumptions. The general feeling was that if the group increased its output above a certain level, the company would raise the formal standard, lay off workers, or put increased pressure on low performers in the group. Therefore, the best thing for the group was to maintain output at what had been informally established as the "acceptable" level. To enforce this group consensus about how much should be produced, there were informal rules. If a worker produced too much, he was a "ratebuster." If he produced too little, he was a "chiseler." A person's position and acceptance by the group depended greatly upon his adherence to these group-imposed rules and standards. In fact, maintaining an "acceptable" level of production (not too high or low) was so important to the workers that they continuously monitored their own output in their heads. Some could even tell the time of day based upon how much they had produced so far that day—"If I have wired seven levels it must be ten o'clock," for example.

3. *The group had developed different relationships with different levels of supervision.* The Group Chief (first-level supervisor) was well liked by the workers and tolerated group behavior such as job trading, misreporting of output, and horseplay that went counter to company policy. Group relations with the Section Chief (second-level supervisor) were pretty much the same as with the Group Chief except that the group did not always obey him and frequently argued with him. Toward higher-level managers, workers were much more formal in their relations. They never argued and were restrained in their behavior when higher-level managers were around. To a large extent, the workers, Group Chief, and Section Chief acted together to keep much information about the group's behavior and production from higher-level managers. With all levels of supervision, there were informal group rules governing one's behavior. For example, any worker telling a supervisor something negative about a co-worker was a "squealer" and unacceptable to the group.

4. *Within the work group, there was an informal social hierarchy.* Inspectors had the highest status within the group while truckers (who serviced the group) had the lowest status. Wiremen and soldermen were in the middle. Inspectors' higher status was partially due to the fact that they were more highly educated than wiremen or soldermen and dressed differently. Inspectors wore coats and ties; wiremen and soldermen came to work in their shirtsleeves and sweaters. In spite

of the differences in status that were widely accepted by the group, individuals were not supposed to be distant or act important. For example, high-status inspectors weren't supposed to act superior even though they were considered superior.

5. *The group could be very forceful in enforcing its informal rules.* Workers who "got out of line" would be subject to sarcasm, ridicule, and even ostracism. The group even went so far as to get one "misbehaving" inspector transferred by sabotaging his equipment, setting him up to take the blame for a slowdown in production, and goading him into making rash statements about the group's behavior to management.

It is undeniable that the Hawthorne experiments represented (or, more precisely, could have represented) a watershed in American management. The scientific management that prevailed at the time and lasted long after the Hawthorne experiments were concluded assumed that workers were totally malleable, that their economic self-interest would ensure that they followed management's dictates. The Hawthorne experiments demonstrated that work and worker/manager relationships were more complicated than that. Work had a social and psychological element. The pay carrot and coercion stick weren't enough to ensure that workers did what managers wanted them to do. Hawthorne could have led us into a different type of labor/management relationship. For reasons we will discuss later, it didn't. What it did lead us into was research on the psychology of worker motivation, the findings of which were then, unfortunately, superimposed over the old scientific labor/management caste system.

The Psychology of Worker Motivation

Worker motivation theory and research, as it developed in the United States, focused on explaining employee behavior in the workplace. What caused, for example, the Relay Assembly Room and Bank Wiring Room employees in the Hawthorne study to behave the way they did? If the scientific manager could not just lay down rules and automatically expect them to be obeyed by employees, then perhaps he could get what he wanted (obedience) by understanding and manipulating the causes of employee behavior. But what really caused employee behavior? Two competing approaches to answering this question arose. One group of researchers (advocates of the cognitive approach) focused upon employee needs and how these needs were met or not met in the workplace. This approach suggested that the behavior we saw from employees was merely their rational effort to meet their needs. A second approach to employee motivation (the behavioral approach) focused not at all on employee internal states (or needs), but rather on the consequences of employee behavior. Behavior, advocates of this approach argued, was determined by its consequences. If management understood the consequences of behavior as perceived by the employee, then it could structure those consequences to produce the desired behavior. Advocates of both the cognitive and behavioral approaches could show evidence that they were right and that those who argued for the competing approach were wrong. As it turned out, both were probably right and wrong.

The key cognitive theorists were Abraham Maslow, C. P. Alderfer, Frederick Herzberg, David McClelland, and (with a slightly different focus) Victor Vroom. Maslow's theory was that all humans have needs and that they fall into a hierarchy of five categories: physiological, safety, love, esteem, and self-actualization. Physiological needs were those for food, liquid, sex, sleep. Safety needs referred to security and freedom from danger. Love needs were social—for affiliation and belongingness. Esteem needs involved the desire for prestige, recognition, to feel a sense of accomplishment or achievement. Finally, self-actualization needs involved the desire to realize one's full potential (to be all one could be). In Maslow's view, employees tried to satisfy these different needs in a strict order. First, physiological needs were important. Once they were satisfied, the employee turned to satisfying his or her safety needs and so on up the hierarchy. Each higher-level need became important only as the next-lower-level need was satisfied. Alderfer's contributions were to reduce the number of need categories from Maslow's five to only three (existence, relatedness, and growth needs) and to suggest that if a person is frustrated in his or her efforts to satisfy a higher-level need, he or she will "regress" and the next-lower-level need will once again become a motivating force. Both Maslow and Alderfer saw an orderly and predictable set of needs that employees tried to satisfy. As it turned out, research on Maslow and Alderfer's theories failed to support any neat and predictable hierarchy of needs. Research did, however, support their contention that employees had needs and that employees tried to satisfy their needs in the workplace. Offering employees the chance to fulfill their unmet needs could be a powerful motivator.

Frederick Herzberg added to the needs theory by suggesting that not all need fulfillment was motivating in the sense of impelling employees toward higher and higher performance. Instead, said Herzberg, there were "satisfiers" and "dissatisfiers." Satisfiers were such rewards (need fulfillers) as achievement, recognition, work itself, responsibility, advancement, and growth. Satisfiers made people feel good about their work and were therefore motivating. Other rewards (things companies could do to fulfill employee needs) were important, but not, in and of themselves, motivating. These "hygiene factors" were such things as company policy, working conditions, supervision, salary, relationships with peers, status, and security. They were important because, if not taken care of, they could cause employees to become dissatisfied. But, said Herzberg, managers should not expect to motivate employees with these hygiene factors alone. Thus, for example, safe and comfortable work conditions were important, but they were not motivating. At most, they kept employees from being unhappy and demotivated. For motivation, management needed also to pay attention to the satisfiers. Considerable controversy surrounded Herzberg's theory, and there is no proof in the research that satisfiers and dissatisfiers are the same to all employees. The important and substantiated part of Herzberg's theory is that management had to go beyond just getting people to feel good or neutral about their jobs if employees were to be motivated to superior performance.

If management had to go beyond satisfying employees to get superior performance, what kinds of needs should management attempt to meet? What really "turned people on," and was it the same thing for everyone? David McClelland, offered an answer to these questions. He said that high achievement (superior performance) was really motivated by one of three possible needs—achievement, affiliation, or power. Some people, said McClelland, got "turned on" by the opportunity for achievement—to take responsibility, set and meet goals, and get feedback and recognition. Others were more interested in being with people and being liked. They wanted the opportunity to coordinate, mediate, sell—affiliation was important to them. Finally, there were those people who were really after power. These people wanted above all else to be in control. They wanted control over their environment, including financial, material, and other resources. And they wanted control over people.

The final cognitive theorist we will discuss here is Victor Vroom. Maslow, Alderfer, Herzberg, and McClelland had all focused on identifying and describing needs employees brought to the workplace and the importance of managers understanding and satisfying these needs in order to motivate employees to superior performance. Vroom added the idea that need fulfillment and motivation was somewhat more complicated than the others had suggested. Vroom and others who expanded upon his "expectancy theory," the motivational power of need fulfillment was a function of a person's preference for an outcome (having the need fulfilled) and of the perceived probability that the outcome would follow a specific act.[3] If we wanted to motivate employees, we had to pay attention not only to employee needs, said Vroom and others but to both how important those needs were to an employee at a specific time and the employee's expectation that the company would (and could) fulfill those needs.

Maslow, Alderfer, Herzberg, McClelland, Vroom, and many other cognitive theorists all made important contributions to the understanding of employee motivation. While each theorist offered a different perspective, they all agreed that employees had needs that they tried to meet in the workplace. Understanding and responding to employee needs was important, something managers shouldn't ignore—not if they wanted superior performance. That point wasn't understood by scientific managers. It will be by managers in *Workplace 2000*.

Earlier, we noted that the cognitive theorists had competition—the behavioralists. Advocates of the behavioral approach weren't concerned about employee needs. They were concerned with just what they could see or hear—behavior. Behavior, they said, is a function of its consequences. Understand the consequences of an employee's behavior to that employee and you will understand his or her behavior. More importantly, understand the relationship between consequences and behavior and you can arrange consequences to get the behavior you want. Behavioralists were well grounded in operant psychology. Their approach had worked with rats and pigeons. They knew it would work with people. It did.

Behavioralists were unrepentant disciples of the celebrated and notorious B. F. Skinner.[4] Skinner was a Harvard-educated psychologist and the founding father of operant psychology. According to Skinner, humans are active organisms who "operate" or act upon their environment in order to change it. It is this "operant" behavior that was of most concern to Skinner since, according to him, it was highly influenced (even controlled) by its consequences. Behavior that elicited a positive response from the environment increased in frequency. Behavior eliciting a negative response decreased in frequency. Behavior eliciting no response or a neutral response first increased and then—provided there was still no response—decreased in frequency. Those were the basic principles of Skinnerian psychology. And he proved that they could be used to explain, predict, and even control behavior. He first proved the concepts worked with animals. Then he tried out the concepts on humans. The latter step got him in trouble. It wasn't that the principles didn't work with humans. They did. But the fact that they did made a lot of people uncomfortable. Among other things, people were uncomfortable with Skinner's theories because he seemed to be suggesting that people weren't that different from animals in the way they responded to their environment. Such an idea was repugnant. People weren't animals, Skinner's critics said. It was grossly oversimplifying matters, said the critics, for Skinner to argue that the behavior of people was "determined" by their prior experiences operating on their environment in much the same way the behavior of animals was determined. After all, the critics said, didn't people have "free will," "freedom of choice," and the ability to determine their own destiny—something lower order creatures didn't have? Not totally, said Skinner, the fact was that by controlling the environment (the kind, level, and frequency of reinforcement people got for their behavior), we could "control" the behavior of people and improve both their lives and society as a whole. This latter idea—the ability to control human behavior—really made Skinner's critics uncomfortable. Control sounded a lot like manipulation to many people. If Skinner was right, worried his critics, by teaching his theories were we giving managers the access to totalitarian power to turn employees into mindless, obedient robots?

In spite of the controversy surrounding Skinner's theories, they were applied extensively in American industry, particularly during the 1960s and 1970s. They were still being taught and used by American managers in the 1980s. Originally called behavior modification or organizational behavior modification, more recently they have been taught and used as "performance management" in order to avoid some of the negative connotations of "modifying behavior." One of the earliest uses of behavior modification was at Emery Air Freight in the late 1960s and early '70s. Another and more refined use of the technique occurred at Preston Trucking Company in the late 1970s. Experiences at both companies are important because they are early examples of what we are likely to see more of in *Workplace 2000*.

Early *Workplace 2000* Motivation—The Emery Air Freight Story

One of the earliest and most successful applications of behavior modification was started at Emery Air Freight in 1969.[5] In the first three years of the program, Emery reported documented savings exceeding $2 million. Essentially, Emery's program involved three steps. First, a performance audit was conducted for a particular department or area to precisely identify ("pinpoint") employee job behaviors that had the greatest impact on performance. Second, the behavior was measured and employees were given specific feedback on their performance compared to the performance goal or desired level of performance. Finally, Emery managers were trained to reinforce desired behaviors as soon as they occurred. To help managers identify ways to reinforce desired behavior, Emery provided a workbook describing 150 types of reinforcers ranging from a nod or smile to specific praise. Interestingly, money wasn't used.

One of Emery's best-known and most successful uses of behavior modification involved efforts to encourage employees to use containers for consolidating small packages going to the same location. Philip Hilts, in his book *Behavior Mod*, describes what happened in this way:

Emery was well known in the air-freight field for one of their packaging procedures, called containerized shipment. Essentially, it meant putting a number of smaller packages headed for the same destination in one large container. The procedure saved time and money.

When the men and supervisors on the dock were asked, they thought their performance was good, and figured that they were using larger containers about 95 percent of the times they were called for. A quick measure of the real situation showed that they were wrong. They used the containers only 45 percent of the time.

. . . [T]he company passed out check lists to the dock workers. The men kept track of their own performance, and thus got immediate feedback. Bosses tacked graphs of performance up on the bulletin board so everyone could watch the action. At the same time, the bosses began applying positive reinforcement to the workers: praise and recognition for performance improvement.

Container use jumped from 45 to 95 percent in offices throughout the country, and in most cases the increase came in a single day.

More Early *Workplace 2000* Motivation—The Preston Trucking Story

Emery was an early and simple example of the use of behavior modification. Preston Trucking began using the technique nearly a decade later. And Preston added a few new wrinkles. As it did for Emery, behavior modification, or performance management, worked. In fact, it worked so well and continued to work so well that Preston won the U.S. Senate's Productivity Award in 1986 and was listed in the top ten of the "100 Best Places to Work for in America" by Robert Levering, Milton Moskowitz, and Michael Katz in their book of the same name.

Preston Trucking wasn't always one of the "100 Best Places to Work for in America." In fact, in 1979 if there had been such a listing, Preston might have ranked among the "100 Worst." Robert Levering, in his book, *A Great Place to Work*, quotes Richie Storck, a teamsters' union shop steward, on the working conditions at Preston before 1979. Here's how Storck described it to Levering: "Everybody was under a microscope. We didn't like the company and the company didn't like us. It was plain and simple. . . . The company, more or less, had the whip on us. You got a ten-minute break, and you didn't dare go eleven minutes because you got reprimanded. You went to lunch for half an hour, and you made sure you were back in half an hour or the boss was standing there waiting for you. . . . It was the bad guys and the good guys. They were the bad guys 'cause they were company. They had the right to discipline us, and we knew it. So we didn't give them a reason to. We used to hide in trucks, and when one of them started coming down the dock, we'd tell them we were working."

How did Preston go from the "good guy/bad guy" conflict between labor and management to becoming one of the best places to work for in America? It did it in much the same way as Emery. Preston provided employees with feedback on their performance and managers used positive reinforcement to encourage good performance. But Preston went further. It created a true partnership with employees—a professional, social, and financial partnership.

To create a partnership, Preston did several things Emery hadn't done when it started. First, Preston initiated weekly and monthly team meetings with employees where managers asked employees for their ideas about how to solve problems and improve performance. Then managers listened to employee ideas and implemented many of the suggestions. The ideas flowed in. For example, in 1987, Preston's five thousand employees submitted nearly six thousand suggestions. Eighty-five percent of these suggestions were implemented and the average suggestion saved the company three hundred dollars.[6] A second partnership-building effort Preston made was to give employees a financial stake in performance improvement and the company's success. Preston was the first trucking company to install a group incentive plan where a share of company profits are distributed to employees under a preestablished formula. Finally, Preston gave employees access to a much wider range of information about the company. At Emery, employees had received feedback on their performance on "pinpointed" behaviors. Preston employees got the same type of information, not just about specific behavior, but about the company as a whole. It even went so far as to share financial information that previously had been restricted to management. As a consequence, when employees made a suggestion for capital expenditure and management couldn't approve it because it cost too much, employees understood why their "good idea" was turned down. And employees could work with management to find an alternative. Thus, a proposal for a twelve-thousand-dollar exhaust fan gets rejected because management can't justify its cost. Instead of blaming managers, Preston employees get together, brainstorm ideas, and come up with a proposal for solving the "exhaust fan" problem at a fourth of the cost—something the company could justify. Partnership, understanding, communication—problem solved.

Workplace 2000 Motivation—Making the Transition

Western Electric's Hawthorne Plant, pre-1969 Emery Air Freight, pre-1979 Preston Trucking, and most other American companies up until the late 1980s operationalized certain common assumptions about American workers. Perhaps the best description of these assumptions was provided by Douglas McGregor in his book, *The Human Side of Enterprise.* McGregor proposed two competing sets of assumptions that managers could hold about their workers—Theory X and Theory Y. Theory X, according to McGregor, could be summarized this way:

1. People, by their very nature, dislike work and will avoid it when possible.
2. They have little ambition, tend to shun responsibility, and like to be directed.
3. Above all else, they want security.
4. In order to get them to attain organizational objectives, it is necessary to use coercion, control, and threats of punishment.

According to McGregor, Theory X assumptions were the most common assumptions held by American managers concerning their workers. They were also incorrect, said McGregor. The average person wasn't indolent, lazy, and lacking in ambition. He or she didn't prefer to be led, wasn't necessarily self-centered and indifferent to organizational needs. More importantly, the average American worker wasn't gullible and stupid. He or she wasn't any of the things the Theory X assumptions said. Sure, said McGregor, the average American worker might act lazy, and stupid—he or she might exhibit at times all of the characteristics that gave credence to Theory X. But, said McGregor, the American worker exhibited these characteristics not because they were natural to him or her, but because of the way he or she was managed. American managers, said McGregor, had created their own self-fulfilling prophecy. By treating workers according to Theory X assumptions, managers got Theory X behavior. There were, said McGregor, a different set of assumptions that were well founded in behavioral research. He called these assumptions Theory Y and described them as follows:

1. The expenditure of physical and mental effort in work is as natural to people as is resting or playing.
2. External control and the threats of punishment are not the only ways of getting people to work toward organizational objectives. If people are committed to objectives, they will exercise self-direction and self-control.
3. Commitment to objectives is determined by the rewards associated with their achievement.
4. Under proper conditions, the average human being learns not only to accept, but to seek responsibility.
5. The capacity to exercise a relatively high degree of imagination, ingenuity, and creativity in the solution of organizational problems is widely distributed throughout the population.
6. Under conditions of modern industrial life, the intellectual potentials of the average human being are only partially utilized.[7]

It is obvious that McGregor's Theory Y assumptions fit nicely with the arguments of the cognitive and behavioral theorists. Also, results at Emery Air Freight, Preston Trucking, and perhaps even Hawthorne seem to be consistent with Theory Y. Given more information, the ability to exercise more control over their own behavior and reinforcement, workers responded. But did they always respond? Was Theory Y right for every work force and every situation? The answer wasn't all that clear.

Numerous researchers throughout the 1960s and '70s tried to answer the question: Which was "best," Theory X or Theory Y? By "best," they meant to establish which set of assumptions when followed led to the highest performance. The best answer the researchers could give to this question was a resounding "maybe" and unequivocal "sometimes." If we were looking for performance, there was just no clear evidence that operating from one set of assumptions was better than operating from another in every instance. Sometimes Theory Y was better. Sometimes it wasn't. Either Theory X or Theory Y was just as likely to be right or wrong depending upon the situation and the individual. Did it matter that neither set of assumptions could be proved correct? We thought it did (thus, all of the attempts to prove one better than the other). As it turned out, it didn't matter very much at all. By the late 1980s, we were being driven to operationalize one set of assumptions and abandon the other.

Up until the mid- and late 1980s, the debate over Theory X and Theory Y was largely academic, and, it could be argued, the results of research on the question of the validity of the two sets of assumptions were colored by the researchers' own personal preferences and predispositions. By the end of the decade, we had moved past this academic debate to the practical necessity of Theory Y. The reality of the American business situation dictated that American workers had to be managed by and made to behave according to Theory Y assumptions, regardless of their true nature. The point was that American business could no longer afford Theory X employees for several reasons:

1. We could no longer afford Theory X management. Theory X employees required an army of manager/supervisor controllers. But we no longer could afford them. The flattening of the organization we discussed in a previous chapter meant that very few "controllers" were left, and they couldn't/wouldn't be replaced. *Workplace 2000* employees had to be, or at least act like, Theory Y self-controlling people.

2. Theory X work didn't exist anymore. Theory X required that we be able to break work down into simple, repetitive, easily learned segments we could tightly "manage and control." But the simple, routine, and often manual work was going away. Robots did the simple, routine and repetitive. What we needed people to do was the complex, ever changing, creative work—the kind of work that could only be performed by Theory Y people who would be self-directing and self-controlling. We couldn't "beat" creativity, good judgment, and initiative out of people.

3. The volatility and chaos of the typical American corporation in the late 1980s eliminated employment guarantees. Under Theory X employees traded obedience (some would say subservience) for the promise of lifetime (or at least long-term) job security. But, we couldn't promise job security anymore, and even if we did promise it, employees wouldn't believe it—not after the layoffs and downsizing of the 1980s.

4. To get the level of performance we needed from workers, work could no longer just be a means to an economic end. There was very little doubt as the 1980s came to a close that competitiveness would require much more than "okay" performance from employees. It would require extraordinary performance. People had to behave as if work meant more to them than a paycheck. If they weren't naturally disposed to behave that way, then we had to create an environment where they would behave that way.

5. Finally, in the 1980s, we came to recognize that quality, customer service, and product innovation—three key strategies for success—couldn't be achieved without employee involvement. We had to build in good quality rather than inspect out defects. Service to customers had to be a continuous, company-wide effort, not just a response to consumer complaints. And innovation required teamwork and sharing of ideas across functions (manufacturing and design engineering working together). Lazy, uncommitted Theory X employees couldn't/wouldn't cooperate to produce the quality, service, and innovation we needed for survival. Only Theory Y employees (or at least employees who behaved like Theory Y) could/would do that.

Workplace 2000 work requires that employees take initiative, respond rapidly to changing circumstances and situations, and be mentally alert and focused on the current organizational imperative. Given those requirements, a Theory X "scientifically" managed work force can't succeed. Scientific management had as its underlying objective control of the worker's body and physical actions. The new workplace demands, if not the control of, at least the organization of an employee's attention.[8]

Motivating *Workplace 2000* Employees— Reenchantment and Commitment

If *Workplace 2000* had to tap the Theory Y nature of employees (or create it if it did not in reality exist), then how could that transition to Theory Y employee behavior be accomplished? The road map for creating a new work force was becoming clear by the late 1980s. Some, such as Robert Howard, a free-lance writer on work-related issues, saw it emerging from California's Silicon Valley in the mid-1980s and called the process the "reenchantment of the work place." Others, such as Richard E. Walton, a Harvard Business School professor, saw, at about the same time as Howard, what he called a "movement from control to commitment in the workplace."[9] Still others labeled the change "participatory management," "democratization of the workplace," or "creating a 'warm' culture." Regardless of its name, the management and motivational techniques were the same.

The movement to *Workplace 2000* represents a kind of watershed of management/employee or corporate/worker relations. Robert Howard describes it this way: "It sets out two antithetical poles of work experience: an antediluvian 'before' of centralized work places and bureaucratic hierarchies, autocratic managers, and workers who are little more than cogs in the industrial wheel; and an incipient 'after' characterized by decentralization, participation, and autonomy where the corporation manufactures not only products but personalities." In *Workplace 2000*, rigid hierarchies will be dismantled, as will the ceremonial trappings of power. Egalitarianism will become utilitarian. The goal will be to create among the work force and between workers and managers, harmony and unity. More importantly, the goal will be to attach people mentally and emotionally to the workplace—to make them feel intimately connected to the corporation even if in reality that connection is transitory.

The differences between the traditional control-oriented,

scientifically managed workplace and the commitment-oriented, "enchanted" *Workplace 2000* are multi-faceted. *Workplace 2000* companies don't just do one thing to promote Theory Y behavior; they do many things, extending from the design of jobs to expectations for performance, to organizational structure, to compensation, and so on. The traditional "control" workplace emphasizes individual responsibility for individual performance. *Workplace 2000* emphasizes shared responsibility for group performance. In the traditional workplace, jobs and job content are fixed. In *Workplace 2000*, jobs are fluid and flexibility is paramount. In the traditional workplace, coordination and control flow top down and are legitimized by status and position. In *Workplace 2000*, control is shared and coordination flows from shared values and goals. Finally, in the traditional workplace, workers and managers are adversaries. In *Workplace 2000*, they are partners.[10]

In *Workplace 2000*, "human resources" or "human assets," as workers have been called in American organizations, become something much more than mere resources or assets that can be counted, tabulated, used, moved, and expended. Why? Because the production and service delivery system can no longer be totally rationalized. Rather, it is chaotic and emotive, and human contribution becomes critical for success in such an environment. Overt domination and control by a managerial elite becomes ineffective and nonutilitarian.

The importance of people as the key ingredient for success in the workplace of the future, particularly versus American managers' traditional preoccupation with technology, is well illustrated by *Manufacturing Engineering* magazine's selections for its Manufacturing Excellence Awards for 1989. In his opening note to the selections, Robert Stauffer, the magazine's executive editor, says, "Increasingly, the focus is turning to the contribution of people as the ultimate key to the success of any enterprise. With that focus have come changes in corporate policies and practices aimed at enhancing the ability of workers to perform, participate, and share in the operation. Companies moving most aggressively along that path have many things in common. One, simply put, is this: they're good places to work. And that's the thrust of the 1989 *ME* Award for Manufacturing Excellence." The change of focus is clearly evident. Stauffer goes on to say, "Last year the award winners were those judged to be tops in the application of advanced manufacturing technology. This year the award is presented to 10 organizations selected as being the best manufacturing companies in terms of employment—the best organizations at which to work."[11] *ME*'s ten selections include such companies as Apple Computer, Digital Equipment, Boeing, AT&T, and Eastman Kodak. The following quotes from *ME*'s descriptions of some of the 1989 award winners reflect some of the common themes of *Workplace 2000*:

About Apple Computer we read:

"The power of the champion is still alive and well in this environment," says Mike Campi, director of Fremont Manufacturing (Fremont, California), Apple Computer, Inc. (Cupertino, California), "because the best way to keep great people is to allow them to feel like they make a difference. At Apple, we've given people the mission to change the world."

And that's what makes Apple a good place to work: the company's commitment to empowering people at all levels of the organization . . .

"It's not the traditional supervisor telling the line operations people what to do," he [Campi] explains. "It's really the line operations people working with the supervisor to make sure that all obstacles that might block their objectives are removed—that means giving them the right tools, working with them. That's what we mean by really giving people responsibility and empowering them with the authority to meet their objectives." . . .

From the CEO on down, the company is very frank about its business directions and new product strategies. While that candor may sometimes result in the competition's learning a bit too much, it also shows Apple's employees that the company is willing to share important information with them, showing them another sign of their power and value . . .

And the result? According to Campi, a lot of great people working in a great environment. "Those may be a lot of superlatives," he says, "but I think that we have products that people enjoy working with and enjoy manufacturing. I think that every individual at Apple, not just the group presidents or senior executives, feels that he or she has the power to make a real difference."[12]

At Digital, the company induced environment is much the same. We read:

A company trust in employees, an open corporate culture, and an energetic, future-oriented work environment make Digital Equipment Corp. (Maynard, Massachusetts) a great place to work.

As Bill Hanson, vice president of manufacturing tells it, "At Digital we feel very strongly that people will do the right thing. That's part of our culture, a piece of our philosophy. People will do the right thing when they're given a sense of vision or a sense of direction, have access to information, are given responsibility. We trust the individual."

. . . [A] Digital orientation [for new employees] isn't just a listing of rules and regulations and an explanation of the employee benefits package. Instead, it's a forum for people to discuss how things get done at Digital, what sort of things are the right things to do, and how they can "buy in."

. . . In Digital's future, contends Hanson, employees . . . will look less like employees and more like partners in the business as the employer/employee relationship becomes similar to that of customer/supplier, with well-defined and obvious benefits and independence for each party.[13]

And finally, at Hewlett Packard, we read that the new management and motivation style is like this:

Harold Edmondson, vice president and director of manufacturing [says], "The heart of the thing is treating people as individuals and trying as hard as you can to satisfy their needs."

The result is an atmosphere where employees are challenged, are urged and expected to be creative, to think individually, to take risks. "We try to make our engineers feel the sky is the limit," Edmondson says. "We give them a substantial amount of technical and intellectual freedom to do the right things."

"We try to create an atmosphere in which employees can

enjoy themselves and prosper and make significant contributions. We also try to be up front about what their future is likely to be, not only in terms of promotion or advancement sequences but also in terms of financial rewards. We all share a genuine desire for the individual to lead a full and rewarding life."[14]

As we said, the preceding examples from *ME*'s 1989 Manufacturing Excellence Awards reflect some common themes we will see more of in *Workplace 2000*. What are these themes? Let's assume we were writing a guide for the *Workplace 2000* manager or executive. What instruction might that guide provide to managers on the "new style of motivating people?" It might go something like this:

1. Make people feel like champions the way Apple Computer does. Create an environment where every employee can feel that he or she can make a difference. Make every person feel personally significant.
2. Give people a mission. Make it not just any mission, but something truly special, such as "changing the world." Make working at the company something much more than just an economic exchange.
3. Empower people through involvement. Make the role of managers and supervisors a "helping" and "facilitating" role. Act on the premise that people want to achieve— that they want to help the company succeed. Instead of having managers and supervisors try to control employee behavior, have them focus on removing obstacles to employee performance. Assume that people can and will do extraordinary things if institutional barriers to performance are removed.
4. Be frank and open about the company's business strategies and direction. Make sure everyone understands what "we" as a company are trying to accomplish. Don't be concerned if a competitor finds out about a particular strategy. Above all else, don't keep secrets. Make sure everyone knows everything.
5. Trust people to do the right thing. Assume that given enough of the right information and enough self-control,

    people will act in the best interest of the company and presumably in their own best interest.

6. Create a unique culture and indoctrinate people from the start to that culture. Don't let an informal social system just develop over time. Visualize what the company should be like, and share that vision. Make sure everyone knows how to behave consistent with that vision, and reward people who do. If someone doesn't act in concert with the vision, express your disappointment and encourage him or her to change or leave.

Such might be the prescriptions for motivation in *Workplace 2000*. But what do they mean for the individual worker? On the positive side, they mean that the workplace will be purposely orchestrated to have greater meaning and significance for each of us personally than ever before. Working will be more than an economic exchange. Regardless of where someone works, he or she will be expected to "sign up," "join up," and "buy into" the corporate vision. Many years ago, Studs Terkel wrote in his landmark book, *Working*, that the Americans he interviewed were looking for something more at work than just a paycheck: "It is about a search . . . for daily meaning as well as daily bread, for recognition as well as cash, for astonishment rather than torpor; in short, for a sort of life rather than a Monday through Friday sort of dying. Perhaps immortality, too, is part of the quest. To be remembered was the wish, spoken and unspoken, of the heroes and heroines of this book." If Terkel was right that Americans seek more from their daily work, they are likely to find it in *Workplace 2000*. To that extent, the workplace will be much better. But being given "daily meaning" in the work one does also carries a price. Robert Howard, whom we quoted earlier, explains the price this way: "The contradictions inherent to this emerging ideology of management make it especially vulnerable to abuses of power and the elaborate manipulation of people and values. . . . The promise of the enchanted work place is promise of meaning, with the corporation as the mediator between work and the self. In order to cash in on the meanings of the enchanted work place, however, the workers must cleave to a set of ends—'superordinate goals,' 'corporate culture,' whatever—that 'like the basic postulates of a mathematical system,' is posited in advance. Workers rarely have the opportunity to influence the content of those ends, let alone play an active role in their formulation."

But suppose an individual American doesn't share the vision—doesn't believe in or fit into the "culture"—doesn't aspire after "changing the world," at least in the way "they" want it changed. What do such Americans do? Howard suggests perhaps the only possible recourse. He writes: "The best they can do is try to search out those firms with superordinate goals they find congenial, picking and choosing among corporate cultures like consumers at a supermarket. The effectiveness of this strategy, of course, depends on their location in the labor market—a possibility for engineers, perhaps, but far more problematic for production workers. As a result, the necessity of allegiance to a set of ends over which one has little control can become a recipe for a dangerous corporate intrusiveness that produces not autonomy and freedom, but enforced conformity, not genuine participation, but a kind of high touch coercion."

And what happens if the fit isn't right? Does the "enchanted" workplace become something less than enchanted? Howard thinks so. He quotes a young worker who described her disenchantment with the "enchanted" workplace after experiencing it for five years. She says: "They are consistently telling you how important you are to the company. You would think that what I'm doing now would shut the company down in a minute, if I took a vacation or something. They try to make you feel that. But, it's insulting. They want you to be the person who shows up on Saturday and Sunday and works until eleven o'clock, consistently. They demand so much from . . . from your life."[15]

At least in respect to the demands of the new workplace, this worker is right. *Workplace 2000* will demand more from every worker—more than ever before. It will also give more—meaning, responsibility, purpose, autonomy, self-control. Each American will have to decide on the value of that exchange.

CHAPTER 5

A Different Type of Pay

For most Americans, *Workplace 2000* will culminate nearly two decades of revolutionary changes in pay practices. As we enter the 1990s, we are halfway through this revolution. Many Americans have already experienced some of these changes. Those who haven't been touched by this revolution in pay almost certainly will be within the next ten years. These changes *are* revolutionary, because they totally alter the financial relationship American workers traditionally had with their employers.

Today, most Americans sit down with their boss once a year to review their performance. As a result of that review, they normally receive a raise in the form of a percentage increase in their base salary that matches or—hopefully—exceeds the raises others in their company have been receiving. Regardless, this raise helps to keep their base pay ahead of, or at least on a par with, inflation. Within the next ten years, most American companies will stop giving these raises or will lengthen the period between performance reviews and raises to as much as two years, or even longer.

While annual increases helped, most Americans knew in

the 1980s that significant increases in pay came to them as a result of their being promoted. After all, their boss made more than they did. Their boss's boss made more than they did, and the president or CEO of the company made more than anyone else in the company. People were paid based upon the position they occupied in the hierarchy—how much responsibility they had and how many people reported to them. Americans knew that performance and skill had little to do with how much people were paid. Most American workers knew people occupying higher-level positions (and therefore getting paid more than they) who didn't have the skills they had and certainly didn't work as hard or produce as much. All that will change in *Workplace 2000*. Pay will be based not upon position but upon skills and performance.

Today, the pay Americans take home is fairly stable. Some workers (not exempt from the Fair Labor Standards Act) are paid extra for overtime they work; some may even receive a cash bonus on occasion. But the base pay of most Americans stays pretty much the same from month to month, at least throughout an entire year until their next performance review and annual increase. That will no longer be the case. Up to as much as 40 percent or more of the average American's pay in *Workplace 2000* will vary drastically from month to month.

Today the typical American works for a company, puts in his or her hours, and is handed a pay check. If the company is profitable, workers don't share in the profits, or if they do, their share is small. In *Workplace 2000*, not only will workers share in the profits in a meaningful way, but each year the average American will own more and more of the company that employs him or her.

These changes *are* happening. If current trends continue—and they are expected to—by the year 2000, most Americans will have to deal with these changes. There is very little doubt that we are moving steadily toward a "different type of pay."

The Evidence of Change

The evidence of change in pay practices surrounds us. It can be found in news reports and research studies. The following items were selected from literally thousands that have appeared in the last few years and that continue to appear at ever increasing rates:

• In October 1988, du Pont announced what chemical industry analysts called a "trend setting" pay plan. Under du Pont's plan, starting in 1989, the salaries of all twenty thousand employees in its fibers business—from group vice president to hourly worker—would be partially tied to the unit's profitability. *The Wall Street Journal* described the new pay plan for du Pont: "After a phase-in period of five years, fibers employees will be paid base salaries that are 6% lower than their counterparts in the rest of du Pont receive. The fibers workers will recoup the 6% difference only if the unit meets 100% of its profit goals. The employees don't collect any of the 6% difference if the fibers group makes less than 80% of its profit goals. At the 80% level, employees get a 3% pay raise. If the unit reaches 150% of its goal, employees receive a bonus that makes their salary 12% higher than their counterparts."[1]

For du Pont, the plan meant a payroll savings of $36 million per year if the profit plan wasn't met and a payout of $72 million in bonuses if actual profits exceeded goals by 150%. How can the company pay an "upside" of $72 million in bonuses with only a "downside" savings of $36 million in payroll costs? Because at much higher profit levels (such as 150 percent of goal), the company can afford to share those profits and pay much greater compensation to employees in the form of bonuses.

• In a Hay Group survey of three hundred U.S. companies conducted in 1987, one out of fifteen reported that they provided lump sum payments instead of salary increases to at least part of their work force in 1986.[2]

• In 1982, merit increases for all workers averaged 9.1 percent. By 1988, such increases had shrunk to 5.3 percent and were projected to shrink further to 5.2 percent in 1989. In the place of large annual merit increases, more and more companies were moving to bonuses, incentive awards, and other forms of variable compensation.[3]

Model Companies

In the last few years, over twenty-five hundred executives and managers from U.S. companies, large and small, have visited Lincoln Electric, a medium-sized manufacturing company in Cleveland, Ohio. These executives were all considering changes in their companies' pay practices. They went to Lincoln Electric to attend a four-hour seminar to learn about Lincoln's pay systems. Ford and General Motors—among other large companies—arranged special tours for their key executives. What has made Lincoln such a mecca for executives throughout the United States who are looking for innovative new approaches to pay? Lincoln's approach works for the company and its employees. And it's done so for over fifty years. At a time when other companies are struggling to compete with foreign competition, Lincoln Electric is the world's lowest-cost producer of welding machines and induction motors. The productivity of Lincoln's employees is as much as 250 percent above the industry average in most years. The company continues year after year to beat its most productive competitors, including the Japanese. The quality of Lincoln's products is equally good. At the same time, Lincoln's employees enjoy total compensation that is extraordinary by any comparisons. In 1987, the average employee made over $45,000 (base plus bonus). Top performing hourly workers in 1988 could earn as much as $80,000 in earnings including bonus. The bonus portion alone has amounted to as much as 100 percent or more of base earnings.

On arriving at Lincoln Electric, visitors find a Spartan plant reminiscent of the 1950s, with painted concrete block walls and tile floors. Then they learn that Lincoln employees receive no company-paid dental insurance benefits, no paid holidays, and have no sick leave. In fact, production employees receive no base salary or hourly wage at all. They are all on a piece rate system. These employees are paid based upon what they produce either individually or as members of small work groups. The more employees produce, the more they make. And there is no limit to what they can make provided the quality is good. The company doesn't pay for bad quality. Bad quality is fixed by employees on their own time, without pay. But in most years, piece rate pay is only half of employee income. The other half comes from sharing in company profits. In 1984, Lincoln's two thousand employees split about $42 million dollars in bonus payments—over $15,000 per person. In 1987, bonuses averaged nearly $19,000 for employees whose average earnings, excluding bonus, was $26,442. Since 1934, Lincoln has never missed a year in making bonus payments. In good years, bonuses doubled employee earnings. In bad years, bonuses still reached as much as 50 percent of earnings. From 1983 through 1987, bonuses averaged 66 percent. Lincoln Electric is a $370 million company with *no* debt and high employee compensation. It hasn't had a layoff in thirty years and virtually guarantees thirty hours per week of work (although not necessarily a particular job) to any employee who has been with the company for more than two years. But Lincoln isn't right for everyone. Twenty-five percent of new employees leave the company within their first three months. Maybe those who leave can't take the weekend work or working extra shifts during busy periods. Maybe they don't like the fact that the company has no seniority policy. Maybe they just don't like working so hard all the time and having to compete for bonus money. Yet those who stay seem to love the company, and many of these employees have been at Lincoln for over thirty years.

Another mecca for executives looking for innovative approaches to compensation is Nucor Steel, headquartered in Charlotte, North Carolina. Like Lincoln Electric, Nucor Steel has been a high-performing company that still manages to offer exceptional compensation to its employees. In 1988, Nucor operated seven steel mills at four sites. It was the ninth-largest producer of steel in the United States. While other larger steel producers had struggled and often failed against foreign competition, Nucor succeeded. During the 1980s, Nucor's sales grew over 850 percent and its profits jumped 1,250 percent. When the labor cost per ton of other steel manufacturers was over $130 per ton, Nucor produced steel at a labor cost of $60 per ton. Nucor's employees produced 980 tons of steel per employee in 1986 at a time when its competitors produced less than 400 tons per employee. As of 1988, the price of steel products from Nucor had remained competitive with the prices foreign suppliers could offer for over fifteen years. Nucor had not laid off a single worker or closed a single plant in fifteen years. And for fourteen years, Nucor had paid a dividend to its stockholders, increasing the amount of the dividend each year. Yet the average employee at Nucor earned over 14 percent more per year than the average steelworker in the United States. At Nucor's Darlington, South Carolina, plant, employees made 200 percent of the average South Carolina manufacturing wage. As we mention elsewhere in this book, Nucor does a lot of things right, like staying "flat" and "lean" and maintaining good relationships with its employees. But one of the things Nucor does most right is how it compensates people. Nucor actually has a range of compensation systems, each tying pay to performance. But as Ken Iverson, chairman of Nucor, said in 1988, Nucor's most important incentive system is probably the one it has for production employees. Here, Nucor organizes its work force into small work groups of twenty-five or thirty-five people. Employees are paid bonuses based upon the production of their work group over a predetermined standard. If the employees produce 50 percent more than standard, they receive a 50 percent bonus. If they produce 100 percent more than standard, they receive a 100 percent bonus. It's that simple. And the standard isn't changed just because people are making a lot of money.

The success of companies like Lincoln Electric and Nucor Steel, and the reason they are sought out by other companies as possible models for future pay practices, has much to do with their use of bonuses as an important component of their pay. American businesses are applying what they learn about pay systems from companies like Lincoln and Nucor. In 1987, the Bureau of Labor Statistics reported that 40 percent of all workers covered by union agreements had bonus payments as some part of their contract. In 1983, bonuses had been so rare that the bureau did not even keep statistics on the number.

More Evidence of Widespread Change

So far, the changes we have mentioned have been just isolated examples. But they are indicative of widespread change. One of the best surveys tapping the depth and breadth of change taking place in pay was conducted by the American Productivity and Quality Center and the American Compensation Association in 1987. They surveyed 1,598 organizations in 40 different industries about evenly split between manufacturing and the service sector. These organizations employed about 10 percent of the civilian working population of the United States. Several key findings from that survey point to the revolution in pay practices. The final report said:

1. "There has been striking growth in the number of firms adopting nontraditional reward systems during the past five years. . . . [M]ore gainsharing, pay-for-knowledge, small-group incentives, lump-sum bonus, and two-tier plans have been adopted in the past five years than all of the prior 20 years."
2. "The more competition a firm reports, the more likely it is to use a nontraditional reward system."
3. "All nontraditional reward systems reportedly have a positive impact on performance."
4. "Many organizations report eliminating or significantly reducing the use of COLA (Cost of Living Adjustments), pattern bargaining, and a variety of executive perquisites."
5. "The use of nontraditional reward practices will grow in the next five years . . . The number of firms using small-group incentives and pay-for-knowledge is projected to double, and use of gainsharing is projected to grow nearly as much. Profit sharing shows the lowest projected increase, perhaps because of its relatively high use now."[4]

These major themes were echoed in a similar survey conducted by the Hay Group.

1. *Lower salary increases.* "With inflation momentarily under control, companies are finding it easier to cap annual salary increases; data . . . indicate that last year's salary increases averaged about one percentage point less than those of the preceding year."
2. *Variable compensation.* "Companies are exuding strong interest in what is popularly known as 'pay for performance'—linking more of the total pay package to actual performance in order to contain fixed costs."
3. *Extended review periods.* "The timing of pay increases has clearly become an influential factor in organizations' compensation programs. Responses from 450 participating companies in the Hay Compensation Report indicate that the average number of months between increases has risen from 12.5 months to 12.7 months—with many companies pushing out to 14 to 16 month review periods."
4. *Lump-sum merit increases.* "Lump-sum merit increases are gaining popularity. Such payments do not increase other salary-related compensation benefits such as life insurance and pensions, and they are not guaranteed from year to year."
5. *Two-tier compensation systems.* "Given the rapidly changing workforce, the tendency towards merger/acquisitions/reorganizations, and the far-reaching concern over rising costs, the greater use of two-tier compensation systems appears to be inevitable. The need for such systems has become especially strong in those companies undergoing a disruptive reorganization process."

The Hay Group ends its report with this note: "Employers and employees alike must understand the new framework for compensation, collaborate on creating good systems of performance measurement, and agree to use pay as a strategic force in moving the organization ahead. The crux of the situation is simple: Workers who enhance their companies' competitiveness and make a direct contribution to profit will be rewarded in kind. Marginal or average employees will be "entitled" only to marginal or average increases—or none at all."[5]

Lance Berger, a Hay Group executive vice president, puts

the matter even more succinctly. He says: "The age of 'entitlement' to automatic salary increases and bigger and better benefits is over."[6]

Why Pay Systems Are Changing

If, as Berger maintains, the age of "entitlement" has ended, why has it ended? What has changed to make traditional methods of compensation no longer viable? Let's look at what is wrong with traditional compensation.

It has been estimated that 95 percent of the major U.S. corporations used a "point-factor" approach to job evaluation and establishing base compensation. Thus, the pay of most Americans has traditionally been established using this practice.

The point-factor approach typically works as follows: (1) a carefully written job description is prepared for each position in the company; (2) each job description is then rated according to common factors such as working conditions, problem-solving requirements, knowledge required to perform the job, accountability for performance; (3) each job accumulates "points" based upon how much of each factor they contain; and (4) the resulting "point score" is then used as a basis for establishing a salary level for each job.

So what's wrong with that? Each job in the company is evaluated and priced based upon the same criteria or "factors." Isn't that fair? Perhaps, but it doesn't fit well with the requirements of business in *Workplace 2000*. For example:

1. A point-factor system is based upon rigid job descriptions that encourage people to do "only what is in their job description." After all, that's what they get paid for. That doesn't fit very well with the highly competitive business climate of *Workplace 2000* where, as Edward Lawler says in a 1987 *Personnel* magazine article, "what's needed is a management approach under which people will do what is right, develop and use new skills, focus

on customer/client relationships, and generally be involved in the business of which they are a part."

2. Since a higher number of points under a point-factor system tend to be assigned to jobs with a higher level of responsibility and broader reporting relationships, a point-factor system tends to encourage bureaucracy and hierarchy. The more people and the more levels reporting to a person under such a system, the higher his or her total point score, and therefore his or her pay. Such bureaucracy and hierarchy run completely counter to the "flattening of the organization" that is required for success in the future. "After organizations have point-factor methods for a while," says Lawler, a professor of business at the University of Southern California, "individuals become quite sophisticated in getting jobs evaluated highly. They realize that creatively written job descriptions can lead to pay increases, as can changed job duties. A considerable amount of time and effort can be spent by individuals on rewriting job descriptions so that they will be scored more highly. And individuals can start grabbing added responsibilities to get points. The added responsibilities can include extra equipment and more subordinates—items that increase the cost of doing business. Overall, in a rather direct although unintended way, point-factor systems actually reward individuals for creating overhead and higher costs. This, of course, is exactly the opposite direction from the current trend toward low overhead, leaner and flatter organizations, and careful expense control. Point-factor job evaluation tends to reward individual managers who increase expense levels and add employees to their staffs."

3. Point-factor systems tend to emphasize paying people for the positions they occupy rather than the skills they possess or their performance. Yet, as Lawler says, "In today's rapidly changing, highly competitive environment, a message emphasizing growth, development, and good performance is more on target than one that emphasizes growing your job or getting promoted." Since significant increases in pay come from promotion to a

job with higher point value, "employees often spend more time worrying about what their next jobs will be than about how well they are performing their present ones."

4. The operation of point-factor systems depends upon the existence of detailed job descriptions. Because rewriting such descriptions is time consuming and costly, organizations with point-factor systems find reorganization and restructuring equally costly and time consuming. Additionally, as Lawler points out, "Most major changes require some individuals to give up responsibilities and accountabilities while others gain them. If the point-factor approach is in operation, change means that some people win in terms of increased pay and others lose. This sets up competition among individuals and often a strong resistance to much-needed changes. In short, point-factor systems often end up as servants of the status quo rather than as stimulants for needed change."[7]

The result of pay practices such as the point-factor approach has been the creation of fixed compensation that is totally out of line with what most companies can now afford. Workers complain that such systems are inequitable because they create managerial- and executive-level compensation excesses. They cite examples such as General Motors, Inman Steel, and Firestone, where top executives received large increases in salary and bonus in the same years their companies lost money, plants were closed, and/or workers were laid off or forced to make wage concessions. They complain about executive compensation packages that result in executive pay a hundred times higher than that of the average worker.[8]

At the same time, executives complain about worker wages that are no longer competitive in the labor marketplace. As a result, companies such as A&P, Boeing, Lockheed, McDonnell Douglas, Giant Food, Safeway, American Airlines, Briggs & Stratton, Pan American, and Dow Chemical, among others, are forced to adopt what are called two-tier or multi-tier wage plans to remain competitive. Such compromise wage settlements protect senior employee wages while allowing these companies to hire new employees at substantially less. While such stop-gap measures help to bring at least entry-level wages into line with that of domestic and foreign competitors, they create their own inequities. Under such schemes, new employees receive significantly less compensation for performing the same job than their luckier peers who were fortunate enough to have been hired prior to adoption of the two-tier or multi-tier system.[9]

Looking for a way to correct these inequities, more and more companies are adopting a four-part approach:

1. Slowing or stopping entirely the growth in base pay
2. Relying more heavily on bonuses tied to group performance
3. Linking base pay to knowledge and skill rather than position
4. Providing expanded opportunities for employees to share in company profits and, in some cases, acquire ownership in the company

Each of these changes has significant ramifications for all Americans.

My Base Isn't Growing

As we noted earlier, the age of entitlement to annual increases is coming to an end. Although such increases are not expected to stop entirely, it is likely they will be stretched out over longer periods—fourteen, sixteen, eighteen, or twenty-four months. Additionally, and perhaps more importantly, rather than receiving the increase as a percentage addition to base salary, many Americans will receive the entire amount as a one-time, lump sum payment. Here is what these changes will mean to the average American worker—let's call him Joe:

If in 1990, Joe's annual salary was $20,000 and he received a 5 percent raise each year, between 1990 and the year 2000, his base salary would increase by 63 percent and he would have been paid over $284,000 in base salary alone (see Table 1). In addition, if Joe worked one hundred hours overtime each year at time and a half, his overtime payments would be

Table 1

Traditional Compensation

(Growth in Base Pay and Overtime with 5% Annual Increase)

Year	Base	Overtime
1990	20,000	962
1991	21,000	1,010
1992	22,050	1,060
1993	23,152	1,113
1994	24,310	1,169
1995	25,526	1,227
1996	26,802	1,289
1997	28,142	1,353
1998	29,549	1,421
1999	31,027	1,492
2000	32,578	1,566
Total	284,136	13,662

$13,662. In base salary and overtime, Joe would have earned $297,798.

Now, consider only one change. Suppose Joe received the same 5 percent raise, but only once every two years instead of every year (see Table 2). Under this scenario, his base grows more slowly, as do his overtime payments. By the year 2000, he collects $258,405 in base salary plus overtime. That's $39,393 less than Joe would have under the traditional compensation plan.

Now, let's take the illustration one step further. Suppose Joe received 5 percent lump sum payments once every two years instead of percentage increases that added to his base salary (see Table 3). Under this scenario, Joe's base salary and overtime pay do not grow through the period since the "lump sum" payments he receives are *not* added to his base, and thus *do not* compound and accumulate. At the end of the period, Joe would have collected $230,582 in base salary plus overtime. Additionally, he would have received $6,000 in lump sum payments. Joe's total compensation for the period is

Table 2

Growth in Base Pay and Overtime Pay

(5% Increase Every Two Years)

Year	Base	Overtime
1990	20,000	962
1991	20,000	962
1992	21,000	1,010
1993	21,000	1,010
1994	22,050	1,060
1995	22,050	1,060
1996	23,152	1,113
1997	23,152	1,113
1998	24,310	1,169
1999	24,310	1,169
2000	25,526	1,227
Total	246,550	11,855

$236,582 or $61,216 less than under the old system. (This is a "worst case" scenario. It is most likely that Joe would receive a combination of lump sum payments and annual increases, perhaps a lump sum every two years and raise every four years.)

Obviously, these changes in base pay have a significant impact on Joe's total income. His employer has saved over $60,000 in base salary and overtime that otherwise would have been paid to Joe. If these were the only changes in compensation the company made, Joe obviously would lose. It would be very much like having Joe take a $60,000 pay cut over the entire period. But these are not the only changes companies are making. From here on, the changes work in Joe's favor.

An Incentive for Group Performance

At least part of the $60,000 potential income Joe will lose through changes in base compensation, he will be able to make

Table 3

Growth in Total Compensation with
5% Lump Sum Payments Every Two Years

Year	Base	Overtime	Lump Sum
1990	20,000	962	1,000
1991	20,000	962	
1992	20,000	962	1,000
1993	20,000	962	
1994	20,000	962	1,000
1995	20,000	962	
1996	20,000	962	1,000
1997	20,000	962	
1998	20,000	962	1,000
1999	20,000	962	
2000	20,000	962	1,000
Total	220,000	10,582	6,000

Grand total 236,583

up through participation in a group incentive program. A wide variety of such incentive systems exist, but it is likely that most companies will adopt an incentive program called gain sharing, since it is rated by companies as being highly effective (81 percent say it has a "positive" or "very positive" impact on performance), and its use is projected to grow rapidly in both the manufacturing and service sectors (projected growth is 68 percent overall, 76 percent in manufacturing, and 168 percent in services).[10]

Gain sharing is a group-based incentive program where employees earn bonuses by finding ways to save money in labor, capital, materials, and energy. The company splits any resulting savings with employees, usually fifty-fifty. Practically every gain-sharing plan is different, so we can't tell exactly how a particular company's plan might work. Let's examine a typical manufacturing example, however.

Suppose Joe worked as an operator in a widget assembly plant. His company might adopt a gain-sharing plan based upon plant-wide performance. The formula for calculating Joe's bonus might look something like this:

a. The sales value of widgets Joe's plant produces each month is $2,500,000.
b. The cost of materials, supplies, energy, and other purchases the company makes from outside sources to produce these widgets is $1,000,000.
c. The value that Joe and his fellow employees add is then $1,500,000 (sales value of $2,500,000 minus cost of materials, supplies, etc. of $1,000,000).

Now, let's assume that historically (over the past five to seven years prior to implementing gain sharing), labor costs at the plant (what Joe and his fellow workers were paid in base pay plus overtime) has run approximately 40 percent of the value added. In other words, historically, when the value added was $1,500,000, labor costs have been approximately $600,000. Joe's company says that if Joe and his fellow workers can improve that ratio (value added to labor costs), a gain will have occurred and the company will share that gain with its employees fifty-fifty—the company keeps half and Joe and his fellow employees split the remainder.

If Joe were in a white-collar or service job, for example as in claims processing in the insurance industry, where there is a countable product (the processed claim), his company might be able to establish a cost associated with what was produced and pay a gain-sharing bonus based upon cost reductions Joe and his co-workers were able to attain. In the case of claims processing, Joe's company would establish how much it has historically cost to process a claim. If employees were able to reduce that cost, the company would pay Joe and his fellow workers a bonus, provided the accuracy rate stayed the same.

If Joe were in a white-collar job that supports a production function (as for example, production scheduling), his gain-sharing bonus might be tied in some way to actual production on the factory floor. In effect, Joe would participate in the plant gain-sharing plan. When they made a gain and received a bonus, Joe and his fellow workers in production scheduling would also receive a bonus, since, presumably, they helped make the gain possible by doing their jobs better.

If Joe's white-collar job is in a profit center, where he actually makes money for the company, his gain-sharing bonus might be tied to the revenue he produced or profits he produced. For example, if Joe and his co-workers provided a professional service and charged for services, the gain-sharing plan might be tied to revenues the service generated above its cost to the company. In retail sales, Joe's gainsharing might be tied to store sales, unit sales in his department, or sales per square foot of space occupied.

If Joe worked in a true "knowledge worker" function such as research, information systems development, or public relations, there is probably no easily countable end product. How, then, can the company calculate whether or not his group has made a gain? One way is for his company to use what is called an "objectives matrix" as suggested by the American Productivity and Quality Center.

Here's how an objectives matrix works:

1. Together with management, Joe's work group identifies a small set (say five to ten) of key measures or indicators of group performance. The key indicators might include such things as ratings by users or clients of their satisfaction with the services the group provides; the group's ability to meet deadlines; measures of service delivery cost compared to budgeted or estimated costs.
2. Once the key indicators are selected, the current or historical level of performance on each indicator is identified.
3. The team earns bonus points (worth a certain bonus percentage of their pay or a certain number of dollars) for improvements in performance on each of these indicators. They may also lose points (but not the "fixed" part of their pay) if performance on an indicator falls below the current, historical, or base level.

In short, regardless of whether Joe works in manufacturing or in the service sector, he will likely participate in a gain-

Table 4

1990–2000 Compensation with Gain Sharing

Year	Base	Overtime	Lump sum	Gain sharing
1990	20,000	962	1,000	2,096 (10%)
1991	20,000	962		2,096 (10%)
1992	20,000	962		3,144 (15%)
1993	20,000	962		3,144 (15%)
1994	20,000	962	1,000	4,192 (20%)
1995	20,000	962		4,192 (20%)
1996	20,000	962		5,240 (25%)
1997	20,000	962		5,240 (25%)
1998	20,000	962	1,000	6,289 (30%)
1999	20,000	962		6,289 (30%)
2000	20,000	962		7,337 (35%)
Total	220,000	10,582	3,000	49,259

sharing plan. But what does that mean to Joe? What type of bonus might he earn? Obviously, there is no guarantee. He could earn a large bonus or none at all. What might he expect to earn? In a well-designed gain-sharing plan, it would not be unreasonable to expect that Joe's payments could start at 10 percent of his base pay plus overtime and reach as much as 35 percent within the decade (see Table 4).

Under this scenario, Joe's total compensation for the period increases to $285,841. With a gainsharing bonus, he recoups over 80 percent of the loss in compensation that resulted when his company stopped giving him regular annual percentage increases. Joe is still nearly $12,000 short of where he would have been during "the age of entitlement," however. Plus, Joe probably would have noticed something about gain sharing that he didn't like. Under the gain-sharing plan we described, Joe received bonuses ranging from 10 percent to 35 percent. But so did John, who doesn't work as hard as Joe does. So did Mary, who tries her best, but—well—just can't seem to produce nearly as much as Joe can. Does it seem unfair that everyone in Joe's work group got the same percentage bonus regardless of how hard they worked or how much they contributed to make gains happen? Remember, we said gain sharing was a group bonus plan. If a gain is made and a bonus is paid, everyone in the group shares equally in the bonus (at least the same percentage). If that seems unfair to Joe, he's not alone. Most people feel it is unfair. Yet, such payments are typical of gainsharing and other group-based bonus plans.

How could that inequity be corrected? Let's look at what really happens. Under gain sharing, each person receives the same percentage bonus (15 percent for example). Now, while the percentage is the same, the dollar amount people receive is different. If Joe's base salary plus overtime is $20,000, then his bonus is $3,000. But if Joe's base salary plus overtime is $30,000, then his bonus would increase to $4,500. In other words, the higher Joe's base salary plus overtime, the higher his gain-sharing bonus in dollars. If Joe could increase his base salary, then he would take home a larger bonus check under gainsharing. But didn't we say that base salaries would not increase? No. We said the "age of entitlement" to annual increases in base salary was over. Base salaries will not automatically increase. There will be a way, however, for Joe to increase his base pay. It won't be automatic. It will come as a result of Joe increasing his value to the company. And it is the third major change in compensation practices we are likely to see.

What About Me? Pay for My Knowledge, Skill, Flexibility

Two primary concerns drive companies to adopt the third major change in compensation practices. First, as soon as most companies adopt a gain-sharing program (and often, even when the concept of gain sharing is first introduced), high performers complain of inequities and having to "carry" low performers. Employees and managers alike are uncomfortable with distributing bonus payments under gain sharing without regard to individual contribution. Yet, as we noted, such a distribution scheme is characteristic of gain sharing (and, in fact, most group incentive plans). Early on, most companies look for some way to correct this built-in inequity in the gain-sharing plan without destroying the group basis of the plan. Frequently, these companies find that a pay-for-knowledge system will, at least partially, offset this inequity. Additionally, pay-for-knowledge addresses a second concern most companies have—the desire to encourage employee flexibility in job assignments.

Pay-for-knowledge and the general movement toward reducing the number of job categories represent a direct attack on the traditional concept of work rules and job restrictions. Traditionally, particularly if a company was unionized, workers have been restricted in the number of jobs they could perform. Workers were forbidden to move from one job to another. Even their supervisor was forbidden by the union contract, for example, to fill in for an employee who was on break. If the employee assigned to perform the job wasn't available, the job simply was not done, even if other employees had to stand around waiting and idle. Under such work rules, a worker couldn't, for example, move a rack of clothes in a retail store if that task was not in his or her job description. If the computer was broken and needed minor repairs, a worker couldn't make them even if he or she knew how. The computer operator had to wait for the person whose job it was to make such repairs. Such restrictions, obviously, cause significant delays, drive up costs, and hurt productivity. In fact, Peter Drucker, the popular management writer, has said that work rules and job restrictions are the main cause of the "productivity" gap between America (and Europe) and other countries such as Japan.[11]

Most simply, pay-for-knowledge is a pay practice that ties base salary to job knowledge and skill rather than position or jobs actually being performed. It is directly aimed at encouraging employees to be more flexible and to give up formal job restrictions. Under such a system, workers have the opportunity to increase their base pay by learning to perform a variety of jobs. Since they learn to perform more jobs, they are more valuable to their company because they are more flexible. In manufacturing, for example, workers might learn to perform jobs "upstream" (earlier) and "downstream" (later) in the production process. In a white-collar or service industry, they might learn to perform the full range of operations to process an order or service a customer. Because of their increased skill and flexibility, their company can use them to help others in case of a bottleneck outside their normal work group. Thus, more product is produced and fewer employees stand around idle waiting for work. According to the American Productivity and Quality Center survey we mentioned earlier, pay-for-knowledge systems are projected to grow by 75 percent overall (63 percent in manufacturing and 122 percent in the service sector). Thus, many American companies will at least experiment with such a system. Fortunately, the rewards for American workers are considerable and will go a long way toward helping them overcome any loss in compensation they might experience from the "end of entitlement" to base pay increases. However, they must "add value" to their company differently than in the past by being more flexible rather than doing one job very well.

Here is how a pay-for-knowledge system works. Again, we will use an average American worker—Joe—as an example. First, Joe's company identifies the tasks performed in existing jobs for an entire work group, plant, division, etc. Then, the skills required to perform these tasks are identified. The number of skills that are identified can vary greatly. For example, plants currently using pay-for-knowledge have identified as few as four or as many as ninety different skills.[12] Regardless of how many skills are identified, Joe's company establishes a number of skill levels and Joe is given the opportunity to apply to be trained in these skills. For each skill level Joe learns (provided he can demonstrate through periodic testing or performance that he is maintaining the skill), Joe is paid a supplement to his base salary or base hourly wage. Thus, Joe can increase his base pay by mastering more skill levels.

Carrying our scenario forward, let's see how a pay-for-knowledge system would affect Joe's total compensation from 1990 through 2000. Assuming Joe started with a $20,000 base salary and was paid a 25 cent per hour pay-for-knowledge supplement for each skill level he mastered and he mastered one additional skill level per year, his annual base salary would increase from $20,000 to $25,210 (see Table 5). (A 25 cent per hour supplement is very conservative. The typical plan could pay as much as $1.00 per hour, or more, per skill set.)

Now, let's see how pay-for-knowledge would impact Joe's

Table 5

Increase in Annual Base Salary with Pay-for-Knowledge

Skill level	Hourly rate	Annual base salary
0	$ 9.62	$20,000
1	9.87	20,530
2	10.12	21,050
3	10.37	21,570
4	10.62	22,090
5	10.87	22,610
6	11.12	23,130
7	11.37	23,650
8	11.62	24,170
9	11.87	24,690
Top	12.12	25,210

total compensation for the period 1990 to 2000, assuming he received a 5 percent lump sum payment every other year and a gain-sharing bonus (see Table 6).

Under this scenario, Joe's total compensation for the period would be $324,728, or almost $27,000 over what he would have received with regular annual increases. Thanks to pay-for-knowledge, Joe has recouped more than he lost as a result of the end of entitlement. In addition, his peers won't begrudge Joe's pay-for-knowledge increases because his flexibility will help them earn greater gain-sharing checks. Joe stands to gain even more, at least in net worth if not in immediate cash, from the fourth, and final, major change in compensation that we discuss next.

An Incentive for My Company's Performance— A Share of the Company

The final major change we see taking place in compensation practices has significant ramifications for every American's

Table 6

1990–2000 Compensation with Gain
Sharing and Pay-for-Knowledge

Year	Annual Salary	Overtime	Lump sum	Gain-sharing bonus	Total compensation
1990	20,000	962	1,000	2,096 (10%)	24,058
1991	20,530	987		2,152 (10%)	23,669
1992	21,050	1,012	1,153	3,309 (15%)	26,524
1993	21,570	1,037		3,391 (15%)	25,998
1994	22,090	1,062	1,105	4,630 (20%)	28,887
1995	22,610	1,087		4,739 (20%)	28,436
1996	23,130	1,112	1,157	6,061 (25%)	31,460
1997	23,650	1,137		6,197 (25%)	30,984
1998	24,170	1,162	1,209	7,600 (30%)	34,141
1999	24,690	1,187		7,763 (30%)	33,640
2000	25,210	1,212	1,261	9,248 (35%)	36,931
Total	$248,700	11,957	6,885	57,186	$324,728

net worth. Here we refer to ESOPs (employee stock option plans). Although we list this "change" last, it may not be a change for some Americans at all. In the late 1980s, there was an explosive growth in the number of companies adopting an ESOP.

Since 1974, when they first became possible, Congress has passed seventeen laws to encourage companies to form ESOPs. Generally, an ESOP works like this. A company sets up a trust fund into which it contributes new shares of stock or money to buy existing shares. Usually, the annual company contribution is about 10 percent of pay each year. In some cases, the ESOP may obtain a loan to buy existing shares of stock and the company contributes money to repay the loan. Regardless, a pool of stock is established. Shares of the stock in the pool are then distributed to individual accounts for eligible employees—usually all employees over the age of twenty-one who work at least one thousand hours for the company in a given year. The stock allocation to an individual account is based upon a percentage of pay or some other formula established in advance. An employee's rights to the shares of stock in his or her account increases with his or her seniority so that after five to seven years the stock is usually his or hers. After that time, when the employee leaves the firm, the company buys back the stock at its fair market value. In a private company, the market value of the stock is determined by an outside valuation performed yearly. In a public company, the value is the market price of the stock. Through an ESOP, employees can eventually acquire ownership of as much as 100 percent of the company. Additionally, employees gain through their stock ownership voting rights on at least major issues (such as a plant closing or relocation) in a private company and most issues in a public company.

Why would a company want to set up an ESOP? The reason is simple. If employees own part of the company, they will most likely take a greater interest in its success. In fact, that is exactly what appears to happen when ESOPs are created. A major study of ESOP companies has shown they grow 40 to 46 percent faster after they set up an ESOP. *Companies that combined the ESOP with a high level of employee participation in decision making grew even faster.*[13] Additionally, important tax and other financial advantages flow to a company when it installs an ESOP. And companies might have other reasons for setting up an ESOP. For example, in the late 1980s, a number of companies created ESOPs to avoid a hostile takeover, reasoning that employees as stockholders would presumably fear a hostile takeover that might result in plant closing or downsizing, thus they would be more inclined to side with management.

In a sense, an ESOP is much like a gain-sharing plan—if company performance is good, part of the financial gains to the company from that good performance are shared with employees. However, an ESOP is different from other types of sharing programs in one important respect. Here is how Corey Rosen, the executive director of the National Center for Employee Ownership, describes that important difference: "In an ESOP, a company makes contributions to a trust fund each year, so employees get some amount of company stock and sometimes cash each year. This is not much different in principle from other gain-sharing programs. Where it differs is that in other variants, the money is either spent or put into a diversified holding unaffected by company performance. In an ESOP, employees build up more and more stock each year, so that each year they receive both the new contribution and the appreciation on the total existing shares, plus any dividends." For example, an employee who earns $20,000 per year and gets a 10 percent gain-sharing bonus, receives $2,000 cash. Under an ESOP, if the employee has a $20,000 (stock) balance, and the stock value increases by 10 percent, then he or she gets not only a $2,000 stock contribution for that year, but another $2,000 from the increased value of the stock in his or her account. In this way, many employees accumulate balances of $50,000 or $100,000 or more over the first five to thirteen years of an ESOP.

Let's see how an ESOP would affect our mythical Joe. If we use Rosen's assumptions about a stock contribution equal to 10 percent of pay each year and a 10 percent annual growth in the value of stock (including reinvested dividends), by the year 2000 Joe would have accumulated stock in his company worth $52,526 (see Table 7). Since he would be "vested" by that time (having been employed by the company long enough to gain ownership rights in the stock), Joe could sell his stock (although he might be required to leave the company to do so) and pocket over $50,000 in cash.

With an ESOP, gainsharing, and pay-for-knowledge, Joe's total compensation for the period is nearly $80,000 more than it would have been with traditional regular annual increases ($377,254 in *Workplace 2000* versus $297,798 with annual increases).

The Positive Side—You Mean I Make More?

The positive side of the four changes in compensation we have just described is that the average American worker has the *opportunity* to make more. Whether he or she actually makes more depends upon the performance of his or her company, its management, fellow workers, and him or her. Remember, as we said earlier, the age of entitlement is over. In developing our scenarios, we made certain assumptions. We assumed:

Table 7

1990–2000 Growth in Value of Stock Under ESOP

Year	Salary + overtime + GS bonus + lump sum	10% stock under ESOP	10% increase in value of stock from previous year	Cum. value of stock
1990	24,058	2,406	None	2,406
1991	23,669	2,367	241	5,014
1992	26,524	2,652	501	8,167
1993	25,998	2,600	817	11,584
1994	28,887	2,889	1,158	15,631
1995	28,436	2,844	1,563	20,038
1996	31,460	3,146	2,004	25,188
1997	30,984	3,098	2,519	30,805
1998	34,141	3,414	3,081	37,300
1999	33,640	3,364	3,730	44,394
2000	36,931	3,693	4,439	52,526
Total	**$324,728**			**$52,526**

- A 5 percent lump sum payment every two years
- A gain-sharing bonus that increased annually from 10 percent to 35 percent of base salary plus overtime
- An increase in base salary by $2.50 per hour over the period as a result of a pay-for-knowledge system
- Participation in an ESOP with a 10 percent stock contribution equal to 10 percent of total compensation per year and a 10 percent growth in the value of accumulated stock (including dividends)

We believe these assumptions are reasonable. In fact, they are conservative. But obviously what happens in a particular company is likely to be different. Some may do better than our scenario represents. For example, some gain-sharing plans will pay out at a higher percentage per year than we assumed. However, a company could do worse. How can an American worker make sure that he or she will be better off, not worse off? Here are some guidelines to follow:

1. One clue to how successful a company is going to be with these new compensation systems, and consequently, how much employees will earn under these new systems, is how the company's management approaches the whole compensation issue. Americans should watch for how their company treats compensation and how consistent it is in applying a compensation philosophy to executives and workers. Carla O'Dell and C. Jackson Grayson, co-authors of *American Business: A Two Minute Warning*, note that successful companies "don't expect a pay system to set strategy or manage people or performance. They use the reward system to reinforce the strategy and philosophy, not create it." Americans should pay attention to how their company approaches executive compensation. Does the practice send the message that "we are all crew members of the same boat?" Or does it send a message that we may be on the same boat, but as O'Dell and Grayson say, "executives are staying in staterooms while everyone else is sleeping on the deck?"[14]

2. Americans should note how their company goes about making these changes in compensation practices. Was the gain-sharing plan, pay-for-knowledge system, and so forth developed by a staff group, an outside consultant, or a group of executives in isolation without employee and lower-level management involvement? If so, there is a good chance the plan won't be successful. Good plans—and more importantly, those that pay out substantial bonuses—are almost always developed as a cooperative, collaborative effort between managers and employees.

3. Personal financial survival under these new pay systems requires that Americans give more attention to developing and adhering to a personal financial plan. All these systems mean that pay will be much more variable. The security of a regular predictable paycheck that constantly gets larger won't exist anymore. Pay may fluctuate as much as 40 percent. If Americans count on the gain sharing, profit sharing, ever increasing value of stocks, they may be disappointed. What spe-

cifically should they consider? They might want to increase their savings, minimize long-term debt (at least the kind where monthly payments increase over time), and maintain higher available cash reserves in case a bonus they are expecting doesn't happen.

4. Since base pay levels impact not only overtime pay but also the dollar amount of gain-sharing bonuses, lump sum payments, and the dollar value of stocks an employee receives under an ESOP, Americans should take advantage of the opportunity to learn new skills under a pay-for-knowledge system. This will likely be the only sure way they have of increasing their base pay level.

5. Every American should learn as much as he or she can about his or her company and its competitive strategy. To a greater extent than ever before, an employee's personal financial fortunes will be tied to the success of his or her company. If the company is competitive—produces a quality product, satisfies its customers, keeps cost down, enters the right markets—then employees may reap significant personal financial rewards. In contrast, if the company makes mistakes—if it wastes money, if the product quality is poor—then not only will the company suffer financially, but employees will share in that suffering. While the average worker may not be involved in making high-level, company-wide decisions, he or she can have a significant impact through participation in decision making and problem solving at the work-group level. Work groups can address needed improvement in such areas as quality, customer service, and cost reduction. In fact, as we shall discuss in a later chapter, most Americans will be required as part of their job to become involved in finding ways to solve such problems and improve performance.

As we said at the opening of this chapter, the changes that are occurring in compensation are revolutionary because they fundamentally and permanently alter the financial relationship Americans have with their employers. In the past, the work contract was to provide a fair day's work for a fair day's pay. In *Workplace 2000*, employees will become—in every sense of the words—"financial partners."

CHAPTER 6

Leadership in the New American Workplace

In the 1980s, most American workers were managed. Few were led. Americans didn't work for leaders. They worked (or more precisely, "put in their hours") for managers. As Burt Namus, author of *The Leader's Edge: Seven Keys to Leadership in a Turbulent World*, has noted, in the 1980s "Effective leadership [was] as rare as an Olympic record, and often as temporary." As a result, American businesses were overmanaged and underled. Such will not be the case in *Workplace 2000*. *Workplace 2000* will require leadership, not management. Stable organizations can be managed. Chaotic organizations must be led. And there is little doubt that *Workplace 2000* will be chaotic. The difference between the 1970s/1980s leadership paradigm and that of the 1990s and beyond is not so much one of content as coverage. A uniquely different style of leadership isn't demanded. What is demanded is more leaders. *Workplace 2000* demands a heightened quantity of leadership, not just a heightened quality.

Accustomed to being "managed," most Americans will find themselves being "led" in the new American workplace. The change from management to leadership will reshape the work environment and the experiences of Americans at work. And the increased demand for leaders versus managers will open exciting new opportunities for those Americans willing and able to develop and exercise leadership skills.

The Difference Between Leaders and Managers

Leaders may be managers. In fact, one of the functions of leaders at times is to manage. But managing is a minor part of what leaders do. Leadership is much broader than and uniquely different from managing. Managers plan, organize, staff, direct, and control. Leaders also do these things, but not exclusively, and when they do them, they do them in a different way and at a different level of purpose. Leaders plan, but their planning, rather than being pedestrian as it often is with managers, is more global in terms of setting the agenda for the future. Leaders organize, but their organizational responsibilities go beyond moving players on an organization chart to mobilizing resources and building institutional arrangements that will enable the organization to achieve its overarching goals. Leaders staff, but their staffing function involves identifying and developing talent rather than merely filling vacancies. Leaders direct and control, but their direction tends more toward defining end purposes and their control leans more toward empowering people and holding them responsible for finding their own means to those ends.

Leaders differ from managers in that they go far beyond the performance of management functions. Typically, managers focus on operating their area of assigned responsibility for efficiency, cost containment, and compliance with delivery schedules. Leaders are also interested in these things, but they go beyond an interest in performance requirements (that, for managers, are usually dictated by others from above) to an interest in the effectiveness of their operation in meeting the larger needs of the organization within which they operate, or society as a whole. Burt Namus puts it this way, "Managers are concerned with doing things right. . . . Leaders focus on doing the right thing and choosing what should be done and why, not just how to do it."

The focus of a leader's attention and interest are different from a manager's. Managers are largely internally focused. They concentrate on mobilizing and deploying capital, labor, and technology to achieve desired purposes. Leaders do too, but their interest extends beyond their own operations. Leaders are "boundary managers." They focus on identifying and acquiring resource and constituent support for their "team's" agenda. In this respect, leaders are much more involved in politics and selling than managers are. Leaders are adept at selling their ideas versus (or in addition to) selling products and services. They are marketers of thoughts, feelings, and emotions, which they connect to concrete action. Leaders are politically adept. They possess and exercise skills to resolve conflict and balance the interests of multiple constituencies to build consensus on both a vision of the future and concrete steps to achieve that vision.

And there are many other differences. Managers have employees. Leaders have followers. Managers command and control. Leaders inspire and empower. The manager's authority is legitimized by his or her position title. The leader's authority is legitimized by his or her vision and ability to communicate that vision to followers. Managers seek stability, predictability, and to be in control. Leaders seek flexibility and change. Leaders accept the world as fluid and constantly changing. They do not respond to change as something to be avoided or minimized as managers often do, but something to be encouraged. Their objective isn't so much to manage or control change as to take advantage of it. To leaders, change provides opportunities, not problems. Leaders anticipate disappointment and defeat. They accept failure as one natural consequence of exploring the unknown. Leaders fully operationalize the kind of belief that appears in Federal Express's Manager's Guide—a sort of bible for leadership at the company—"Fear of failure must never be a reason not to try something new."[1]

Managers and leaders think in different ways. Managers are analytical and convergent. Leaders are intuitive and divergent. Managers make decisions and solve problems for their employees. Leaders set a direction and then empower and enable followers to make their own decisions and solve their own problems. Managers emphasize the rational and tangible. Leaders emphasize intangibles such as vision, values, motivation. Managers think and act for the short term. Leaders think and act for the long term. Managers accept organizational structure, policies, procedures, and methodology as they exist. Leaders constantly seek to find a better way.

What It Is Like to Work for a Leader

As might be expected given the differences in leadership and management we have just cited, working for a leader is quite different from working for a manager. Leaders behave differently and have different expectations. What might Americans expect from their bosses in *Workplace 2000?* In what ways will bosses act or behave differently? Here are some of the qualities we can expect from our *Workplace 2000* leader:

Workplace 2000 Leaders Will Have a Vision

Workplace 2000 leaders will have a vision of the future. What is a vision? What does it look like, smell like, taste like? How does an American know when what he or she is hearing or reading or (more aptly) being asked to live for is a vision? Well, it isn't "build market share" and certainly not "make money." A vision is much broader and more compelling. It's a dream and an ideal. It's nothing less than "changing the world." The leader visualizes an ultimate purpose or mission for the organization that is so inspirational followers will voluntarily suspend rational judgement about the probability of success. For example, "perfection" might well be rationally judged to be both indefinable and impossible. Yet under the spell of the leader, "perfection" becomes not just desirable, but seemingly imminently definable and attainable. Leaders visualize a larger reality and transmit that vision to others.

A vision is more like the following goal Steven Jobs had in mind for his company Next. Jobs said:

We wanted to start a company that had a lot to do with education and, in particular, higher education, colleges, and universities. So our vision is that there's a revolution in software going on now on college and university campuses. And it has to do with providing two types of breakthrough software. One is called simulated learning environments. You can't give a student in physics a linear accelerator. You can't give a student in biology a $5 million recombinant DNA laboratory. But you can simulate those things. You can simulate them on a very powerful computer.

It is not possible for students to afford these things. It is not possible for most faculty members to afford these things. So if we can take what we do best, which is to find really good technology and pull it down to a price point that's affordable to people, if we can do the same thing for this type of computer, which is maybe ten times as powerful as a personal computer, that we did for personal computers, then I think we can make a real difference in the way the learning experience happens in the next five years. And that's what we're trying to do.

. . . We're doing this because we really care about the higher education process, not because we want to make a buck."[2]

Jobs isn't going to just build a computer or "make a buck." At least that's not the way he conveys his vision. No, Jobs is out to change the world of higher education, to change the way people learn—fundamentally and forever. Notice also that Jobs doesn't talk about how the vision will be achieved, just that it is there and worth achieving. The details will come later. The vision isn't complicated. It's simple, but inspiring. But also, Jobs is very clear about the future state. We may not be able to visualize from Jobs' description what his Next computer would look like, but we can visualize what it would do, or at least (and more importantly) what it would mean to people who used it. Jobs's vision is broad, societal, far-reaching. But do all visions have to be so grand? No. The new American workplace will need different types of leaders with different levels of vision. Small business units (the predominant organizational structure of *Workplace 2000* as we explained in an earlier chapter) will require leaders with Steven Jobs's kind of broad vision. But there will also be a need for leaders at a different level—reporting to the business unit leader. These lower-level leaders (such as division managers and department heads) are interpreters of the grand vision and arbiters of values for their own units. They "visualize" how their unit can contribute to realizing the company leader's vision.

A vision is a powerful tool for mobilizing people to action. Leaders know that and use it. Charles Garfield, a computer scientist, worked on the Apollo program for NASA. He described the power of the "vision" leaders had and used for the Apollo program: "I saw men and women of average capabilities tapping resources of personal energy and creativity that resulted in extraordinary accomplishments. I saw their excitement and pride come alive, affecting everyone around them, building their imaginations with the possibilities that arose from what they were trying to accomplish. One thing became very clear to me. It is not the goal but the ultimate mission that kindles the imagination, motivating us toward higher levels of achievement."[3]

The pride, excitement, and extraordinary accomplishments Byrd refers to came in response to what was obviously a grand vision. But what about the more mundane vision of a lower- or middle-level leader—not the leader of a business unit itself? Can the challenge of realizing a "less than grand" vision motivate people to extraordinary effort? Apparently so. John Stack, selected by *Inc.* magazine in the late 1980s as the person it would most like to have as a chief operating officer on its "Dream Team," tells the following story about what happened to him while he worked at International Harvester:

I remember, we had to ship out 800 tractors to the Soviet Union, and I was in charge of scheduling the parts. At the time there was a severe shortage of the parts we needed, but without those parts the tractors wouldn't go to Russia, and our department would get killed. As I recall, we had until November 1, and this was October already. On paper, it couldn't be done. So I put up a big sign, saying "OUR

GOAL: 800 TRACTORS," and I explained to my guys exactly what was going on, what was at stake . . .

[My guys] . . . were amazing. They went into the factory each night and crawled over those tractors and figured out what parts were needed and how many tractors were short those particular parts. They got the parts any way they could. On October 31, we hit 803. Boy, did we send up the balloons . . .

. . . [I]t showed me what people could do. I saw these guys get hungry. I saw them push and accomplish things they never thought were possible. I saw satisfaction on a daily basis. I mean these guys didn't know they were working! I thought, My God, if I can get people pumped up, wanting to come to work every day, what an edge that is! That's what nobody else is doing. Suppose I could run the right numbers so that a guy wakes up in the morning and says, "Man, I feel like shit, but I really want to go in there and see what happened." That's the whole secret to increasing productivity.[4]

Steven Jobs and John Stack both had a vision. Jobs's vision was to change the world. Stack's was a little more mundane—just do an impossible thing right and on time. But for both Jobs and Stack, the vision was key. Vision, as we have said, is the foundation of leadership. Without a vision, one cannot be a leader. Where, then, does vision come from? In *The Charismatic Leader: Behind the Mystique of Exceptional Leadership*, Jay Conger suggests that "vision is very much an incremental process spurred on by past experiences, creative insights, opportunism, and serendipity." He identifies six stages of experiences or development that lead to the development of a vision and leadership:

1. Early adulthood or early to mid-career interests such as Donald Burr's childhood love of airplanes, John De-Lorean's early interest in the automotive industry, Steven Jobs's high school interest in buying, selling, and trading electronic equipment, and Mary Kay Ash's interest in selling.

2. Early and broad exposure to a type of product/service or

a particular industry that enables the future leader to detect shortcomings and emerging opportunities in his or her chosen field of interest. For example, Jan Carlzon held a number of positions in the travel industry before becoming head of SAS, and Louis Gerstner had been a McKinsey consultant working in the financial services industry before becoming head of the credit card and traveler's check businesses for American Express.[5]

3. Exposure during his or her career to innovative ideas and/ or tactics. For example, Mary Kay Ash developed her idea for home "parties" to sell cosmetics as a result of her experience as a salesperson with Stanley Home Products, which used the same technique to sell household cleaning products.

4. Personal experiences that heightened the future leader's sensitivity to constituent needs or market demands. For example, Ross Perot, founder of Electronic Data Systems (EDS), developed his idea for EDS as a result of his personal experiences working for IBM and his observation that many of the IBM customers he dealt with couldn't use their computers effectively.

5. A period of experimentation in which the future leader is able to try out and refine his or her idea. Conger notes, "It would be wrong to think that somehow, quite miraculously, the leader's vision simply appears one day. The process is much more gradual. . . . Visions tend to be in constant evolution. . . . The leader may experiment with the initial ideas to test their possibilities and the receptivity of the organization and marketplace . . ."

6. Seizing a market, resource, or technological opportunity. The key here is the future leader's unique ability to take advantage of an emerging trend or need. Conger tells the following story of the development of Steven Jobs's vision for the Next computer:

> Shortly after he stepped down from Apple Computer, Steven Jobs contemplated the possibility of new ventures. He spent days reading books on science in search of ideas. He had been reading microbiology texts and became intrigued by DNA and how it replicated itself.

He phoned Paul Berg, a Nobel prize winner in biochemistry at Stanford, and over a 2-½ hour lunch, Berg explained the recombination of DNA in a laboratory and how it was a time-consuming process of trial and error. Jobs was curious whether Berg had ever attempted to speed up these experiments by simulating them on a computer. Berg had, but the computer hardware to manage such complex simulations was extremely expensive and the existing software was primitive. With a burst of enthusiasm, Jobs exclaimed that he wanted to start a new computer company and that this might just be the product. For Jobs, this meeting would open the door to his next opportunity: the Next computer company.

Conger notes that vision—the spark of leadership—derives from two sources. First, the leader has the unique ability "to synthesize diverse information, weeding out the irrelevant, and then conceptualizing it into a coherent picture," and then the leader is willing to take the risk of taking action to realize his or her vision.[6]

Workplace 2000 Leaders Will Be Able to Communicate Their Vision

Having a vision is one thing. Communicating that vision to others in a way that is exciting and compels followers to action is another. Leaders are great communicators. In fact, communication may be a prerequisite skill for leadership. Leaders create a verbal picture of the future state they envision and demonstrate through stories and anecdotes how persistence, perseverance, cooperation, determination, commitment, etc. on behalf of followers can and will lead to the desired future state. Leaders must therefore be adept at communication. Conger notes, "The task of leadership . . . becomes a matter of infusing day-to-day work with a larger sense of purpose and intrinsic appeal. To accomplish this, the leader must not only be able to sense meaningful opportunities in the environment but also to describe them in ways that maximize their significance." Part of "visioning" is explaining. The vision interprets the past and present and explains the future (or at least a version of the future). John Gardner, in his book *On Leadership*, describes "explaining" and its purpose in this way: "Explaining sounds too pedestrian to be on a list of leadership tasks, but every leader recognizes it. People want to know what the problem is, why they are being asked to do certain things, why they face so many frustrations. Thurman Arnold said, 'Unhappy is a people that has run out of words to describe what is happening to them.' Leaders find the words."

Leaders certainly do "find the words." In fact, they find eloquent words. Listening to a leader is quite different from listening to a manager. Consider the following contrasts of listener reaction to leaders and managers as provided by Jay Conger:

> About the leader: "I enjoy listening to him—it can be very exciting at times. . . . He's so visionary when he speaks. . . . He presents a tremendous challenge."

> About the manager: "He can often be very detailed in his speeches covering a lot of ground. . . . He generally reads them from a prepared manuscript so there's not a lot of dynamism."

> About the leader: "He fills the room with ideas, challenges . . . hell of a job stimulating, exciting, you and the group. He's very engaging. He puts the force of his personality behind his ideas, and he gets you moving toward an idea as quickly as he can. . . . He engages by building to a crescendo."

> About the manager: "He speaks in a businesslike tone. It's really a monotone. . . . For example, he'll explain current capital budgeting plans or sales trends in different markets or the company's general strategy."

The leader engages, excites, and mesmerizes his or her audience. How? With stories, with common and easy-to-understand language, with repetition and rhythm in his or her pattern of speech, with direct and powerful words, and with expressive body language, all of which create the sense of a common enemy to be conquered or common values to be preserved and extended. The leader also communicates by matching his or her words with action.

John Gardner says this about the ability leaders have for "getting their message across": "Effective leaders deal not only with the explicit decisions of the day . . . but also with that partly conscious, partly buried world of needs and hopes, ideals and symbols. They serve as models; they symbolize the group's unity and identity; they retell stories that carry shared meanings. Their exemplary impact is great. There are messages for followers in what leaders pay attention to, in how they deal with critical incidents, in the correspondence between their words and acts, in the ethical tone of their behavior."

The *Workplace 2000* Leader Will Build Trust

In addition to having and being able to communicate a lofty vision, the *Workplace 2000* leader will also have the capability to get his or her followers to trust in his or her ability to turn that vision into reality. The leader's followers will act to accomplish the leader's vision because they will believe the leader's vision—with his or her guidance—is imminently attainable. How does the leader build such trust? First, the leader has or creates the illusion of a track record of success. Attaining the vision is believable to his or her followers because the leader says, "Look at what I have been able to accomplish before. You can believe in me because I have demonstrated I have the knowledge, skill, determination, etc. to see something like this through to a successful conclusion. Sure there are risks. But I can minimize those risks and keep them at an acceptable level." Not only does the leader have a history of success to imbue confidence, but he or she exudes confidence enhancing personal characteristics. He or she is (or at least appears to be) smart, quick witted, knowledgeable, perceptive, and talented. To be around him or her is to be around someone obviously destined for greatness.

Other ways leaders build trust and faith in their abilities are:

- Through self-confidence. The leader never seems to doubt his or her own capabilities or, for that matter, the capabilities of his or her "team" of followers. "We can do it," the leader says. "I know we can. I have no doubt."
- Through steadiness and predictability. Followers know where the leader stands on those issues that are important. He or she will, they know, respond to events in concert with the vision and known values. Above all, he or she can be relied upon. John Gardner says, "The need for reliability is not only ethically desirable, it is generally a practical necessity. A leader who is unpredictable poses a nerve-wracking problem for followers. They cannot rally around a leader if they do not know where he or she stands."
- Through unconventional behavior. The leader is predictable, but he or she is also different. He or she is noisy and expressive where others (mere managers) are quiet and reserved. He or she is informal and reachable where others (the managers) are formal and closed to all but their peers. The leader stands out from the norm as a welcome, refreshing change. "Something," his followers say, "is really different here."
- By possessing and demonstrating (or appearing to possess and demonstrate) values, beliefs, and aspirations in common with those he or she leads. The leader is different in many respects from his or her followers, but fundamentally, he or she isn't different. To his or her followers, the leader's words and actions send the message, "We are alike. I'm one of you. I think like you think. I want what you want."
- By a total personal commitment. The leader demonstrates his or her total commitment to the "cause." He or she will and does put personal reputation, financial security, and whatever else it takes "on the line" (or at least appears to do so). Frederick Smith risked several million dollars of his own money to start an overnight air delivery service. At the time, few "experts" thought a market existed for such a service. But Smith persevered. In 1988, Smith's company, Federal Express, had revenues of $3.8 billion.

The *Workplace 2000* Leader Will Empower People and Hold Them Accountable for Performance

The leader of the future American business will trust his or her subordinates and reject the possibility that the organization can be successful as a result of command and control. Obtaining employee commitment will be seen as the only option for securing success. The leader of the future will push responsibility and accountability down to the lowest ranks of the organization. He or she will rely upon people at every level to do the right thing as they understand it. If the people fail, the initial assumption of the *Workplace 2000* leader will be that perhaps he or she is at fault—not his or her employees. "Perhaps," the *Workplace 2000* leader will say, "I have failed to communicate the vision, or I haven't created the right environment, or I haven't adequately shared the social and financial rewards that can flow from success." "First," he or she will say, "I must look to my own behavior—what I have said and done. Then, and only then, will I look to the behavior of my employees."

The *Workplace 2000* leader will expect uncompromising excellence in performance and assume that it can and must be achieved. Excellence will be viewed as not an option, but a necessity. To enable excellence, leaders of the future will search diligently for the best way to do things right the first time and will be devoted to training and coaching every employee in the details of performance. Nothing will be insignificant enough to be left to chance, particularly if it involves such critical matters as product quality or customer service. In respect to the search for "one best way," the organization of the future will share characteristics of the "scientifically managed" organization of the past. But there will be one critical difference in *Workplace 2000*. In the past, the "one best way" was defined by engineers or professionals charged with that responsibility. Employees weren't expected or allowed to join in the search. *Workplace 2000* leaders will insist upon the organization finding and following "one best way," but then the new leader will be equally insistent that employees be "empowered" to find a better way.

"Empowering" will be the chief motivational tool of *Work-*

place 2000 leaders and the primary way they get things done. People feel empowered when they feel confident and in control. Leaders empower people. And empowerment is an emotional and motivational high. No task seems too difficult. No outcome seems too impossible or, at least, unworthy of valiant effort. The leader's efforts at empowerment are varied, but all aimed at the same outcome—followers who have ever increasing faith in their own abilities. What are the leader's empowering strategies? He or she uses all of the following:

- Building confidence through winning. The leader firmly believes in the philosophy that "winners win." Therefore, he or she structures situations wherein winning is never totally certain, but highly likely. The challenge exists, but it is an attainable opportunity. "Small success by small success," reasons the leader, "I will build their confidence in their own innate abilities to the point where they will finally believe they cannot just possibly or probably, but certainly meet and conquer any challenge no matter how imposing it might be."
- Makes performance (success) really matter. The leader is effusive with reinforcement. Accomplishment, success, even improvement is lavishly praised and meaningfully recognized. Success—even getting better—is made really important and a cause for celebration with noise and pageantry. But the praise is genuine—not fake. It is earned, not given. The leader is well aware of the dangers of insincerity. Leaders are in touch with people. Intuitively, they understand the psychological, social, spiritual, aesthetic, and physical needs most people in the culture hold. Leaders are not reluctant to utilize their understanding and sensitivity to these needs and their ability to arrange the environment to meet these needs in order to redirect follower behavior in concert with the common good. The leader doesn't question whether such redirection is manipulative since he or she assumes the "rightness" of the overarching goal.
- Making work fun. The leader occasionally does something totally outrageous to relieve the tension. He or she believes in the irreverent sign on the wall, the silly memo,

the joke in the middle of the serious project review meeting. The leader carefully times and orchestrates an "event" designed to reduce the stress. "After all," the leader reasons, "tense people, people under stress, people who aren't having fun and enjoying what they do can't produce—at least not as well."

- Finally, and most importantly, the leader coaches. He or she doesn't control, order, demand, or criticize. The leader asks people what they want to do—what they think they should do—to solve their own problems. The leader creates experiences and opportunities for his or her followers. He or she says, "Why don't you make the presentation at this month's meeting? I know you can do it. You're ready. It will be good for you." The leader sets people up for success then, if it happens, tolerates their occasional failure. He or she doesn't blame. The leader corrects or, more precisely, guides the failed employee through a learning experience. "What did this teach you?" the leader says.

The leader understands that, left on their own, people don't necessarily like to solve problems. Solving problems is hard work. What people prefer to do is engage in what Ronald Heifetz, a professor at Harvard's School of Government, calls "work avoidance mechanisms." Heifetz provides the following example of what can (and usually does) happen in most organizations when a problem is presented: "Say we're in a senior staff meeting, and the financial guy announces that we're losing market share. One possible reason, he suggests, is poor packaging. The first thing that happens is the packaging guy becomes furious and rebuts the charge. The two of them start going at each other, and maybe others join in."[7]

In such a situation, the focus of discussion is on everything and anything but the problem. In a leaderless group, a manager might step in to end the conflict and even offer a solution. A leader would step into such a situation to refocus the group on the problem (the loss of market share) and facilitate the group's efforts to deal with the problem and develop consensus on a course of action.

On occasion, a leader may exercise authority. Typically, the leader will coach and facilitate people in the hope and expectation that, with proper guidance and support, they will find ways to solve their own problems. On occasion, however, the leader will step in with a solution or, at least, specific direction—"Okay, now this is what we are going to do . . ." When does he or she provide such direction? When the environment or situation has become so confusing and complex that people are unable to think straight or organize themselves to engage in problem solving or take action. In such situations, the leader calms and reassures.

Here is how one *Workplace 2000*-type leader described her management style according to an April 1989 *Fortune* article by Walter Kiechell III: "I make sure that my people have the training and resources they need. We sit down and talk about what has to be done, the general direction we want to go in. Then I pretty much give them free rein. If they run into trouble, they can come back to me and we'll renegotiate."

Perhaps one way to examine what it is like to work for a leader is to examine a leader. Let's take the case of one Patricia M. Carrigan. In 1982, Patricia Carrigan became the first woman assembly plant manager in the history of General Motors. Her first assignment was to take over GM's Lakewood Plant, which had a history of labor trouble. In the first two years, Carrigan cut absenteeism from 25 percent to 9 percent, reduced sickness and accident costs by two thirds, and brought the number of grievances to nearly zero from a high of fifty-five hundred cases. In April 1989, *Boardroom Reports* explained Carrigan's leadership style: "Carrigan involved the workers in making changes and spent time explaining why new performance standards were necessary, asking for workers' ideas, and training them to meet the new requirements. When Carrigan was eventually reassigned to another plant, the union local gave her a plaque that said, in part, 'we, the members of Local 34, honor Pat M. Carrigan for her leadership, courage, risk-taking and honesty . . . we will always warmly remember Pat M. Carrigan as one of us.' "

Notice what Pat Carrigan did. She involved people. She explained why change was necessary. She asked for help and others' ideas. She made sure people were trained to respond in new ways. She was courageous. She took risks. She was honest. And, perhaps most importantly, she was "one of us." Carrigan led.

The Problems in Working for a *Workplace 2000* Leader

Working for a leader rather than a manager can be an exhilarating and ego-enhancing experience. It is frequently fun and exciting. But working for such an individual also has its problems. By definition, a leader gains much of his or her uniqueness from an ability to envision a future quite different from the present and to sell his or her followers on the importance and value of obtaining that vision. Fine, as long as the vision is the right vision. But what happens when the vision is wrong? Leaders are human. They make mistakes. They have been known to dream things that can't be or shouldn't be. Perhaps their vision is right, but they are trying to force into reality something neither the organization nor the market is yet prepared to accept. Leaders are typically ahead of their times. But they can also be too far ahead. They can squander time, energy, valuable resources, and emotions on striving (and having their followers strive) for something that can't happen soon. Worse, in their enthusiasm for achieving the vision, they may be unable to see that it is unattainable. Their self-confidence and conviction that anything is possible may blind them to the reality that the technical problems really can't be overcome (at least not within the time frame they envision); that the market cannot be convinced of the value of the new product or service no matter how "good" it might be; or that the organization can't (or just won't) change as rapidly as the leader demands. Also, the leader's vision may not be right for the company, its customers or employees, but only right for the leader personally. Knowingly or unknowingly, the leader may sell a vision that sounds good, but benefits only one—the leader himself or herself. By its very nature, working for a leader is working for a person obsessed with an idea or agenda. Obsession has its bright and dark sides.

Leader/follower relationships are inevitably emotional. The leader designs them to be that way. Followers (and leaders themselves) experience tremendous emotional highs. In this respect, being under the spell of a leader is like being under the influence of a powerful mood-altering drug. The highs are great! Followers feel energetic, confident, enthusiastic, and never more alive. But like a drug-induced euphoria, eventually the leader-inspired high may come to an end. When, and if, the vision turns false or isn't accomplished, the failure of the dream can come as a crushing blow to leader and followers alike who have invested so much of their lives into making the vision a reality. The personal attachment to realizing a dream future state can, in extreme cases, become so powerful that everyone associated with the endeavor can feel a real sense of emotional loss—even a debilitating loss—when the struggle ends. This feeling of loss may occur not only when the vision isn't realized, but also when it is. Success brings a brief euphoria followed by a true sense of purposelessness until somehow another vision can be found.

Another problem in working for a leader is the isolation that can occur. The power of a unique, driven, "oh so different" team led by a strong personality may, and often does, alienate other people and groups. Team members bond with their leader in search of a common goal. A "we/they" spirit develops. Those not part of the team feel left out and frequently are jealous of the team's camaraderie and/or accomplishments. When the jealous "outsiders" are important constituents of the team (senior executives or other teams whose help or approval is needed for team success), then the alienation and isolation can become dysfunctional for the team and the organization.

A third problem in working for a leader is that, at some point, it may become impossible for followers to convince the leader that he or she is wrong. Leaders can become seduced by their own rhetoric and unwilling (even unable) to admit that their vision is flawed. Less forceful, less certain, and less articulate followers may find it impossible to challenge the leader. Those who do may find themselves banished from the team or, at least, denied further access to the leader, who no longer wants to hear from detractors.

Finally, there is the problem of empowerment and its darker side. To be empowered is to be given the opportunity to succeed, to grow, and to develop—to gain greater and greater confidence in one's abilities. Empowerment also entails being given the opportunity to fail. The occasional failure of a team member is tolerated by the leader and by other team members. Repeated failure isn't. Leaders create the expectation for success if not always, most of the time. Successive failure detracts from the vision and challenges the invincibility of the team. That can't be tolerated. Those who fail and don't rapidly redeem themselves risk outright dismissal or, at a minimum, being treated as outcasts. Leaders want only bright, energetic people on their team and they hold those people responsible for results. Here is how one *Workplace 2000*-type leader described her approach to managing people who work for her in Kiechell's April 1989 *Fortune* article: "I used to do things for people because I would try to protect them, but I realized I was doing them a disservice. I was not giving them the opportunity to fail or achieve success, which was something my bosses had always given me."

And leaders don't like being taken off guard. They maintain open lines of communication—anyone can come to them at any time—and they want their people to exercise initiative. But they also want to be informed. This is how another leader quoted by Kiechell put it, "I don't mind people going off in their own direction. . . . What I can't stand is when they don't tell me about it. . . . The thing that bothers me most is being blindsided, when somebody changes something at the last minute, goes against the confidence you put in him. I don't like playing games."[8]

Recognizing "Good" and "Bad" Leaders

In *Workplace 2000*, most Americans will work for a leader. But that doesn't mean they will work for a "good" leader—one with noble intentions. Leadership carries with it no requirement for good or evil. Leaders may use their skills to ennoble or tyrannize, even terrorize. James Hodges, a history professor at the College of Wooster in Ohio, notes: "So many leaders want to sanitize leadership, make it sound clean and noble. But it's really a messy proposition that can involve manipulating people and getting them to do what they don't want to."[9] How, then, does one distinguish the "good" from the "bad"—the "moral" from the transgressor—the "manipulator" from the motivator? In *On Leadership*, John Gardner suggests that we judge leaders in a framework of generally accepted American values.

"Bad" leaders

- Are cruel to their followers
- Encourage their followers to do immoral or illegal things
- Motivate with appeals to bigotry, hate, revenge, fear and/ or superstitions
- Diminish their followers, rendering them dependent and childlike
- Destroy or diminish the processes established to protect freedom, justice, and/or human dignity
- Lust for power as an end in itself
- Uses propaganda to distort reality
- Betrays the trust others have in his or her judgment

Morally acceptable leadership

- Accepts, but isn't hungry for, power (at least power is not the sole end)
- Serves the common good in addition to that of special interests (including his or her own interest)
- Uses persuasion rather than coercion (in those rare instances where coercion is used, it is circumscribed by carefully designed and followed custom and procedure)
- Is "first among equals," not just "first"
- Treats followers as ends in themselves, not as objects to be manipulated
- Fosters individual development; believes that there are great untapped reservoirs of energy, talent, creativity, capability in all people; seeks to release human possibilities for the common good
- Understands that the individual is dependent upon the group and the group is dependent upon the individual; seeks to balance the needs of the group and individual to the common benefit of both

- Respects and operates within the confines of law, custom, and traditional values
- Encourages individual initiative; pushes personal responsibility and involvement to the lowest levels

Working for a leader is different from working for a manager. An inept or corrupt manager may do harm but little lasting harm. Not so a leader. Inept and/or corrupt leaders, particularly those who place their self-interest above those of the organization or their followers may do real lasting harm not only to their institutions but personally to their followers as well. Consequently, followers must be ever watchful for signs of the leader's abuse of power—both institutional power and the power to persuade. John Gardner has noted two failures of followership we are all prey to: "First, there are qualities such as apathy, passivity, cynicism, and habits of spectatorlike noninvolvement that invite the abuse of power by leaders.... Second, there is the inclination of followers in some circumstances to collaborate in their own deception. Given the familiar fact that what people want and need often determines what they see and hear, the collaboration comes easily. But a citizenry that wants to be lied to will have liars as leaders."[10]

Not only may leaders be "bad," but good leaders can go "bad," or at least become ineffective. Leaders may go bad because they get bored or they give up. They can also go bad because they become intoxicated with their own power.

Earlier we noted that leaders occasionally step in to provide specific direction when confusion reins. Such occasional direction and control are fine, but the danger for the leader, followers, and the organization is that the leader will become so intoxicated with solving problems (being the hero) that he or she will be unable to move back to a coaching/facilitating role when such is called for. Also, followers may become addicted to the "white knight." Ronald Heifetz, quoted in the October 1988 issue of *Inc.*, notes that entrepreneurs are particularly susceptible to becoming "white knights" versus leaders. He says, "Because the entrepreneur is inclined to accept responsibility and to see himself as a hero or heroine, he's also inclined to say, 'Okay, I'll do it for you again. I'll pull the rabbit out of the hat like last time. In fact, I pulled it out the last two times. And watch, I'm going to do it this time, too.' The entrepreneur is energized by those expectations. And if he does save the day, he's reinforced the expectation that he'll be able to do it again and again. But, it's a losing game. . . . Because he's a human being. Because he's a jerk like everybody else—with his own failing and his own blind spots. And because the landscape eventually gets too complicated, even for him. . . . [Eventually], there's no one around who has any capabilities. Every time he pulls the rabbit out of the hat, he generates more dependency and weakens his constituency, his own company. That's the trap in becoming the hero. If people keep expecting you to restore equilibrium, what they're actually doing is looking for you to help them avoid work."

Will *Workplace 2000* Leaders Be Found or Made?

Where will the leaders of the twenty-first century come from? Will they be found or made? Can anyone develop the capacity to lead? The answers to these questions are mixed. It seems clear from the available research that not everyone can lead. We cannot pick *Workplace 2000* leaders at random, nor even as cavalierly as we have traditionally tapped the next available employee for management or supervision. Yet it is apparent that we can create the opportunity for more people to exhibit leadership qualities and we can supplement natural and early ingrained talents with specific leadership skills.

Let's start with attributes. What does it take to be a leader? What are the personal characteristics or skills a leader must possess? Research on leadership would suggest that the following, at a minimum, are required:

Attributes or Personal Characteristics

Positive Self-Regard. "Positive self-regard" is a term used by Warren Bennis and Burt Namus in their book *Leaders: Strategies for Taking Charge.* Basically, Bennis and Namus say leaders have the capacity to recognize their strengths (and weaknesses), nurture and develop their strengths, and discern and establish a link between their strengths and the organization's needs. Positive self-regard is more than just "confidence," or "feeling good about oneself," or "maturity." It is also the ability to act on those feelings to find the right "fit" in life—to seek out and do the kinds of things they enjoy doing. It is also positive feelings about others. Leaders approach their dealing with others with the same kind of confidence, maturity, and good feelings as they approach their dealings with themselves.

Optimism. Leaders are optimistic. It is not that they reject the possibility of failure. It is just that they don't dwell on failure. They expect to win. And they expect others to win. There may be minor (even major) setbacks along the way. But ultimately, the leader expects success.

Inquisitiveness. Leaders are learners—lifelong learners. They are interested in the past, present, and particularly the future. Not only are leaders learners, but they are quick learners and they enjoy learning.

Action orientation. Leaders act on the world to change it more to their liking. They aren't passive. They believe that through their action (their behavior) they can effect change.

Empathy. Leaders are empathetic. They understand and relate to people. They intuitively appreciate the feelings, perspectives, desires, and needs of others almost as well as they understand their own, and they are willing and able to act to influence the behavior of others based upon that understanding.

Value laden. Leaders have a clearly defined set of values. They have firm notions about what is prudent and courageous; about the importance (or unimportance) of honesty, fairness, and civility; about what are (or should be) "desired end states"; and about the proper relationship between means and ends and what means can (or should) be used to achieve what ends. It is clear to leaders what is acceptable and unacceptable, if not to society as a whole, at least to them personally, and leaders act in accordance with these values. The leader's values define and limit their conduct.

A need to achieve. Leaders are "driven people." They are obsessed with doing something, accomplishing something, being something, and perhaps even proving something to themselves or others. This "need to achieve" is so strong that leaders are willing to endure hardship, make personal sacrifices, and generally "do whatever it takes" to fulfill their need. Interestingly, in many (and perhaps most) cases the "need" leaders wish to fulfill never really can be fulfilled. Yet they persist anyway—at least they do as long as they are leaders.

Leadership Skills

Attributes are the personal characteristics leaders (or would-be leaders) bring to the leadership task. Some are genetic. Others are learned. But the learning of attributes occurs over a lengthy period of time (and often early in life, as we shall see). Skills are different from attributes. First, at least relative to attributes, skill learning occurs over a much shorter period—days, weeks, months or, on occasion, a few years. Second, and more importantly, skills are "teachable." With proper training, most people can (and eventually will) learn the skills of leadership. But not everyone can develop the attributes of a leader.

What are the key leadership skills? We think there are eight.

Communication skills. Earlier we noted that the ability to communicate could be considered a prerequisite for leadership. By communication, we mean the ability to read, write, speak, and listen—to acquire and disseminate knowledge and ideas. Communication skills are widespread in the population (although as will be seen in Chapter 9, less widespread than they should be). The difference in communication skills required for leadership and that required for the normal population is one of degree, not content. Leaders need the skill to read rapidly with high comprehension; to write clearly; to speak persuasively; and to listen effectively.

Political skills. By political skills, we mean those of negotiation, conflict resolution, and consensus building. All of these are teachable. Unlike communication skills, they are not widely distributed within the population.

Motivation skills. Here we are talking about knowledge of the cognitive and behavioral approaches to motivation (as discussed earlier in this book) and how to put that knowledge to use to get people to change their behavior.

Change-management skills. Leaders are, if nothing else, change agents. To be effective, they must understand the human response to change and have the skills to implement change in a way that overcomes predictable resistance.

Trust-building skills. We include "trust building" as a skill because we believe it is teachable. We can teach people how to express commitment, how to demonstrate self-confidence, how to share values, how to demonstrate sensitivity, etc. Obviously, the effectiveness of such training would depend upon the match that existed with personal attributes.

Empowerment skills. Here we refer to training we could offer perspective leaders on how to delegate, hold people responsible and accountable for performance, build teams, facilitate employee problem solving, and so on.

"Farsightedness" skills. We borrow "farsightedness" from Burt Namus. Namus defines "farsightedness" as "keeping the eye fixed on the far horizon, even as one takes steps toward it. . . . The mental process is more like that of a historian skilled in collecting facts and then interpreting change by tracing cause-and-effect relationships as they played out over a period of time. Using his imagination to fill the gaps, the historian tries to describe what 'really' happened, why it happened, and why it was important. . . . Like the historian, the leader has a mental model of cause-and-effect relationships. . . . Using this mental model of how the world works, he can evaluate current trends and possible developments for their long-term significance."[11] We see farsightedness as a particularly critical skill for *Workplace 2000* leaders not just because of the chaos and turbulence we are likely to see in the business community (thus making the skill to recognize patterns and trends ex-

tremely important), but for another reason. Business in the twenty-first century will be (as it already is) a global enterprise. Most businesses will compete globally in a rapidly changing world. In *On Leadership* John Gardner states the leadership skills for global competitiveness this way: "Leaders must have some grasp of economic realities and some comprehension of the basic framework within which scientific and technological change takes place. They must gain an understanding of the political process. They must comprehend the pitfalls of power and the sources of human conflict. Corporate executives must understand the relationship between government and the private sector and must comprehend the national and world economy. In this interdependent world, leaders should come to know some culture other than their own, and all high-level leaders must understand international issues in depth."

We agree. And we incorporate that type of knowledge and skill under the general heading "farsightedness."

It is obvious from our list of attributes and skills required of *Workplace 2000* leaders that finding or creating a sufficient number of such leaders will be difficult. First, it will be difficult because many (and perhaps most) of the attributes we listed are genetically acquired, learned early in life, or learned over such a lengthy period that "attribute training" would probably be impossible. Second, "leadership" training which has been attempted to date has not been very effective.

There was an explosion of interest in leadership training in the late 1980s in spite of a continuing debate over how "leadership" should be defined and whether people could be trained to be leaders even if we knew what leadership was. Most of the training conducted to foster leadership was either "awareness" training or "skills" training. Awareness-training programs focused on exposing managers to the need for leadership, providing some common leadership vocabulary, providing an opportunity for managers to assess their own leadership "style" or "potential" (using one of various types of survey instruments), and, not infrequently, providing a "leadership-building" or "trust-building" experience. The latter "touchy-feely" exercises garnered the companies providing such training considerable criticism from the press. For example, *The New York Times* in 1988 described some of the exercises used in the General Motors Leadership Now program (begun in 1986), such as the one where two executives stretch a rubber band between each other (in order to learn to trust each other) and commented, "One wonders what Alfred Sloan (the company's authoritarian patriarch) would have said."[12]

The second approach to leadership training typical of the late 1980s was "skills" training. Rather than approaching leadership as a "state of being" or something participants in the training had to "become aware of," "skills" trainers focused purely on behavior. Identify the behaviors exhibited by leaders, they reasoned, teach people the skills necessary to behave the way leaders do, and you'll create leaders (or you will at least make the normal manager behave in a more "leaderlike" fashion).

Both the "awareness" approach and "skills" approach to leadership training had their advocates. However, what became evident in the late 1980s was that neither approach was sufficient to produce leaders, particularly if the training was "generic" and delivered out of the context in which the participants worked. Training, even specific skill training, was just a minor part of leadership development. Future leaders need to learn some fundamental leadership skills and *Workplace 2000* companies will offer skills training (at least for those employees targeted as having leadership potential). But skills training wasn't sufficient to develop leaders in the 1980s and it won't be sufficient to produce leaders for *Workplace 2000*. Consequently, *Workplace 2000* companies will go far beyond training to identify and develop the leadership talent needed. Here are some of the additional things companies will do in the future to attract, develop, and retain leaders:

- Selection and early identification of employees with leadership attributes. In *Workplace 2000*, more emphasis will be placed on recruiting employees for their drive, ambition, and personal characteristics than their education or training in a speciality. *Workplace 2000* companies will be looking for flexible generalists, not specialists. Breadth of knowledge will be more important than technical proficiency. In respect to education, we are likely to see greater interest in those with a liberal arts background rather than business, science, or engineering. How much exposure a perspective employee has had to literature, art, religion, drama, history, sociology, and psychology will likely be considered a better indication of leadership potential than his or her technical knowledge or industry experience.

- Provision of a wide range of experiences and opportunities to exercise leadership early on. *Workplace 2000* companies will recognize that the potential for leadership isn't leadership. It must be demonstrated. Consequently, twenty-first-century companies will push responsibility, accountability, and the performance of leadership tasks further down the flattened hierarchy. Not only will this be a necessity given the structure of the new workplace (flat and lean), but it will give new and low-level employees an opportunity to demonstrate their leadership potential. Additionally, *Workplace 2000* companies will rotate potential leaders through a wide variety of jobs to give them exposure to all functions of the enterprise—marketing, sales, design, engineering, manufacturing. These rotations will include at least one and possibly several international assignments. Breadth of experience will be necessary not only to identify leaders (can they lead in a variety of situations?), but also to provide them with the knowledge base they require to be effective.

- Mentoring and shared experiences. Mentors are friends, advisors, coaches, teachers, and exemplars. *Workplace 2000* companies—once they identify a potential leader—will make every effort to place that person with a leader/mentor within (or even outside) the company. In effect, potential leaders will be expected to intern or apprentice with established leader role models. Additionally, potential leaders will be brought together at conferences or on special task forces to share experiences such as the five-week exercise the University of Michigan School of Business conducted for twenty-one senior executives for the U.S., Japan, Brazil, Britain, and India in 1989. Jeremy Main described the experience in *Fortune*: "The executives attended lectures and seminars at Ann Arbor, built rafts and climbed cliffs on a blustery Atlantic island, got briefed in Washington, survived a simulated press ambush, traveled in fact-finding teams to Brazil, India, and China, and gave one another nicknames like 'Country Boy Iron Belly.' " What was the purpose of the University of Michigan experiment? The hope was that the thirty-five days would give these executives a new perspective and better enable them to function as leaders. While *Workplace 2000* leadership building "experiences" may not be the same as the University of Michigan experiment, they are likely to be similar.

- Finally, *Workplace 2000* companies will invest in "leadership renewal." At different points in their careers, established leaders will be expected to take a sabbatical to further their education and broaden their experiences. These sabbaticals may last months or even years as leaders go back to school for "refresher education."

While none of these steps to develop leaders are necessarily new (many, particularly larger, companies have done them in the past), what will be new is the number of companies engaged in such practices and the number of employees who are provided with such opportunities.

The demand for leaders in *Workplace 2000* and our difficulty in finding or creating leaders has important implications for Americans who aspire to leadership roles. On the whole, Americans can expect increased opportunities to play significant leadership roles in *Workplace 2000*, particularly those segments of the population that have found themselves shut out of such roles in the past. Foreign nationals, women, and minorities will find greater opportunities open to them than ever before. Two developments will dictate this expansion of opportunity. First, as we noted in Chapter 2, the continued flattening of organization and movement to push responsibility lower in the organization will create the need for more leaders. Instead of a single CEO, we will have a multitude of small business units run by men or women with executive level responsibility and accountability for performance. Second, there will be a shortage of "white males"—the traditional "leaders" of the past—with the experience and qualifications to assume such roles. All Americans will have a greater opportunity to become leaders. Those who don't or can't will at least work for one.

CHAPTER 7

Experiments in
Workplace 2000

In a 1982 article for *National Productivity Review*, Frank Ruck described what he termed a Catch-22 of the American workplace of that time. He said:

Today, most job design in the United States is better suited to robots than mature adults because enhanced technology and automation have simplified work, making it more standardized and routine. Work organizations have become larger and more bureaucratic; at the same time, economic prosperity has increased the affluence, education, and the aspiration level of many Americans.

Many people want jobs that allow them to make greater use of their education and that provide intrinsic work satisfaction. The problem or catch is that most organizations function in ways that are in conflict with the abilities and aspirations of the people who work in them . . .

When it comes to organizing for effective action, American-run businesses appear to be locked into some kind of cultural trance.

So we were. And we lived in a trance throughout most of the 1980s. We stared directly at the solution to our problems and all but ignored it while continuing to moan about our precipitous fall from competitive grace. We needed employee cooperation, but maintained institutional policies that encouraged competition. We needed collective effort toward the common good, but organized in a way that encouraged specialization and fragmentation. We needed flexibility, but kept rigid hierarchies. We needed employee commitment, but alienated employees and treated them as adversaries. We needed maximum performance from everyone, but adopted and maintained management practices that ensured average performance. We needed employees to take initiative, but controlled their every action. When we reluctantly tried something new, we did it in isolated plants, departments, or divisions and kept the results largely secret. More often, we opted for the quick fix or the solution offered by the management guru of the month. Alternately, we decided that "happy" employees would be productive or productive employees would be "happy." We neglected the reality that committed employees would be productive and "happy"—at least we did until the late 1980s. At the close of the decade, we came to the conclusion—nearly twenty years after it had been proven with American workers in American plants—that "participative management," "employee involvement," "teams" (and we used all of these terms) were our salvation. Eighty percent of the Fortune 1000 companies were doing at least something about installing "employee involvement" or "team" systems in 1989 according to the American Productivity and Quality Center.[1] Still only 20 to 30 percent of these companies were using such an approach with a substantial number of their employees. That will change in *Workplace 2000*. In the new American workplace, practically all Americans will work in a "team" where they and their co-workers will largely manage themselves. Here is how the American "team" system evolved and what it means to the average American worker.

The Early Experiments

Throughout the 1970s and 80s, American business experimented with new management practices and new organizational designs. Some of these experiments were reported widely in the media. Others were reported only in specialized "productivity" or "quality" newsletters or academic journals. Other experiments were conducted entirely in secret, often in plants of large companies tucked away in small rural towns. Some of the workplace experiments conducted throughout the nearly two decades were revolutionary, fundamentally changing the nature of the relationship between labor and management with surprising, often stunning results. Others were more evolutionary—merely the attempt of American companies to adopt practices of the Japanese or other successful American companies. Some of these experiments were heartfelt and courageous attempts to find a new way. Others were just fads. Yet taken together, these experiments led us to the new American "team" system. Below is a limited chronicle of what happened, where it happened, and—when information is available—why it happened. Our chronicle is representative, but as we said, incomplete. Hundreds of stories of other experiments—some more important and some less important than the ones we present here—are left out. Our purpose here is only to provide some examples. We will start in 1971.

1971—General Motors Assembly Plant: Tarrytown, New York

One day in April of 1971, the plant manager of the General Motors Assembly Plant in Tarrytown, New York, approached several key union officials and made an extraordinary suggestion. "Why not," he said, "find a new way of doing things? Why not find a way to work together instead of fighting each other?" If the union would do its part, the manager said, he would put pressure on his own managers to get them to change their ways. The reason the Tarrytown plant manager's suggestion was extraordinary was that in the late 1960s and early 1970s, labor and management didn't cooperate. They didn't work together. They fought. Here is how managers and union leaders described their relationship prior to that fateful day in the spring of 1971 according to an article in the *Harvard Business Review*:

> Manager: "Management was always in a defensive posture. We were instructed to go by the book, and we played by the book. The way we solved problems was to use our authority and impose discipline."

> Tarrytown plant general superintendent: "For reasons we thought valid, we were very secretive in letting the union and the workers know about changes to be introduced or new programs coming down the pike."

> Union officer: "We were always trying to solve yesterday's problems. There was no trust and everybody was putting out fires. The company's attitude was to employ a stupid robot with hands and no face."

> Union committee chairman: "When I walked in each morning I was out to get the personnel director, the [union] committeeman was shooting for the foreman, and the [union] zone committeeman was shooting for the general foreman. Every time a foreman notified a worker that there would be a job change, it resulted in an instant '78 (work standards grievance). It was not unusual to have a hundred '78s hanging fire, more than three hundred discipline cases, and many others."

> Union committeeman: "My job was purely political. It was to respond instantly to any complaint or grievance regardless of the merits, and just fight the company. I was expected to jump up and down and scream. Every time a grievance came up, it lit a spark, and the spark brought instant combustion."

In 1970, the explosive relationship between labor and management at Tarrytown was so bad that Tarrytown had the poorest labor relations and worst production record in GM. Absenteeism, turnover, and operating costs were all high. With thirty-eight hundred employees, at times Tarrytown had two thousand labor grievances. Workers hated their management and their jobs. Management acted as if it hated the workers. Warnings, disciplinary actions, and firings were commonplace. The plant was dirty, crowded, and noisy. Foremen were seen by employees as insensitive dictators who treated them no better—and often worse—than they did the parts being assembled. One worker put it this way: "They number the parts and they number you." It was within this atmosphere that the Tarrytown plant manager made his suggestion to the union for a change in relationships. In part, the plant manager's desire for a change was dictated by a change in the composition of the work force. Young people were being hired who were part of the counterculture revolution of the late 1960s. The plant manager described the need for change this way to Robert Guest, author of the *Harvard Business Review* article: "The young people in the plant were demanding some kind of change. They didn't want to work in this kind of environment. The union didn't have much control over them, and they certainly were not interested in taking orders from a dictatorial management."

Nothing might have come of the plant manager's suggestion to the union officials that spring day in 1971 had GM not decided to stop assembling trucks at Tarrytown and had two production supervisors at the plant not made an unusual suggestion. GM's plan to stop assembling trucks at Tarrytown carried with it a decision to renovate the truck assembly area of the plant and to move two departments into the newly renovated area. As always, management called in manufacturing and industrial engineers to design the layout for the newly renovated area. It was when the engineers presented their proposals to plant supervisors that two supervisors made an extraordinary suggestion. "Why not," they suggested, "ask the workers themselves to get involved in the move?" After all, the two supervisors reasoned, the workers "are the experts in their own right. They know as much about trim operations as anyone else." If the suggestion of the two supervisors wasn't unusual enough, then management's agreement to accept the suggestion certainly was. Over the doubts of many supervisors and managers—and the suspicion of the union—workers were involved in making decisions about the change. Workers who were to be moved were shown charts and diagrams prepared by the engineers. Worker suggestions were sought for ways to improve the proposed layout. The workers responded with hundreds of ideas and, oddly enough, management accepted and implemented many of them. The result? The move was completed on time with few grievances. The training director remarked that something had happened that had never occurred before. He said, "Although it affected only one area of the plant, this was the first time management was communicating with the union and the workers on a challenge for solving future problems and not the usual situation of doing something, waiting for a reaction, then putting out the fires later."

In 1972, GM decided to rearrange another major area of the Tarrytown assembly plant—the chassis department. Department employees were again involved in making decisions about the department's new layout. That same year, Irving Bluestone, vice president of the General Motors department of the United Automobile Workers Union (UAW), made a speech. He said in part: "Traditionally management has called upon labor to cooperate in increasing productivity and improving the quality of the product. My view of the other side of the coin is more appropriate; namely, that management should cooperate with the worker to find ways to enhance the dignity of labor and to tap the creative resources in each human being in developing a more satisfying work life, with emphasis on worker participation in the decision-making process."

In 1973, the UAW and General Motors negotiated a national agreement. In the contract, both parties committed themselves to establishing a formal mechanism at the top levels to consider ways to implement Bluestone's "Quality of Work Life" ideas. At Tarrytown, management and the union took this agreement as a signal that it was okay to continue and expand their cooperative efforts. A Tarrytown union official said: "We as a union knew that our primary job was to protect the worker and improve his economic life. But times had changed and we began to realize we had a broader obligation, which was to help workers become more involved in decisions affecting their own jobs, to get their ideas, and to help them improve the whole quality of life at work beyond the paycheck." At about the same time, Delmar Landon, director of organizational research and development at General Motors, began sending professionally trained "communication consultants" to Tarrytown and other GM plants to meet with supervisors and work groups to help them solve problems in interpersonal communication.

In April of 1974, Tarrytown management hired a consultant to work with supervisors and workers in joint problem solving programs. While suspicious that somehow management was trying to trick them, union officials eventually agreed to go along with the program. Working together, the union, consultant, and management representatives proposed a series of Saturday training sessions on problem solving. Thirty-four workers on two shifts volunteered to participate in the Saturday training. Management agreed to pay the participating workers for six hours of the training. The remaining two hours the workers agreed to participate without pay. The problem-solving sessions began to generate ideas for fixing problems such as water leaks and glass breakage. Top management was impressed.

In November of 1974, because of the oil crisis, disaster struck Tarrytown. General Motors eliminated the second shift at the plant and laid off half the work force. Many workers participating in the plant's problem solving sessions were affected. As a result, the problem solving group was reduced to just twelve members. Yet the group continued to work on problems. Plus, employee involvement was spreading to other departments. Rumors circulated among workers in the plant that something unusual was going on. The crisis-dictated layoffs resulted in surprisingly few grievances.

In 1975, a union/management joint policy group was formed at the Tarrytown plant to administer a formal employee involvement effort and to evaluate ideas generated by problem-solving teams. The policy group decided that employee participation in problem-solving efforts would be voluntary and that the formal effort would begin in two departments. In a survey of interest, 95 percent of the employees in the two departments volunteered to participate in the program; 570 of the 600 people in the two departments participated in twenty-seven hours of instruction in problem solving on their own time and began meeting to work on solving problems. Plant managers and the union were once again impressed with the results of employee problem-solving efforts. Unfortunately, later that year the program had to be put on hold. GM had decided to return the plant to a two-shift operation. While hundreds of new workers were being hired and trained, there wasn't time to continue the employee problem-solving efforts.

By early 1977, Tarrytown was back at full capacity with a work force of nearly 3,800 workers. Plant managers and the union agreed to take the Quality of Work Life effort plant-wide. Plant management agreed to train over 3,000 workers in problem solving at a cost of over $1.6 million. Throughout 1977 and 1978, all managers and supervisors and more than 3,300 workers took part in the training program. Many workers were skeptical. But most eventually responded—adopting the philosophy of the worker who after years of fighting with his foreman approached his foreman after the second day of training and said: "Listen, you and I have been butting our heads together for a long time. From now on I just want to be able to talk to you and have you talk to me."

Commenting on the results of the Tarrytown experiment in 1979, the Tarrytown production manager said, "From a strictly production point of view—efficiency and costs—this entire experience has been absolutely positive, and we can't begin to measure the savings that have taken place because of the hundreds of small problems that were solved on the shop floor before they accumulated into big problems." Union officials went further. They maintained that Tarrytown had gone from being one of GM's poorest-performing plants in quality to one of its best and that absenteeism and grievances had been cut substantially from previous Tarrytown levels:[2]

1975—The Kemper Life Insurance Company Corporate Offices: Suburb of Chicago

In 1975, Jerry McCann, vice president of operations for Kemper Life Insurance's corporate offices just outside Chicago, was meeting with his managers to discuss problems the corporate office was having in processing an increase of life insurance applications. A new on-line, real-time computer system that had been installed in the hope of speeding up processing of applications didn't seemed to be helping. Applications still moved at a snail's pace in assembly-line fashion from screening to underwriting to issuance. It took the same time to process an application from a healthy twenty-three-year-old as it did to process an application from a high-risk fifty-nine-year-old, since every application had to move through the same approval process. Then, in McCann's meeting, someone suggested an innovative approach to the problem. "Why not eliminate the assembly line? Wouldn't it be simpler if a small team of employees could handle all of the needs of a specific agent or group of agents? A small team would be more like a small company. And, like a small company, they could make quick decisions." Such an idea had never been tried before, but McCann took the risk. A small three-person "company" was set up to do everything for a specific group of agents. The "small company" team consisted of an underwriter and two service representatives and was provided with computer terminals, files, and all current information the team required to respond quickly to the needs of "their" agents. The underwriter led the team and was charged with full authority to approve or disapprove applications. McCann's experiment with the small "company" worked so well that all of underwriting operations were soon reorganized into small "company" teams. Eventually the small "company" team system was expanded to other areas of operations. By 1986, 45 percent of policies were being processed in twenty-four hours and an additional 10 to 15 percent within one week—a turnaround time that would have been impossible under the old assembly line system according to John Scott, Kemper's vice president of operations in 1986.[3]

1975—Delco Remy: Fitzgerald, Georgia

In 1975, Delco Remy, the battery manufacturer, opened a new plant in Fitzgerald, Georgia. Instead of organizing the plant along traditional lines, practically all production and support people were assigned to teams. The plant manager, plant superintendent, production manager, engineering manager, personnel manager, comptroller, and quality control superintendent made up a "support team." Electricians and mechanics comprised a "maintenance team." Production employees were assigned to "operating teams" of five to twenty-five employees each. Each "operating team" was given wide responsibility and accountability for self-management. In his book *Thriving on Chaos*, Tom Peters provided the following laundry list of duties "operating teams" performed (and still perform) at the Fitzgerald plant:

- Handle all quality control
- Do all maintenance and make minor repairs on machines
- Keep track of their own time; there are no time cards (no clock)
- Handle the "housekeeping" (no janitors)
- Participate in a pay-for-knowledge program (for learning almost every job in the plant)
- Engage in regular problem-solving activities
- Are responsible for safety
- Have full-time access to the lock-free tool room
- Do budget preparation and review (capital and operating)
- Help determine staffing levels
- Advise management on equipment layout and generate requirements for new equipment
- Are in charge of all recruiting and run the assessment center for new recruits
- Decide on layoff patterns (whether to lay people off or have everybody work shorter hours, for example)

In 1985, the Fitzgerald Plant won Honda of America's Quality Performance Award for excellence as a supplier.

1976—TRW's Oil Well Cable Division Plant: Lawrence, Kansas

TRW's Oil Well Cable Division opened a new plant in Lawrence, Kansas, in 1976 which, in the words of Gino T. Strippoli, vice president and general manager of the division, was designed "to avoid all the traditional bugaboos, such as authoritarian policies, rigid work rules, and adversarial labor-management relationships that inhibit an organization's effectiveness." To avoid the "bugaboos" of the past, TRW eliminated time clocks at its Kansas plant and made all workers salaried. It eliminated job classifications and organized workers into teams. Workers participated in production scheduling, problem solving, and hiring and training new workers. Teams evaluated worker performance, recommended new equipment, and were given the power to take disciplinary action against their co-workers when needed. The approach was somewhat unconventional, to say the least. Many in the community and other managers throughout TRW thought the approach was just "weird" or worse. "They often think," said Strippoli in 1982, "we're running a country club; we've relinquished responsibility for managing; employees can make sweeping organizational changes at whim; and anarchy prevails. . . . Most emphatically, that's not the case. Our division does have managers. But they are managers with a difference—people who don't automatically embrace the old, counterproductive ways of doing things, who are willing to strike out in new directions to gain the cooperation of employees. Perhaps most importantly, our managers treat employees as problem solvers, as first-echelon managers. That frees our managers from constantly putting out fires; instead they can perform bona fide management tasks: directing, organizing, coordinating, and motivating. And I'm able to plan and think about tomorrow; our teams of employees are taking care of today." Rather than being a "country club," Strippoli argued, more was asked of workers at the Lawrence, Kansas, plant than at other TRW plants. "As management, we ask a lot of our teams. Participation doesn't mean less of a workload for them, but more. We ask them to think, to make decisions, to take initiative in handling the minute-by-minute operations—all of which are more taxing than just pressing a button on some machine."[4]

Worker output at the Kansas plant increased by 80 percent over a period of six years.

1978—Polysar Gulf Coast Plant: Orange, Texas

In 1978, John Ludwig became the new general manager for Polysar Gulf Coast's synthetic rubber production facility in Orange, Texas. Polysar Gulf Coast's Orange, Texas, plant was noted for its efficiency and the quality of its production. The plant was also noted for its autocratic management. Decisions were made at the top. Independent thinking was discouraged. Employees were to follow rules and regulations. And there were many rules and regulations. Employees were told, "You aren't paid to think, just do your job." From start-up in 1967 until 1978, employees described the management style as a "reign of fear." Then, in 1978, Ludwig arrived. He called a general meeting with all employees to explain his management style. Ludwig said his beliefs were different from the previous management. He believed the best way to motivate employees was to "treat them like grown human beings." And, said Ludwig, he wanted participation at all levels. A few months later, Ludwig's philosophy was put to the test. Polysar corporate made a decision to shut down a unit at the Orange, Texas, plant and instructed Ludwig to lay off one hundred workers. Ludwig called another meeting with the workers. He explained the dilemma. Then he announced he wasn't going to make the decision on what to do alone. Instead, he would appoint a committee of foremen, operators, and managers to study the problem and recommend a solution. The committee met and developed a plan to reorganize the plant's production divisions and the work force. The plan, which achieved corporate objectives without layoffs, was implemented almost exactly as the committee proposed it.

By 1980, Ludwig's participative management style had spread throughout the plant. Managers and supervisors were communicating with and listening to employees more than ever before. Still, there was no formal employee involvement program at the plant. The quality assurance coordinator proposed to remedy that. Why not, he suggested, start a quality circle program patterned after the kind of thing the Japanese were doing? Although there was some resistance from old-line managers, Ludwig agreed to the experiment. Employees were hand picked for six circles, trained, and encouraged to solve problems in their work areas. Each circle was composed of three to ten workers who worked for a common supervisor. After receiving training in problem-solving techniques, circle members met one hour per week on company time to attempt to solve work-related problems identified by circle members themselves or suggested by management. Initially, supervisors led the meetings. Later, employees took over the role of circle leader after receiving training in how to lead the meetings. Circles adopted names for their groups: "The Belligerent Bunch," "The Awesome Analysts," "The Pits," "The Problem Boys," and "A Perfect Circle." Between 1981 and 1987, the number of circles grew from the original six to twenty-seven, involving 65 percent of employees at the plant. Commenting on the results of the Orange, Texas, experiment in 1987, Polysar management reported significant improvements in product and service quality, improved employee job satisfaction, and lower employee turnover and absenteeism.[5]

1979—The New York City Department of Sanitation

In 1979, Ron Contino was given responsibility for the Bureau of Motor Equipment (BME) of the New York City Department of Sanitation. The BME was in trouble. On any day as many as half of the department's trucks were out of service for needed repairs. The overtime budget for BME had grown to $4 million. Working conditions in the department were poor and employee morale was low. Contino brought in a new management team and took steps to gain control of the overtime budget. Then he did something else. He approached BME's trade unions and asked them to recommend candidates for a "labor committee" whose members would be detached from their regular duties, report directly to Contino, and devote themselves full time to solving problems. With union agreement, the committee was formed. It consisted of three auto mechanics, a sanitation man, and two foremen. Members of the committee circulated among the BME shops and gathered suggestions from employees. Once a week, they met with Contino and other top managers. Initially, suggestions from the labor committee were for workplace improvements—heat, shop ventilation, lighting improvements. When Contino and his managers acted on these suggestions, the labor committee began to bring ideas for productivity improvements and cost reductions. A committee suggestion to change the brand of tires the BME was using saved the department $300,000 a year. Another suggestion to remove doors on landfill unloading carts saved the department $750,000 per year. In total, the committee suggested improvements generating $2 million in savings over the first two years.

In 1982, workers in the Central Repair Shop expressed concern over the productivity improvements being generated by Ron Contino's labor committees. Traditionally, repair shop managers monitored work performed by employees by applying union-negotiated work standards, which specified the time allowed for completion of tasks. What happens, employees complained, when productivity improves? Won't management just raise the standards? Contino responded to the employee concerns with a policy change. No longer, he said, will we monitor performance using the work standards. Instead, we will treat each shop as a "profit center." We'll compute the value of the output of the shop based upon what it would cost the department to purchase the repairs outside. The value of input will be the cost for operating the shop—salaries, benefits, supplies, etc. The difference will be the shop's "profit or loss" and we will discuss each shop's "profit/loss" performance at weekly committee meetings. In 1986, *Commitment-Plus* reported the results of BME's "profit centers" as follows: "Spurred by the profit motive, the shops tackled problems with a vengeance. They found cheaper vendors. They discontinued production of items that were cheaper to buy on the outside. They bought machinery to improve output. And the results were impressive. In 1981 the shops had a productivity factor of 1.4, meaning that they yield $1.40 of services for every dollar invested, and a resulting $2 million profit. By 1983, the productivity factor was 1.6, and the 'profit' was $3.6 million."[6]

1979—General Motor's Cadillac Engine Plant: Livonia, Michigan

In 1979, GM nearly doubled the size of its Cadillac Engine plant at Livonia, Michigan, and installed sophisticated new equipment at the location. It also undertook what was called the Livonia Opportunity—a labor/management agreement to work together to improve productivity, quality, and the quality of work life at the plant.

Key to the Livonia Opportunity were what GM called "business teams." Each "business team" consisted of twelve to fifteen employees who had complete responsibility for a product, service, or completion of a major step in the production process including responsibility for monitoring and controlling quality (the position of quality inspector was eliminated). Everyone in the plant was assigned to a "business team." To encourage employee flexibility, forty-five job classifications were eliminated and a pay-for-knowledge system was implemented whereby employees could earn higher base pay by learning to perform more jobs in a team or by moving to another team and a suggestion system was installed that provided employees with the opportunity to earn cash awards for suggesting ideas for productivity improvement.

As established, business teams were designed to be relatively self-managed. Each team had its own set of performance measures for quality, safety, productivity, and so on that it could use to monitor its own performance. There was very little in the way of traditional management and supervision. For example, the position of general foreman was eliminated and replaced with the position of team coordinator. Team coordinators performed functions quite different from traditional foremen. Instead of supervising the business teams on a day-to-day basis, team coordinators focused on budgetary control, productivity improvement, and overall coordination of the teams. Day-to-day coordination of activities within teams and leadership of weekly, one-hour problem-solving team meetings were assigned to an assistant team coordinator (ATC) who was elected by team members. To prepare employees to work in teams, management and the union jointly developed a five-day training program covering areas such as problem solving, teamwork, and statistical process control. Additionally, team coordinators and assistant team coordinators were trained in public speaking, work design, and how to hold effective meetings. The results of the "Livonia Opportunity" were impressive. For example, between 1982 and 1983, labor and overtime costs were cut by 50 percent, average per engine costs dropped 25 percent, quality improved, warranty costs were reduced, and labor grievances were one third of what was typical for GM plants.[7]

1981—Digital Equipment Corporation Plant: Enfield, Connecticut

In 1981, Digital Equipment Corporation began work on designing a new manufacturing facility to be located in Enfield, Connecticut. From the beginning, the Enfield facility was intended to be an experiment in a totally new technological and work-system design. Instead of a traditional organization, the Enfield facility was designed around what are called "operating teams." Each operating team consisted of twelve to eighteen employees with skills and responsibility for completing all steps in the production process. Each operating team was, in effect, a small business. Instead of dividing the twenty assembly steps of the assembly process up among as many as twenty-six specialists, each member of an Enfield operating team was trained and certified to complete all twenty steps. To encourage this employee flexibility, a pay-for-skill system was installed whereby employees earned pay points for completing training and certification through a series of skill blocks.

In addition to having responsibility for completing all steps in the production process, operating teams are also given responsibility for many traditional managerial or supervisory functions, such as

- Selection and discipline of team members
- Salary and benefits administration
- Training of team members and certifying skill acquisition
- Budgeting
- Material planning, receiving, and distribution

- Shipping of the end product
- Developing performance "contracts" and conducting performance reviews
- Equipment maintenance
- Safety and first aid
- Performance problem solving
- Development of work schedules

Very little in the way of traditional management and supervision was retained. Instead, three operating team support groups were created. A technical support team provided information systems, technical, and engineering support to the operating teams. An administrative support team handled such matters as payroll, accounts payable, purchasing, and employment sourcing. Finally, a management team handled resource allocation, team training, and long-term planning, resolved conflicts between teams, and generally managed relationships internal and external to the plant.

In its first two years of operation compared to other Digital plants, Enfield cut product assembly time by 40 percent, reduced scrap by 50 percent, and reduced overhead costs by 40 percent.[8]

1983—AT&T's Hotel Billing Information System: Tempe, Arizona

In 1981, Ed Murdock, then district manager for operator services for AT&T in Phoenix, Arizona, attended a company-sponsored seminar on innovative work systems. Most AT&T managers at the seminar found the descriptions of employee involvement and self-managed team systems they heard at the conference interesting. But most agreed that such systems would never work at AT&T and certainly not with operators. Murdock disagreed. Not only did Murdock disagree, he did something about it. At the time, AT&T was planning to open a new office for its hotel billing information system (HOBIS) in Tempe, Arizona. Returning from the seminar that had sparked his imagination, Murdock convinced his boss to let him open and operate the new Tempe office without supervisors. Such a change was drastic—even revolutionary—for

AT&T. Here is how three authors writing about the HOBIS experiment for the Winter 1987 issue of *Organizational Dynamics* explained the significance of Murdock's proposal:

> HOBIS . . . bore a superficial resemblance to most other operator offices across the country. Operators, sitting in front of video display terminals, had to provide charges to hotels on customer-dialed long-distance calls, arrange refunds for customers who lost money in pay phones, and give credit on incorrectly dialed long-distance calls. The office handled roughly 11,500 calls each business day. A computer monitored the operators' actions and printed daily reports on speed, volume and mix of calls by type (hotel or pay phone).
>
> At most traditional facilities of comparable size [to Tempe], eight to ten first-level supervisors and one second-level manager would be on duty. . . . Strict work rules, heavy supervision, and narrow spans of control had been deeply rooted in 100 years of Bell System history and tradition. Bell archives were filled with pictures of indistinguishable operators working under the watchful eye of a supervisor, who walked back and forth behind them, recording their every movement. The supervisors, in turn, were closely watched by their managers. Each level of management in the pecking order was expected to compile numerous performance measurements and indexes and file frequent reports, which were used for internal comparisons between different Bell offices. Supervisors randomly listened in on calls from a remote location to check whether operators were greeting customers with standard protocols and to ensure that no call lasted longer than 30 seconds."

Given the culture of AT&T and the devotion of the company to its tradition of close supervision, Murdock and Murdock's boss were taking a tremendous risk. In fact, Murdock's boss approved the plan provided *his* boss wasn't told until the results were in. And there was much that could conceivably go wrong. Murdock himself drew up a list of twenty-seven possible problems such as "What if the employees demand management pay?" "What if an employee comes in drunk or 'high' on drugs?" "What if someone gets hurt on the job?" In spite of these potential problems, Murdock was convinced that a self-managed, supervisorless office could work. Of course, the office would not be without some management. Murdock decided that there would be one manager in the office to handle administrative and personnel matters. He selected for this role Hilda Ortega, who was new to AT&T and thus, as Murdock put it, didn't have a "Bell-shaped head." Ortega explained her role as "that of a resource person and mentor rather than that of the traditional overseer. I'll ultimately be responsible for administration and bottom-line results. I can help guide them (the operators) in their decisions, but the final choices will always be theirs." As she indicates, Ortega's role was to be primarily advisory. Day-to-day operating decisions were to be made by a six-person office committee. Initially, the members of this committee were the first persons hired for the new office. The committee then selected the remaining hundred operators. In addition to selecting operators to work in the office, the "office committee" (after receiving training in teamwork, communications, problem solving, and how to lead meetings) developed a statement of purpose (a kind of mission statement for the office); assigned operators to administrative duties, subcommittees, and task forces; undertook problem solving; developed training programs for new employees; and generally performed all of the duties normally performed by supervisors and managers. The HOBIS experiment lasted nearly three years, from early 1983 to late 1985, at which time AT&T closed the Tempe office and moved it to a centralized location. While the HOBIS experiment didn't last long, it was generally considered a success—absenteeism among operators dropped, there were fewer employee grievances during the experiment, customer complaints declined, and HOBIS met or exceeded all measurements on call volume and customer satisfaction. Also, HOBIS employees reported increased job satisfaction and less stress than they had experienced in their previous jobs. Interestingly, in spite of some problems such as a continuing difficulty in training new office committee members (who rotated every six months), a few bad decisions by the committee that caused morale problems, and the tendency of some more aggressive committee members to dominate weekly committee meetings, few, if any, of the twenty-seven problems Murdock feared might occur actually happened.[9]

1983—TRW Ramsey Piston Ring Division: St. Louis, Missouri

In 1977, Ruben F. Mettler, an aeronautical engineer who had been executive vice president of TRW's Space Technology Laboratory since 1958, became chairman of the board and chief executive officer of TRW. In 1980, Mettler distributed to all TRW managers, supervisors, employees, and members of key constituencies within and outside the company "TRW and the 80s," a kind of key guidebook to the strategies, goals, and objectives TRW would follow under Mettler's leadership into the 1980s. The importance of "TRW and the 80s" was that it spelled out clear objectives and productivity improvement strategies that provided the impetus for employee involvement and team systems implemented at TRW Ramsey starting in September of 1983. Two of TRW's objectives and the productivity strategies laid out in "TRW and the 80s" are particularly relevant to the TRW Ramsey story:

1. TRW seeks to achieve superior performance as an economic unit, with special emphasis on high-quality products and services.
2. TRW seeks to achieve high quality in its internal operations, with special focus on its many relationships with employees.[10]

According to "TRW and the 80s," TRW's corporate productivity strategies were to:

1. Keep abreast of developing techniques of measuring and increasing productivity and use new technology and management innovation effectively to improve the efficiency of . . . operations;
2. Improve . . . product design, manufacturing engineering, and quality control techniques;
3. Make capital expenditures directed toward the most ef-

ficient use of . . . facilities and toward improving . . .
manufacturing and design systems and techniques;

4. Engage in effective cost reduction programs at all levels
of the company;

5. Design job assignments and . . . work environment with
an understanding and awareness of the importance of
fostering productivity;

6. Promote effective two-way communication between employees at all levels to understand better the problems
and concerns that affect productivity;

7. Maintain challenging, achievable, and measurable productivity objectives for all employees;

8. Communicate . . . productivity objectives to employees
and make them the subject of regular and meaningful
review; and

9. Employ programs that will motivate employees to produce products and provide services more effectively and
efficiently.

Recognition of the need to improve productivity and quality
and to involve employees in the process was not unique or
new to TRW. And TRW, like a number of other companies,
had previously established a high-level steering committee to
oversee such efforts. What made TRW different was that it
recognized the failings of its previous efforts and decided to
do something different. As in many other companies, TRW's
steering committee—composed of top-level executives—had
been too large and unfocused to get results throughout the
organization. Also, training programs that had been undertaken in the past (such as training designed to teach managers
how to measure productivity) had been a case of too much
too soon. TRW managers weren't aware of the need to improve
productivity and were confused about just how to define productivity in different divisions and at different levels. To remedy this confusion, provide coordination, and develop a long-
range plan for carrying out the spirit and letter of "TRW and
the 80s," TRW recognized it needed one person who could be
in charge of its productivity improvement effort. That one
person turned out to be Henry P. Conn, co-author of this book.
Conn held a master's degree in mechanical engineering and

an M.B.A. He had served in several operating positions at Ford and was corporate director of manufacturing engineering services at Allis-Chalmers, where he had implemented a cost-cutting program that had saved that company about $100 million. Conn was brought into TRW as vice president of productivity reporting to Mettler. After spending his first year touring TRW's many sites and visiting with universities, productivity centers, other companies, and a number of productivity consultants to gather information, Conn took a number of actions including:

1. Reorganizing and streamlining the corporate steering committee (Conn chaired this committee)
2. Establishing a forty-member productivity council composed of representatives of all operating groups and staff functions, which met quarterly to plan and direct productivity improvement efforts and report to the steering committee on progress
3. Developing a network of four hundred (later twelve hundred) productivity coordinators who were responsible for improvement efforts in their own plants and divisions
4. Initiating a "seed money" program whereby corporate would provide 50 percent of the funding for pilot productivity-improvement programs operating units wanted to undertake
5. Establishing a three-day "Productivity College" to provide participants with state-of-the-art information on productivity improvement and measurement techniques including providing participants with a methodology for measuring their own unit's productivity improvement efforts
6. Developing a set of macro productivity ratios that would be used to measure productivity corporate-wide

Conn's objective in undertaking these actions was unusual for someone in a top-level management position of a large company. Other U.S. companies had created a top-level productivity management position and/or corporate division responsible for productivity improvement. Often, these divisions became large corporate staff functions that designed and developed productivity or cost-cutting programs and then pushed them out to the rest of the organization. Conn's approach was different. William Ruch and William Werther, in their 1983 review of TRW's productivity improvement efforts, describe it this way: "From the beginning, Conn said his objective was 'to work myself out of a job.' His overriding concern is to build productivity into the framework of the organization and into the thinking of every operating manager so that productivity becomes a line function and staff support is no longer necessary. In short, Conn is aiming to make productivity management an integral part of each manager's job."[11] Conn's Productivity College exposed TRW line managers and executives to innovative productivity-improvement ideas in the hope that they would find one or more interesting and worth pursuing when they returned to their divisions. The corporate "seed money" offered by TRW was an inducement to divisions to try something different. Finally, the four hundred productivity coordinators were intended to serve as line advocates for pilot productivity-improvement efforts in their own plants and divisions. TRW corporate efforts to educate line managers and supervisors about the need to change and corporate support for pilot programs resulted in a number of divisions undertaking improvement efforts. One of these was TRW Ramsey.

Ramsey had been founded in 1919 and was one of the oldest piston and retaining ring manufacturers in the United States, supplying parts for gas, diesel, and jet engine manufacturers plus manufacturers of small appliances. The company was bought by TRW in 1950 and became a wholly owned subsidiary of TRW at that time. Throughout its history, Ramsey had ranked as one of the top three companies in market share among piston and retaining ring producers. However, conditions changed for Ramsey between 1978 and 1983. As the production of automobiles by domestic manufacturers fell due to foreign competition, Ramsey lost orders. At the same time, its normally good labor/management relations turned sour over issues such as cost-of-living adjustments resulting in two strikes by the International Association of Machinists (IAMS). It was in this climate that Eugene Kutcher, vice president-general manager of TRW Ramsey, decided to make some changes, including closing Ramsey's two older manufacturing facilities and consolidating operations in St. Louis; installing new automated manufacturing equipment; and implementing a structured employee-involvement system.

Ramsey's employee-involvement system consisted of two principal components: management-directed work teams and advanced problem-solving teams. Work teams were nonvoluntary employee problem-solving groups that met weekly or monthly to work on performance improvement projects. Work team meetings were facilitated by managers and supervisors who were required to attend two three-day training sessions and receive one-on-one follow-up coaching from consultants to learn team leadership skills (measurement, feedback, behavior management, group decision making, conflict resolution, listening, creative problem solving, effective meetings). Advanced problem-solving rings were voluntary employee problem-solving groups that met weekly to work on particularly difficult or critical problems that were outside of the control of work teams. Where only managers and supervisors had received training and coaching for the work teams, at least half of the membership of problem-solving rings were required to have received formal training and coaching in team skills. In addition, ring members were provided with more advanced training and coaching in problem solving (brainstorming, consensus decision making, cause and effect diagrams, Pareto diagrams). Ramsey began its involvement system in September 1983 and completed training/coaching activities in October 1984. Writing in 1985, Don Schilling, a senior consultant for Tarkenton Conn & Company who worked on the Ramsey implementation, and Tom Bremer, the manufacturing manager at Ramsey, described the results of the Ramsey experiment: "The general productivity effort and climate have improved significantly . . . The productivity ratio of hours earned to hours worked . . . has increased by 17 percent. . . . With respect to quality, the cost of scrap per standard hour decreased by nearly 15 percent. . . . In addition, the latest data on the percentage of rings rejected at final inspection reveals a gradual reduction of nearly 17 percent. . . . There has also been a hint of improvement in the employee-relations environment. With over 80 percent of the eligible union membership voting a labor agreement was overwhelmingly ratified in May of 1985 by a margin of 273 to 58."[12]

1984—New United Motors Manufacturing Inc. (NUMMI): Fremont, California

In March of 1982, General Motors finally gave up and closed its Fremont, California, assembly plant and laid off the last twenty-five hundred of Fremont's remaining workers. Opened in 1963, Fremont had become a symbol of much that was wrong with American automotive manufacturing—strikes, sickouts, plant shutdowns, high absenteeism, employee sabotage, low employee morale, poor quality, and atrocious inefficiency. A little over two years later—in May of 1984—the Fremont plant reopened. In organization, management practices, labor-management relations, and a host of other ways, the new Fremont plant was totally different from its former self. Once a symbol for all that was wrong with American manufacturing, by the late 1980s Fremont (or NUMMI as it was called) was being touted as a model for the 1990s.

Fremont's turnaround came as a result of a joint venture between Toyota and GM plus an historic agreement with the United Auto Workers that emphasized labor/management cooperation and mutual trust. The first page of the NUMMI-UAW agreement signed in 1983 spelled out the nature of labor/management relations intended for the new Fremont plant: "(B)oth parties are undertaking this new proposed relationship with the full intention of fostering an innovative labor relations structure, minimizing the traditional adversarial roles and emphasizing mutual trust and good faith. Indeed, both parties recognize this as essential in order to facilitate the efficient production of a quality automobile at the lowest possible cost to the American consumer while at the same time providing much needed jobs at fair wages and benefits for American workers."

Under the NUMMI/UAW agreement, the NUMMI Fremont plant would be organized and managed quite differently from the old GM Fremont plant even though it would employ many of the same production workers. Chief among the differences between old plant and new plant were the following:

1. A formal organization chart, as such, wouldn't exist. Instead, workers would be organized into teams of four to eight persons each, with one team member acting as team leader.
2. Teams would be largely self-managed (no traditional managers or supervisors).
3. Workers on the production line would be responsible and accountable for their own quality (no inspectors) and would have the authority and duty to stop the line by pulling a cord should they get behind or detect a problem that might result in a quality defect.
4. There would be no executive dining room, executive parking spaces, or private offices. Executives would wear the same uniforms as workers and the few executive and support personnel who remained would work side by side in open offices (no partitions).
5. When a decision had to be made, all parties likely to be affected by the decision would be consulted and a decision would be reached by consensus.
6. Highest priority would be placed on maintained job security. Before considering lay-offs in times of reduced demand, managers agreed to first terminate contract employees and then, if necessary, take pay cuts themselves.
7. Employee teams would be charged with responsibility for continually finding ways to improve efficiency and quality and would meet on a regular basis to assess the methods they were using and to find a better way to perform the work.

The NUMMI experiment was extraordinary not only because of the changes in management practices and labor relations, but also because of the cooperation that occurred between what were traditional competitors and adversaries. Yet all three parties to the agreement—GM, Toyota, and the UAW—had something to gain and, in fact, were under intense pressure to undertake an experiment such as NUMMI. A December 1985 *Management Review* article explained the pressures faced by the three players in the NUMMI experiment in this way:

1. General Motors. GM and other U.S. auto makers faced a crisis in their declining share of the world auto market. There was significant pressure from the U.S. government and labor unions to retain jobs for U.S. workers rather than to increase outsourcing. Relations in the industry between labor and management remained adversarial and often inflexible. GM's CEO, Roger Smith, realized that organizational transformation of GM's U.S. manufacturing operations was essential if it was to compete successfully with Japan and other foreign entrants in its global markets. . . . What was needed was a model from which GM's transformation could spring and provide much-needed hands-on learning of a new way . . .

2. Toyota. Other Japanese automakers Honda, Nissan, and more recently Mazda—were turning to the development of subsidiary operations in the U.S. There was increasing pressure from both the U.S. and Japanese governments to address balance of payment issues by shifting manufacturing activity to the U.S. There was mounting pressure in the U.S. Congress to authorize various protectionist measures against Japanese products. Toyota had little experience in overseas manufacturing and needed to establish a viable manufacturing presence in the U.S. as quickly as possible . . .

3. United Auto Workers. The UAW was no less frustrated with its threatening environment than the corporations involved. Thousands of its members were already unemployed, and prospects for the future were bleak. U.S. auto manufacturers were threatening to increase their parts outsourcing or to manufacture entire automobiles in cheaper labor markets abroad. . . . What was needed was an environment unfettered with an adversarial past to show that the UAW can play a positive role in helping [the] U.S. auto industry regain its world leadership position."[13]

By all accounts, the NUMMI experiment of the mid- to late 1980s was a success. Various estimates suggested the plant was 20 to 40 percent more efficient than comparable GM plants. Absenteeism at NUMMI was less than at the typical plant and much less than historically at the old Fremont plant. Perhaps more importantly, the quality of cars assembled at the NUMMI plant was significantly better. The NUMMI as-sembled Chevy Nova, ranked number two of cars sold in the U.S. in customer satisfaction during the first ninety days of ownership according to a 1986 survey. No other GM car made the top fifteen that year. Yet NUMMI was not without its detractors. Dissident union workers complained that NUMMI and other plants like it created "management by stress," "a worker hell," and excessive peer pressure where management and union leaders alike discouraged workers from filing griev-ances about safety and work load issues. Other workers agreed that workers at NUMMI did have to work hard since workers had more responsibility and there were fewer less-demanding jobs. But, they noted, at least the workers had a say in how things were done and the work was distributed fairly with fewer opportunities for "select" people to hold a monopoly on the "good" jobs where they could just coast all day.[14]

1985—Hanes Knitwear Plant: Sparta, North Carolina

(*For further information on this study, see page 351 in the Notes.*[15])

In the late 1970s, Hanes Knitwear's Sparta, North Carolina, plant was like many American manufacturing plants—a good place to work in a small American town. The plant belonged to a large American corporation. Plant management was friendly and supportive. Pay and benefits were good, even ex-cellent by local standards. Many workers had been employed at the plant for most of their lives, as had their friends and relatives. There was a secure and predictable rhythm to work. The atmosphere was relaxed with little pressure for perfor-mance. Working on an individual incentive, high performers could make their quota by noon with plenty of time to socialize in the afternoon. Workers took pride in their company, were comfortable with their management, and were confident that they gave a "fair day's work for a fair day's pay." They were secure in a good job with a good company. It was a life that would last forever. Then it all ended.

In the early 1980s, the world of work at Sparta underwent a drastic change. Hanes brought in new plant management, changed performance standards, changed work methods, and initiated a wave of determined efforts to improve plant performance significantly. But these efforts weren't working. By 1985, not only was the safe, secure, predictable "family plant" gone, but the plant was in turmoil. Employees hated their jobs, distrusted their management, and were beginning to turn against the company they had loved. Performance wasn't improving. Sparta was Hanes's highest cost domestic plant. The situation seemed hopeless for management and employees. But something significant happened at Sparta starting in 1985.

In the spring of 1985, it was obvious that something was terribly wrong at Sparta. Recent employee relations surveys had reached an all-time low—significantly below the crisis point in practically every area. Employees were dissatisfied with their pay, lacked confidence in their management, felt insecure about their jobs, were disgruntled with their supervisors, and had lost pride in their company. Hard performance measures were equally as bad, or at least not getting any better. But these measures had to improve. The company was facing stiff competition and losing market share. Its major competition produced 400 percent more product with just 150 percent more people, enjoyed a $2.00 to $2.50 per hour labor cost advantage, and paid significantly less for fringe benefits when compared to the Sparta plant. Hanes could close Sparta and move production offshore. After all, offshore wages were 10 to 15 percent less, productivity was higher, there were significant tax advantages, and even with higher shipping cost, the unit costs of finished goods arriving at distribution centers from off shore facilities was less than the unit cost of similar goods shipped from Sparta. But Hanes management didn't want to close an American plant and put long-term employees out of work. Something had to be done to try and save the plant. In order to determine what could be done, Hanes management sent an assessment team to the Sparta plant in May of 1985.

The 1985 assessment was conducted by a team of consultants from Tarkenton Conn & Company, an Atlanta-based consulting firm specializing in performance management, organizational change, and innovative compensation systems. Over a period of four days during May of that year, the assessment team interviewed all of the managers and supervisors, and approximately one third of the employees at Sparta. In addition to reviewing general management practices, interviewers questioned managers, supervisors, and employees about three issues of concern to Hanes senior management: (1) employee reaction to changes in work methods and performance standards (the work wage equity program); (2) employee response to the employee involvement/quality circle program (the S.T.E.P.—success through employee participation—teams); and (3) validity of the employee survey results. The assessment findings from those interviews provided a basis for sweeping changes in management practices implemented at Sparta over the next few years. Additionally, the assessment results provided a snapshot of employee response to the changes implemented at Sparta prior to 1985 and the deteriorating state of management/employee relations at that time. The following summary of assessment findings is taken with permission from the May 1985 Assessment Report and recent interviews with Hanes management and assessment team members.

Work Wage Equity

A significant issue addressed by the assessment team was employee reaction to Hanes's work wage equity program. Don Eppert, director of human resources at Hanes, explained work wage equity in a recent interview:

> In the early 1980s, we undertook a significant revision in our engineered time standards for work performed and individual incentive pay at Sparta and other sewing plants. We recognized at that time that we had not kept up with

revisions to time standards over the years to keep them in line with changes in methods and product design. We let the standards remain the same so long that by the early 1980s we were faced with having to undertake a significant adjustment all at one time if we were going to begin to bring our labor cost situation back in line with that of our competitors. Based upon new studies undertaken by our industrial engineers, we were faced with the need to hike our engineered standards by as much as 30 percent. Obviously, such a drastic revision created a significant amount of tension at the plant. It was a catalyst for a lot of the problems we were seeing with employee relations. But given our competitive situation, we had no choice. We just couldn't get that message across to the people. Their perception was that we just wanted them to do more work for less pay.

During assessment interviews, employees described their response to Work Wage Equity. They saw themselves as a work force under siege from a heartless, uncaring, even evil management. "Hanes," they said, "was just trying to get rich off the bodies of their people." Employees couldn't understand why their once paternalistic management had turned against them. "Now," said employees, "they work us like dogs. They work us like slaves. We're under constant pressure. We used to love coming to work, now we dread it. This is management by fear."

The resentment voiced by employees was not just directed at the new rates, but also at how the rate change was implemented. In their report, the assessment team said: "A large part of the resentment against work wage equity came from the way it was implemented. Operators were not told all the reasons for the change, nor how the new rates would be calculated. When employees questioned or voiced complaints, they received little response. . . . When people complained to engineers about the rates, the engineers responded (according to employees): 'We will change the rates when we feel they need to be changed.' . . . Employees described their perception of management's attitude as: 'That's the way it is; if you don't like it, leave.' [Employees said] We are treated like dirt under their feet. They call us morons. They act as if we are stupid."

With little information about the real reasons for changing rates, employees invented their own reasons. The assessment team reported numerous rumors, such as "Management was trying to punish all employees because a few employees had complained about inequities in the old rates," or "Management was speeding up rates to try to get rid of people, particularly older employees." While some employees attributed the speed-up to the need to respond to foreign competition, many saw the foreign threat to be three to five years off. "Why," they asked, "did they have to work harder now to meet a threat that was still in the distant future?" Few, if any, employees understood the real reason they were being asked to change: to meet an immediate competitive threat by correcting a labor cost situation that was grossly out of line.

S.T.E.P. Teams

Like many American companies in the early 1980s, Hanes had created its own form of quality circles. Called S.T.E.P. teams, this employee involvement system could have served as a vehicle for communicating the reasons for major change and for engaging employees in a cooperative effort with management to ease the transition. Yet as the assessment team found in its interviews, S.T.E.P. teams at Sparta were an almost total failure. The Assessment Report summed up the attitude of most employees toward the teams as follows: "Most employees considered S.T.E.P. a waste of time. They saw the S.T.E.P. representatives as being able to get out of work and talk while others had to work hard to make their quota. People complained that the process was 'just a gripe session.' . . . Team members admitted that occasionally the meetings turned into gripe sessions, [but] felt that they were much better informed [as a result of attending the meetings]."

Everyone agreed that S.T.E.P. teams failed as a vehicle for communication. Team members were supposed to report back to nonmembers of team activities and what they had learned. Yet few did. Some employee groups had no representatives on

S.T.E.P., therefore no one to keep them informed. Even when a group had a representative, seldom was there time for the representative to inform his/her group of S.T.E.P. activities prior to returning to work.

The Employee Survey Results

Senior management was particularly concerned about results from the most recent employee surveys. As we reported earlier, scores on these surveys had reached an all-time low. Based upon survey results, employees were apparently unhappy with the company and almost every aspect of management. But were they really this unhappy?

In response to the most recent survey, Sparta managers and supervisors had conducted follow-up interviews with employees to validate and expand upon the written survey. What managers and supervisors reported from their follow-up interviews was completely different from the survey results. Employees weren't that unhappy. The survey had been taken at a particularly low point for the plant. Employees just vented their frustrations on the survey. Everything was different now. If the survey was repeated, Sparta managers and supervisors were confident the results would be much more positive. But were things really better? Was the original survey correct? Had employee opinions changed since the survey as Sparta managers and supervisors thought they had?

When asked by the assessment team, employees unanimously said no. Conditions had not changed. Employee opinions had not changed since the written survey. If the survey were repeated, results would be the same. Why, then, did employees tell their managers and supervisors something totally different during the follow-up interviews? The employees' explanation was:

- "It wouldn't do any good [to be honest with them], I couldn't be honest when I was there one-on-one."
- "My supervisor was just writing down what she wanted to write down versus what I said."

Apparently, many employees did not volunteer to go to the one-on-one interviews. They "didn't think it [the interviews] would do any good."

General Management Practices

A fourth set of questions asked of employees during assessment interviews covered general management practices: recognition of good performance; consistency of enforcing personnel policies; management response to employee ideas, suggestions, and questions, and so on. The Assessment Report summarized responses to these questions:

Responses the assessment team received [to questions about performance feedback and reinforcement] were mixed. The amount and quality seemed to depend upon the individual supervisor. Some supervisors gave much more feedback and encouragement than others. Most operators said they received lots of feedback [while they were] in training, but once on the floor, it depended upon the supervisor. [On the floor, they said] ". . . you hear about it if you sink below 100 percent [efficiency], but if you do well, you aren't likely to hear about it." "If you are a slow performer, supervisors are always watching to catch you.". . . Some operators didn't understand how their totals [performance efficiencies] were calculated by the computer. Feedback to non-operators, i.e., material handlers, was non-existent.

When we asked employees what reinforcement there was for [doing] a good job, most responded, "More money, but it isn't worth it"; "If you do well, managers push you to do more to make up for slower workers." The high performers felt that they were taken advantage of [by management].

Many [employees] were confused and angry [about management's seeming inconsistency in administering personnel policies]. "Management [said employees] publicized that they follow the seniority policy on filling jobs, but that is not always the case. An hourly employee with little seniority got promoted to management." Operators also misunderstood the job posting policy. They cited an example where temporaries had been hired to fill in . . . instead of posting the job and letting people with seniority bid on it.

Operators also said that managers never responded to their ideas or suggestions. When employees gave suggestions, managers listened, but the suggestions went nowhere. The usual response was "we'll work on it," but nothing happened. [Anyway] operators claimed, the supervisors were always in meetings and doing paperwork so that they were never available.

[The attitude that employees perceived managers and supervisors had toward employees was also a problem.] Employees said, "Managers do not respect the operators. They treat us like children or morons, as if we are stupid." [Employees also complained that] the quality of the product they produced was slipping and more and more expensive outside "experts"—engineers, motivation consultants, physical therapists, etc.—were being sent into the plant to "gawk at us." Employees felt they were "watched all the time."

Such was the situation at Hanes's Sparta, North Carolina, plant in the spring of 1985. The assessment team's report was disheartening to plant management and Hanes senior management. The assessment team provided a series of specific findings and recommendations to address Sparta's problems. However, no one could be sure if by implementing these recommendations the plant could be saved. Could performance be improved to the level the company required? Could relations between employees and management at the plant be restored? Performance did improve. Employee/management relations were restored. Before we discuss how this was accomplished, let's turn to the spring of 1988—three years later.

Spring 1988. The plant that was in trouble in 1985 has grown. The direct labor work force is up by 60 percent over 1985 levels. Hanes management would like to expand further. But few people are unemployed in the community, partially because of the growth at Hanes's Sparta plant. More and more, new employees are recruited to Hanes from other companies. People want to work for Hanes. It's not an easy place to work, they will tell you, but it is a good place to work.

The labor force has grown at Sparta. So has production. It is up by nearly 90 percent. More people, but a much faster increase in production. Unit costs are way down. The Sparta plant—Hanes's highest-cost domestic producer in 1985—is now Hanes' lowest-cost domestic producer. The direct labor work force has grown, but it is also much more productive. That keeps costs down. Something else keeps costs down. Hanes Sparta—the troubled plant in 1985 with a work force that had to be watched and controlled—hasn't had growth in its managerial, supervisory, and other indirect staff. It has the same number of managers and supervisors—managing many more people. The direct-to-indirect ratio at Hanes Sparta is the best in the company. People at Hanes Sparta are talking about getting better—becoming the world's low-cost producer of T-shirts. Managers, supervisors, and employees all believe their plant can get there.

Something else has happened at Sparta. You see it when you walk through the plant. The clutter, disorder, material handlers pushing and shoving their way through narrow isles, the stacks of material, the chaos of 1985 are all gone. Teams of operators now sit in a neat, orderly, clean space. Between each row of operators, a conveyor belt delivers brightly colored trays of material to each work station. No operator waits for material to sew. A full tray is always waiting. Material handlers monitor lighted boards at the end of each aisle. A light goes on—an operator needs to be supplied. The material handler takes two steps backward to retrieve another tray of material to feed the line. The new tray glides into the correct space, waiting to be used. The material handler has only moved a few feet. The operator never paused. Production continued.

Something else is different at Sparta. Flags fly from operator station after operator station announcing membership in "clubs." There are a lot of bright green flags—the Director's Club. In smaller numbers—scattered throughout the rows are silver flags—the Vice President's Club. Still fewer—but not infrequent, are gold flags—the President's Club. Each flag represents a level of production—green flags a 120 percent average, silver flags a 130 percent average, gold flags a 140 percent average. These are given for not just a one week av-

erage, but a twenty-six-week average. There are other flags—
a Zero Defects flag, a Perfect Attendance flag. A lot of operators have a green, silver, gold, or some other type of flag.
Many operators have more than one flag. A lot of operators
have 120-, 130-, or 140-production averages for twenty-six consecutive weeks. In 1985, few operators could be forced past
115 percent performance. Then, many were struggling to
maintain 100 percent. Many of these were afraid of failure.
That was 1985.

You don't hear talk about "failure" or "fear" at Sparta today.
You do hear about operators coming out of training and "going
for" the Director's Club. Then, you hear, they want to get in
the Vice President's Club, then the President's. You do hear
talk about "pressure." But it is a different type of pressure than
you heard about in 1985. Then, managers and supervisors
pushed employees. Now, employees push themselves. A
Sparta manager preaches in an interview: "You can't go out
and push people and get them to perform. They just push back.
You can coach, but you can't push. The better you are to them,
the better they will be to you. Now twice as many people
work for me as before [back in 1985]; the difference is we work
together as a team. We stress teamwork. We help each other
out."

Something has happened at Sparta. You hear a lot about
teams and teamwork. You hear a lot about team meetings at
Sparta. Once a month employees, their supervisor, and the
plant manager come together to talk about performance, share
information, recognize good performance, and communicate.
A manager says: "The team meetings—they were important.
They help a lot. We sit down with employees and talk. They
get a lot of information about what is happening and why.
They give us a lot of information. We can explain why we did
something—why we had to do it."

Don Eppert, Hanes's director of human resources, describes
the Sparta of today: "Today? Today, Sparta is completely different from what it was like in 1985. In 1985, plant management was reeling under the blows. We were getting nowhere
and the employees' perception was that we didn't care. Today,
the plant manager is very much in control. The work force is
focused and directed. Communication, management, and su-

pervisory skills have vastly improved. The work force is more knowledgeable than they have ever been about business needs and customer needs. They know where they fit in and what they have to do. And they do it not just because we want them to, but because they want to. They are very data conscious now and more wired into productivity, quality, the importance of training, and customer service. It is a totally different plant from the mess we found ourselves in just three years ago."

What made the difference? How did a plant in trouble become a high-performing plant with good management/employee relations in just three years? It started with the findings and recommendations from the 1985 assessment.

Tarkenton's 1985 Assessment Report presented seven major findings concerning management policies and practices at the Sparta Plant. The following is taken from the Assessment Report:

To introduce our findings, it is useful to put them in the perspective of the Sparta Plant's transition. . . . In the old culture, the Sparta Plant was . . . a family. The plant manager was a second father, a respected figure who had a personal relationship with all the employees. He was from Sparta and knew everything about the employees and their families. Everyone had access to him. The "floor ladies" [supervisors] were the mother figures who doted over the operators and were at their beck and call. The workers were friends and relatives. Hanes was known as a good place to work. Pay and benefits were good and people took pride in quality, their plant, and Hanes. People worked their own method [of sewing] and there was little pressure for production.

The new culture was formed in reaction to domestic and foreign competition, external forces outside of the plant's control. Changes resulted from outsiders impacting the plant—Hanes management, external consultants, special interest groups, and other plants. Where there used to be stability, now there is constant change. High priced "experts" come to "gawk" at them. There is extreme pressure for production and keeping costs down. Toward that end, more structure has been imposed, and one uniform [sewing] method is required. Operators have much less control over their own lives, so they feel like machines. There had been a change in management styles. People have less time to talk with their supervisor, and much less with the plant manager. Employees feel they are being watched all the time.

Quality [once a source of pride for workers] is now perceived by employees as subordinate to meeting production quotas. The environment has changed to one of suspicion. Operators feel managers do not trust or respect them. People feel under pressure to produce every minute.

From this perspective, we have seven major findings:

1. Employees do not understand the need to change. They know little about the business in general. They are naive about the competitive environment. Because people don't know why changes are necessary, they resist the changes and rumors are rampant.
2. Part of employees' misunderstanding is due to the lack of a structure for two-way communication. Management does not have a regular forum to educate and inform employees. Instead, an outside consultant (the motivation consultant) talks to employees. And what he tells them is not always consistent with Hanes's management positions. As a result, employees receive mixed messages. When employees ask questions, supervisors listen. But there is no management follow-up. Employee questions go unanswered.
3. Plant management has less opportunity to motivate and control due to the number of outsiders influencing the plant. Employees feel like animals in a zoo being "watched" by outsiders who measure their performance and set the standards. As a result of these outside influences, employees have even less trust in their own plant management.
4. Managers and supervisors do not exercise the communication and leadership skills necessary to deal openly with employee problems. This is partially due to the fact that outsiders attempt to manage for them.

Supervisors lack the skills to involve employees in solving problems.
5. There is little team problem solving. Employees have little input on matters that directly concern them. They are told to perform and not ask questions. The emphasis is on individual, not team, performance.
6. Employees at the plant are experiencing a "change overload." Changes came too fast and hit them all at once. There was no easing into the changes, and employees had no input or control over the process. They feel under constant pressure. They fear not making the new higher performance standard and losing their jobs. The fear itself is probably the main hindrance to their performance.
7. The manner in which "Work Wage Equity" was implemented, the concurrent changes, and the impact of outsiders has seriously impaired the credibility of plant management with employees.

In summary, we believe that most employee complaints and much of Sparta's problems stem from the manner in which changes have been introduced and the general lack of management and communication skills among managers and supervisors at the plant.

The key to improvement both in management/employee relations and performance, said the report, was the involvement and participation of the nonmanagement work force in making change happen. Hanes and Sparta managers and supervisors had been trying to force change from the outside. The more they forced, the more employees resisted. To make matters worse, as resistance mounted, more and more outsiders—engineers, motivational consultants, ergonomics specialists—were being brought in to apply increased pressure. Rather than helping, these additional outsiders just further undermined plant management's credibility—a credibility that was already suffering. What should Hanes do? The report listed eight specific recommendations.

First, remove the external influences to the maximum extent possible. If Sparta was to survive and performance was to improve, Sparta managers, supervisors, and employees had to make the necessary changes themselves. They would need support, but Sparta people should run the plant—not outsiders.

Second, employees were not likely to change unless they saw a need to change. Employees at Sparta lacked an understanding of the business. They had to be educated on both domestic and international competition. And they had to be kept informed on a regular basis about changes in the competitive picture and performance expectations. Employees, said the report, needed to know the basis of competition— how Hanes competes and who its competitors are. Employees needed to know the wage differential and how that impacted unit labor costs. In short, employees needed to know the facts as Hanes management and plant management knew the facts. To educate the work force, the assessment team recommended a series of plant-wide or unit-wide meetings where this information should be shared. "It is particularly important," said the report, "that these meetings be led by Sparta management, not by an outsider, in order that local management gain credibility and build employee trust." Additionally, these meetings had to be held not just once but regularly to update employees as new information became available.

Third, communication up and down the chain of command within the plant had to be strengthened. A formal structure had to be created to ensure that vital information could be communicated from the top level of Hanes and Sparta management to every employee *and* that questions and concerns of employees could be raised, dealt with, or passed upward to higher levels for answers. How could this be accomplished? The assessment team recommended that the plant institute a series of interlocking team meetings. Every manager and supervisor should meet with his or her employees on a bi-weekly basis to share information on performance, recognize good performance, and ensure a free flow of communication— management to employees and employees to managers.

Fourth, said the report, if Sparta managers and supervisors were to conduct these meetings successfully, they had to be trained in participative management skills—how to listen, provide performance feedback, reinforce good performance, lead employees in problem solving efforts. But, said the report, training alone would not be sufficient. In addition to attending training classes, Sparta managers and supervisors needed follow-up assistance in applying these skills. A major focus of this training and follow-up coaching should be to change the culture at Sparta from one where managers monitored and controlled to one where managers coached and rewarded.

Fifth, the assessment team recommended that Hanes consider making some concessions to employees—backing off to some extent or slowing down the process of change. Employees were being asked to change too much too quickly. They were under extreme pressure and the pressure itself was impairing performance. They needed some relief—some "pressure valve" to release the tension. Management, the report said, needed to respond in some way to employee concerns— to provide at least some temporary respite. The report suggested several alternatives such as letting individuals set their own goals, changing the method of calculating and reporting performance against standard to more closely approximate the old method, and even the possibility of suspending or eliminating performance rates entirely. The specific alternatives should be selected by Hanes and Sparta management. The important point, said the report, was that Hanes should take some positive and dramatic action to shore up credibility, release the "pressure," and dispel the resentment that employees felt.

Finally, the assessment team recommended a significant change in the mandate of S.T.E.P. teams. S.T.E.P., said the report, was not and could not be an effective vehicle for communication. Too few employees were involved. However, S.T.E.P. could serve an important role for involving employees in in-depth problem solving. Normal employee teams (as suggested in recommendation three) would not have the time in their team meetings to engage in in-depth problem solving. Such problems should be given to S.T.E.P. teams, and team members should be given training and follow-up coaching in problem solving skills.

Not surprisingly, neither Hanes nor Sparta management immediately accepted the assessment team's recommendations. The recommendations were "risky," "revolutionary." Not only Sparta, but no Hanes plant was managed in the way proposed for Sparta in the Assessment Report. And it wasn't just Hanes and Sparta. Few American companies were managed in the way the assessment team proposed in 1985.

In effect, what the assessment team was proposing was that Sparta adopt what the American Productivity and Quality Center has called "natural work teams"—a "high order" involvement technique. John Belcher, a vice president at the APQC, describes natural work teams: "Natural work teams represent true participative management. Supervisors conduct regular communications meetings in order to keep their subordinates fully informed regarding business conditions, organizational performance, and competitive challenges. Employees engage in problem solving as problems arise. Supervisors solicit employee ideas for performance improvement and informally recognize employee contributions. There is a sense of common objectives and employee commitment is high."

Tarkenton's Assessment Report was delivered to Hanes and Sparta management in May 1985. In June, Sparta's plant manager and personnel supervisor attended a two-week course in Atlanta to learn more about the management technique the assessment team had proposed. Finally, in early July, Hanes and Sparta managers sat down with Tarkenton consultants to plan the implementation. The assessment team's recommendations would be followed.

As worked out by the planning group, changes in management practices at Sparta would involve a series of activities— training sessions and follow-up coaching for Sparta managers and supervisors, educational sessions for employees, a concession to employees to re-audit performance standards, and the installation of a new, automated performance feedback system. Implementation would take at least six months, culminating in fully operational work-unit teams.

The following highlights of the implementation process provide a chronological record of Sparta's transition as reflected in detailed month-by-month summaries prepared by the Tarkenton consultant Don Schilling and others assigned to the implementation. The period covered by detailed records is July 1985 through the fall of 1986.

July 1985

1. Sparta managers and supervisors attend four days of management/supervisory training on performance-management skills, problem-solving skills, and team meeting skills.
2. S.T.E.P. team members attend three days of training on problem-solving techniques.
3. Training classes are supplemented with follow-up individual coaching for attendees to ensure application of the skills.

August 1985

1. The plant manager begins educational meetings with all employees to share information on "the competitive picture." Part of these meetings include employees' hands-on examination of swatches of material from garments produced at Sparta and garments produced by Hanes' major competitor in a "blind" quality test (employees did not know which garment was from Hanes Sparta). Employees are asked to touch the cloth swatches and examine the quality for themselves. Employees say their garments aren't as good as their competitor's. Their quality has slipped. (In later meetings with employees after a quality-improvement effort was initiated, this exercise was repeated. In these later blind tests, employees identified the Hanes Sparta garments as being of superior quality. They could feel the improvement.)
2. Plant management announces that, in response to employee concerns about the new engineered performance standards, an independent (non-Hanes) consulting firm would reexamine the standards. The industrial engineering consultant makes his report of findings to Hanes and Sparta management. Then, at their request, he presents his findings to employees. Most of the standards, says the consultant, are correct. But some are, in fact, out of line. Sparta management says that the incorrect standards will be changed.
3. Hardware and software are acquired for a new performance reporting system for the plant. The new com-

puterized system will track performance on critical measures for each work group or team against goals and objectives they set. Positive and negative exception reports will be prepared on a regular basis to provide feedback to managers, supervisors, *and* employees on key measures. These reports will be used in team meetings and posted later.

September 1985

1. Team meetings begin. The plant manager attends and conducts *every* team meeting—as many as six meetings every two weeks. Initial meetings are devoted to continuing to share competitive data and to providing a forum for general communication. Employees are involved in drawing up a code of conduct for their team meetings. The code specifies rules for attendance, participation, and so on. Drawing up the code is the first step toward involving employees in determining how the business will be conducted.
2. A consultant attends every team meeting and evaluates the plant manager's team leadership skills against preestablished criteria. During the first team meetings, the plant manager scores 89 out of a possible 100 percent. This is the highest score the consultant has ever given any manager for his or her first series of meetings.
3. The production manager attends a two-week training course in Atlanta on leading work-unit teams.

October 1985

1. Team meetings continue with the plant manager leading most meetings. The production manager takes over leading other teams. The personnel supervisor takes over leadership (or facilitation) of the S.T.E.P. team meetings.
2. Sixty meetings have now been conducted. All were held on schedule. The plant manager's score on team leadership skills is reported by the consultant as 97%—the best any manager has ever attained.
3. Teams decide to focus on improving plant quality at the suggestion of plant management. The plant manager

says, "We decided not to focus on performance/productivity to begin with. The people already felt under tremendous pressure for performance. What they were concerned about—and we were concerned about—was improving quality. So we picked quality for the teams to work on. Later, we did get to the point where we could talk about performance also. But not in the beginning."

4. Teams set their own quality goals.

November 1985

1. Team meetings continue with supervisors beginning to take over responsibility for running their own teams. The plant manager continues to attend team meetings and they are monitored by the consultant.

2. Quality as measured by percentage of defects begins to improve. The consultant reports: "Percentage Defects continue to improve as shown by a noticeable reduction in variability and level. This suggests the degree to which the Hanes's quality image has been translated into the daily workmanship and motivation of operators—a predisposition easily triggered by data-based performance information. Such improvements are known to yield swift results, but are somewhat unusual this early and prior to the initiation of problem solving."

3. Interviews conducted by the consultant with a sample of twenty-four employees elicit a positive response to team meetings. Employees say they particularly like the feedback on performance, the recognition they receive during the meetings for good performance, the general information sharing, and the follow-up action managers take to their ideas, suggestions, and questions. Employees feel closer to the plant manager and production manager, their unit's performance has improved, management seems more "interested" in them and that "feels good," their jobs are more interesting, they feel "big"—better about themselves, they have less need to rely upon rumors, and they can voice their opinions/ideas. One fourth of the employees surveyed say there is "nothing" they dislike about the meetings. Others say

they don't have enough time to ask questions, they fear a negative response from their peers if they speak up, the meetings interrupt performance when they are "on a roll," and sometimes they are embarrassed by individual compliments from managers in public.

4. The consultant makes the following comments about implementation progress:

   a. Employees have become extraordinarily "performance driven." Not only is the level of plant activity representative of extremely hard work, but employees are exceptionally "numbers" conscious now. They are interested in comparing their performance with that of other plants, can recall exact performance levels from nearly a month previous, and seem sincerely interested in how "the numbers" make each individual and unit look.

   b. Management and supervisors have begun to view performance measurement as a useful tool rather than a burden. Non-sewing units—indirect units—are beginning to develop their own measures.

   c. Hanes middle and senior management are beginning to show a "refreshing" interest in the results from the implementation.

   d. Employees are responding to the recognition and verbal reinforcement. The power of such "non-contract" incentives at Sparta paints an optimistic picture of success.

December 1985

1. Supervisors take on increased responsibility for conducting team meetings.

2. Plant managers and supervisors begin to use token reinforcers to recognize teams with quality improvement or other noteworthy accomplishments. All six sewing units receive an extra half hour for lunch as a reward for achieving their quality goals the first time. Members in three units receive gift certificates for meeting their goal four consecutive weeks. Free coffee and doughnuts are pro-

vided in one unit and for quality inspectors to recognize performance. One sewing unit treats their supervisor to a free dinner. They wanted to "express their appreciation to her for her efforts." The people pay for the dinner themselves.

3. Measures are developed for indirect areas. These teams begin to set goals.

4. Written and verbal communication between the plant management and Hanes management about the results of the implementation increases. Hanes management begins to visit the plant to demonstrate interest in the effort and performance improvement.

5. Performance feedback extends beyond team meetings as plant-wide graphs and charts are posted on the main bulletin board and in the cafeteria.

6. The quality of team meetings continues to improve. Team leadership scores reach 100 percent. Employee participation in meetings (as measured by counts of significant comments or contributions) increases.

7. All sewing units have lower defect rates than prior to the start of team meetings. Some units are hitting their quality goal 88 percent of the time.

8. A new corporate employee survey at the Sparta plant shows the following compared to the previous survey:

   a. Employee evaluation of top management's willingness to listen to them—17 percent improvement
   b. Employee rating of the fairness of top management—18 percent improvement
   c. Employee evaluation of management's consideration of employee interests—14 percent improvement
   d. Employees stating they feel free to tell their department manager anything—8 percent improvement
   e. Employee rating of plant manager—20 percent improvement

9. Concern is expressed by the consultant, plant managers, and employees that supervisors are not providing feedback, reinforcement, and so on outside of team meetings. Supervisor-led team meetings are not being conducted

as effectively as they were when managers led the meetings. Training does not seem to have been as effective with supervisors.

January 1986

1. Team meetings continue.
2. Employees continue to display, in the words of the consultant, "a competitive spirit which is fueled by performance data." The consultant describes employee behavior: "The drive [on the part of employees] to hit goals set by the team is evidenced by embarrassment from not hitting commitments, inquiries regarding the integrity of the numbers, and an emerging willingness to pinpoint operator related obstacles."
3. Concern continues about the inability of supervisors to fully assume their roles in making the team system work. The consultant notes: "It is very important that supervisors play a larger role in the team meetings in order to prevent management burn-out and to enhance the system. However, there are several indicators that supervisory development has not progressed as far as the development of the managerial team. For example, employees continue to comment about the failure of supervisors to practice feedback, reinforcement, and provide training on-the-floor. An item from the recent corporate survey shows an 8% decline in employee ratings of supervisor fairness and absence of favoritism. Additionally, supervisors have a key role in supplementing formal operator training and reinforcing performance of what is inherently boring and repetitious job content. Yet supervisors are not performing this role consistently."

   The consultant recommends additional training and coaching for Sparta supervisors to upgrade their supervisory skills.

February–March, 1986

Team meetings continue, with performance being sustained at approximately January levels. Hanes and Sparta managers continue to discuss options for upgrading supervisory skills, which is seen as critical if further performance gains are to be made. Several options are considered for providing the necessary training. The two options with the most support are either to purchase a predesigned, prepackaged course on basic supervision or design a customized course specifically for Sparta supervisors.

April 1986

Hanes and Sparta management decide to provide Sparta supervisors with customized training with several unique components:

1. Supervisors will participate in the design of the course. In conjunction with managers and trainers, they will determine which of dozens of supervisory skills are most relevant to meeting their needs.
2. A supervisory/employee interaction survey instrument will be developed and administered to employees on a regular basis in order to provide ongoing feedback to supervisors on the quality of their relationships with employees.
3. The training will be delivered in short (two- to three-hour) modules. Each module will cover a specific skill and will be followed by frequent one-on-one contact with the trainer to clarify skill content and encourage application of the skill.

May 1986

Five groups of managers and supervisors participate in sessions to determine skills to be taught in the planned supervisory training. The nominal group technique is used to brainstorm, vote, and rank the skills in which Sparta supervisors were perceived to have the greatest need for improvement. Combinations of these ranks yielded the following four skills as the group consensus:

1. Motivating improved performance (correcting problem performance and shaping performance)

2. Overcoming resistance to change
3. Reinforcing/recognizing positive work habits
4. Handling chronic complainers

June—July, 1986

1. Supervisory training sessions are conducted in the four skill areas followed by extensive one-on-one coaching on the application of each skill.
2. The supervisor/employee interaction survey form is designed and administered. The final version is a simple, one-page, check-off form. Employees are asked to rate their supervisor on a ten-point scale in the following areas:

Friendliness—degree to which supervisor is likable and respectful in his/her relations with others

Concern—degree to which supervisor is sensitive to the employee's feelings and shows understanding and trust

Fairness/consistency—administers policies, rules, and recognition consistently

Openness/flexibility—encourages employees to talk about themselves or their concerns and will change his or her approach based on others' input

Confidence—supervisor indicates he or she is comfortable relying on the employees to do the job

Recognition/encouragement—notices when an employee is doing well and attempts to motivate lower performers

Calmness—supervisor responds to problems without getting too emotional and does not take everything too seriously

Trust—the degree to which one can rely on the supervisor to be truthful and committed to following up on employee concerns

Helpfulness—the degree to which the supervisor assists the employee in doing a better job

Direction—the degree to which the supervisor clearly states his/her expectations

The rating form is designed with a twofold purpose in mind: to provide supervisors with feedback on their personal interaction style as perceived by employees and to evaluate the effectiveness of the supervisory training.

Ratings are to be collected every two months. Individual ratings will be shared with each supervisor and his or her boss. Average plant-wide ratings will be posted.

The interaction survey form is introduced to employees in team meetings. The first survey, to establish baseline data, is conducted immediately.

A second survey is administered in July. Plant-wide results are very favorable—average 73.6 percent positive. Employees and supervisors are more favorable toward this "mini-survey" than the yearly "corporate" survey. The mini-survey is seen as more accurate because it is administered more frequently and covers items that are "more relevant."

3. The consultant notes considerable changes in supervisor behavior following the training modules and coaching sessions:

a. There is an extremely high rate of compliance with "homework" assignments supervisors are given during training.

b. Supervisors express the belief that they now feel recognition is a much more effective way to motivate employees than sharp criticism. Many note a favorable reaction from employees they reinforce and a noticeable improvement apparently resulting from the recognition.

c. A number of supervisors demonstrate what the consultant calls "exceptional ability" to redirect em-

ployees' undesirable work habits and then immediately recognize positive performance.

d. Plant management recognizes supervisors and other
support staff for their contribution toward improvement.

4. Sparta begins the installation of a new conveyor system
designed to streamline work flow. Team meetings are
used as a device to communicate the need for the system,
answer questions, report on progress, and "sell" the new
system. There is some initial concern on the part of
supervisors and employees, but a willingness to "wait
and see" how the installation on the first line works.

August 1986 to Present

1. Employees and supervisors are pleased with the results
from the new conveyor system. The vast majority of
employees, says the consultant, are eagerly awaiting the
time when the entire plant utilizes the system.

2. The flag system is installed to recognize individual
performance.

3. Senior Hanes management visits Sparta to address all
employees. The message delivered is: "All of the changes
have been absolutely necessary to keep Sparta alive. Continued changes will be necessary to build capacity to the
level required to be competitive. In addition, everyone
will have to do better. So get ready because we'll all be
doing more, particularly management."
The employee response to the address is:

- "He told it like it was."
- "It was sincere—a shot in the arm."
- "It was future-oriented with no false promises."
- "It was the truth."
- "He honestly answered our questions about the
future."
- "We got the message."

Between the spring of 1985 and fall of 1986—a period of approximately eighteen months—Hanes and Sparta managers were able to totally reverse what seemed to be an impossible situation. Because of what happened during those months, a plant was saved and a troubled plant became a high-performance plant.

1986—Beaumont *Enterprise*: Beaumont, Texas

In 1984, George Irish, the newly appointed chief executive officer for the Beaumont *Enterprise*, was conducting a "state of the business meeting" with employees in the newspaper's editorial department. He finished his talk and then asked if there were any questions. Assistant news editor Mamie Meek, a sixteen-year veteran of the Beaumont *Enterprise*, stood up and said: "What are you going to do about the parking problem?" Meek's question changed her life and launched one of the few employee-involvement systems in the newspaper business.

George Irish had arrived at the Beaumont *Enterprise* to take over as publisher and chief executive officer after the Hearst Corporation purchased the paper from Jefferson Pilot Publications in 1984. Irish had been publisher of the Midland *Daily News* of Midland, Michigan, just before coming to the Beaumont *Enterprise*. Before that, he had been a personnel manager for a small group of newspapers. For Beaumont, Irish was a refreshing change, since he believed in participative management. Irish's predecessor, in contrast, had been authoritative and dictatorial. It was the former publisher who had created the "parking problem" Meek referred to in her question. In an effort to ensure that outside salespeople had a parking space as they came and went during each day, the former publisher had dictated that parking spaces would be assigned with the best spaces going to advertising sales personnel. For the rest of Beaumont's employees, the assignment of spaces was a symbol that, as far as the publisher was concerned, they were less important. That was the parking problem. Given their experience with their previous publisher, Irish's response to Meeks's question came as some surprise. Instead of ignoring the question or saying he would "look into it," Irish responded that he would appoint a committee of employees to study the problem and recommend a solution. And, he said, "Meeks, you are going to chair the committee."

Meeks did chair the committee to study the parking problem, which ultimately recommended that parking assignments be eliminated. More importantly, Meeks became interested in the process of group decision making and employee involvement—so much so that she checked a book out of the library on how to run effective meetings. As it turned out, the book covered not only meetings but was, in fact, a guide to quality circles, an employee-involvement system many American companies had adopted from the Japanese. As a result of reading the book, Meeks became fascinated with the idea of quality circles and approached Irish with the idea of starting quality circles at the *Enterprise*. Irish agreed and gave Meeks a three-month leave of absence to design a plan for implementing circles at the newspaper. In January of 1986, Beaumont launched its first circles in the production department, where papers were printed and prepared for distribution. Production department circle members, who called themselves the Ink Spots, soon found a way to improve color registration and the quality of printing for color photographs and advertising while simultaneously reducing newsprint waste. The savings to the paper were estimated to bc $47,000 over five years. Eventually, Beaumont established employee quality circles in advertising, circulation, the mail room, and even in the editorial department, where writers and editors worked. The following are some of the projects undertaken by Beaumont's employee problem-solving circles as reported by the American Productivity and Quality Center in 1989:

1. Mail room workers worked with representatives of the accounting department to find a way to improve the legibility and timeliness of forms they received from accounting informing them of subscriber address changes and addresses of new subscribers. As a result, the paper was able to reduce the number of papers returned on outdated subscriptions and new subscribers got their papers earlier.

2. Classified advertising salespeople recommended to the

paper and got approval to hire a part-time "runner" to deliver sample ads to advertisers for their approval. As a result, the salespeople were freed to spend more time developing new accounts.

3. An editorial circle developed a method for improving the taking and delivery of telephone messages to reporters while they were on assignment, thus ensuring that reporters didn't miss important calls during their absence.

4. Following recommendations from an employee circle, the paper purchased an answering machine to speed the taking of calls on wedding and engagement announcements and set up a special sports hotline to provide callers with up-to-date information on scores.

5. Writers, photographers, and mid-level editors developed guidelines for selecting stories to appear in the paper and for ensuring that late-breaking stories were included even if a page had to be remade at the last minute.

As a result of its experience with quality circles at the Beaumont paper, the Hearst Corporation installed circles in a number of other locations, often with the assistance of Meeks, who became the human resources development manager for the Beaumont paper. Commenting on the experience with quality circles, Irish, who became a group publisher overseeing several Hearst papers, said, "It's an exciting process. . . . The time I spent in quality circle work . . . I really found to be invigorating. There was a lot of productive people coming up with ideas that management, just sitting around in a board room, would never have come up with."[16]

1987—Aid Association for Lutherans (AAL): Appleton, Wisconsin

At noon on August 14, 1987, five hundred managers, clerks, and technicians of the headquarters offices of the Aid Association for Lutherans (AAL) insurance company in Appleton, Wisconsin, picked up their chairs and personal belongings, said good-bye to their former colleagues, and reorganized themselves into self-managed work teams. As a result, in less than two years, AAL headquarter's employees increased their productivity 20 percent and cut the time it took to process cases by 75 percent.

Founded in the early 1990s, AAL is a nonprofit fraternal organization associated with the Lutheran church. Part of AAL provides charitable services, the other part sells insurance to members of Lutheran congregations and their families. In 1988, AAL's insurance arm ranked among the top 2 percent of U.S. life insurance companies in asset holdings. Long a small insurance provider, AAL saw explosive growth between 1982 and 1986, resulting in a 40 percent increase in its work force. To cope with its growth, AAL brought in Richard L. Gunderson, an experienced insurance and financial manager, to replace its retiring president and chief executive officer. Gunderson immediately launched studies that convinced him that AAL had to significantly reduce its operating costs if it hoped to be competitive. Consequently, Gunderson ordered a number of staff reductions and transferred practically all of AAL's top managers to other jobs, replacing them with new managers who would be less resistant to change. One of Gunderson's management changes was to bring in Jerome Laubenstein as the new vice president for the insurance department. Laubenstein, along with five new regional managers and two hundred employee volunteers, spent several months studying ways to reorganize the department and "do more with less." The conclusion the study team reached was that the department should be reorganized into self-managed teams of twenty to thirty employees each and that each team should have the responsibility, accountability, and skills necessary to service all the needs of policyholders for a group of sales agents or district representatives. In effect, the teams would provide "one-stop shopping" or "one-team processing" for agents. Instead of dealing with "faceless bureaucrats" and having policy applications or change requests flow through as many as three different sections, agents would deal with one team of headquarters employees who could provide all necessary services and who would get to know them on a first name basis.

As we noted earlier, AAL's movement to self-managed teams resulted in a 20 percent increase in employee productivity and a 70 percent reduction in processing time in less than two years. But that wasn't all. Self-management allowed AAL to cut management significantly and eliminate three layers of supervision, resulting in a 10 percent reduction in payroll costs at a time when the teams were handling 10 percent more work. Managers and supervisors weren't fired. They were reassigned to new jobs elsewhere in AAL.

AAL's movement to self-managed teams met with a mixed response from employees. On one hand, they liked the fact that they didn't have a supervisor watching over them every minute of the day, that they could learn more jobs and get paid extra for their increased skills (under a pay-for-knowledge system); and that they could have more control over their work environment. Yet most felt increased stress, many resented being separated from their former co-workers and friends so abruptly and some disliked being forced to assume responsibility for traditional managerial functions such as hiring and firing. As one AAL employee noted: "I wasn't hired to be a manager."[17]

What We Learned from Those Interesting Experiments

As we noted at the beginning of this chapter, our examples of workplace experiments conducted by American companies are incomplete. There were many more examples we could have cited. Yet we feel Tarrytown, Digital Equipment Enfield, TRW Ramsey, GM's NUMMI Plant, and the others are representative of the variety of experiments we were seeing throughout the 1970s and 1980s. Each of the experiments described in this chapter was unique. Some began because a farsighted or courageous individual decided to go against the sometimes long-standing tradition of his or her company and do something different. Thus, we had a plant manager at a General Motors plant in Tarrytown deciding to find a new way of working with his union; we had Ed Murdock at AT&T deciding that self-managed teams could work with operators even though the tradition of AT&T said otherwise; we had John Ludwig at Polysar Gulf Coast who was willing to change management practices at a plant that was already successful and risk tampering with something that seemed to be working because he thought there was a better way. In other cases, it wasn't a single or small group of individuals at an isolated location but a company's top management that decided to try something new. Thus, we had TRW experimenting at Ramsey, Lawrence, Kansas, and a host of other locations. We had GM joining with Toyota for an experiment at its NUMMI plant in Fremont, California; Delco Remy conducting much the same kind of experiment at Fitzgerald, Georgia; and Digital Equipment setting up a similar "self-managed" plant at Enfield. Regardless of how these experiments got started, most led to the same conclusion—"employee involvement" or "team systems" worked. When we changed the way we managed people—when we stopped trying to manage people—productivity improved, quality improved, service to customers improved, employee morale improved and grievances, absenteeism, and turnover were all reduced.

By the end of the 1980s in general, American business had decided to stop experimenting and to put what it had learned from two decades of experimentation to use. *Business Week* summed up what we had learned in this way in its July 1989 cover story on employee involvement:

> This growing body of evidence suggests strongly that the old system of assumptions, beliefs, and practices relating to work has been disproved as a pattern for modern factory and office jobs. . . . [T]he old paradigm involved the division of production work into simple, repetitive tasks performed by unskilled workers under close supervisory control.
>
> In the new paradigm, workers will be multi-skilled and to some degree will manage themselves through teamwork. Management will train workers, share business information with them, and develop specialized "gainsharing"—or bonus—plans to allow workers to cash in on the gains of increased productivity. Jobs will be protected by long-term security plans.
>
> American companies are now discovering what the Japanese learned long ago: that people—not technology alone or marketing ploys—are the key to success in global competition.[17]

So they were. By the end of the 1980s, the list of American companies with strong employee-involvement efforts underway was growing longer and longer. It included:

AT&T	Honeywell
Chaparral Steel	IBM
Cummins Engine	Johnsonville Foods
Dana	Lincoln National Insurance
Delta Airlines	Stew Leonard's Dairy
Disney	3M
Domino's Pizza	McDonald's
Donnelly Mirrors	Motorola
Federal Express	Nordstrom
Fel-Pro	Nucor
Florida Power & Light	Procter & Gamble
Ford	Sara Lee
W. L. Gore & Associates	Texas Instruments
Harley-Davidson	Xerox
Herman Miller	Wal-Mart
Hewlett-Packard	

Thousands of smaller companies

In the 1970s and 80s, few Americans had the opportunity to work in an environment such as that at NUMMI, Aid Association of Lutherans, or TRW Lawrence, Kansas. In the 1990s, more Americans will have that experience. In *Workplace 2000*, most Americans will.

CHAPTER 8

Employees Take Charge

Experiments in the American workplace conducted throughout the 1970s and 1980s led us to one conclusion—quality, innovation, service to customers, and competitive performance in general were significantly enhanced when the workplace was redesigned and employees took charge. Additionally, employee involvement led to improved trust between management and labor, better organizational procedures and processes, improved decision making, and less resistance from workers to the introduction of new technology.[1]

The effectiveness of employee-involvement approaches can largely be attributed to the alignment that resulted between employee needs and workplace design when employee involvement and team systems were implemented. Writing in 1984, Lyman Ketchum, a consultant specializing in workplace redesign and formerly operations manager for General Foods' Gaines Pet Food business, noted what he saw as the emergence of a "new paradigm" for the redesign of the American workplace that would satisfy the psychological needs American workers sought from the work itself. Ketchum argued that the new American worker sought to fulfill the following needs in the workplace:

1. To join with others in a common task
2. To have the latitude to make decisions about how work was performed
3. To receive recognition for his or her contributions to work performance from his or her peers, supervisors, and support personnel
4. To learn and continue to learn
5. To make reasonable use of his or her intellect
6. To receive information about how he or she is doing and what was going on in and beyond the immediate work area
7. To feel that his or her contribution was important and part of a logical whole

The problem with traditional workplace design, said Ketchum, was that it created what was, in effect, a "psychological slum." Employees needed to join with their peers in completing a common, whole task. Yet in the traditional workplace, work was designed so that employees were limited to the performance of a discrete, narrowly defined task and were discouraged and, in some cases even forbidden, to seek knowledge about the whole task, product, or service they were producing. Thus, two workers engaged in mutually dependent activities and located physically close to each other might never discuss the work process, their interdependency, or the need for mutual cooperation to make their lives easier and work performance better.

Employees needed, said Ketchum, some degree of autonomy and the ability to make their own decisions. Yet in the traditional workplace, information was tightly controlled and compartmentalized. Employees and quite frequently even first-line supervisors lacked access to information upon which they could make decisions. Consequently, not only strategic but also day-to-day operating decision making was pushed up the organization to overburdened middle- and upper-level managers who bemoaned the incompetency and lack of initiative of their subordinates. Employees sought recognition for their accomplishment and contribution. Yet in the traditional workplace, job content was simple and there was little for which an employee could be recognized. Instead of recognition, supervisors focused on controlling workers—looking for and documenting rule infractions.

Finally, said Ketchum, employees need to learn and go on learning and to make reasonable use of their intellect. Such intellectual growth was impossible in the traditional workplace and even in the traditional American culture. In the American tradition, formal learning was preparatory to work and not a part of the work experience except as narrowly defined training experiences. Learning, education, and intellectual growth in most cases were restricted to the period from childhood to young adulthood. At that point, learning ended and work began. The corporate objective in designing the workplace was to simplify jobs and by doing so to minimize training and its associated costs.

In contrast to the old paradigm, Ketchum foresaw back in 1984 the emergence of a new type of workplace almost completely opposite from what we had known before. In the new workplace, employees would not be assigned specific jobs, but rather would become members of teams. Teams would be given complete responsibility and accountability for producing a complete product, delivering a complete service, or at least completing some logical step in the production of a product or delivery of a service. Teams, to a much greater extent than traditional organizational units, would have a clearly defined "mission" to service the needs of an equally well-defined customer or group of customers, either external or internal to the organization. Within teams, team members would be expected to be flexible. Over time, each member of the team would be expected to learn and, when the occasion demanded, perform all of the jobs within the team and, most likely, would be paid extra for doing so. The need to learn a variety of jobs would mean that team members would be continuously learning new skills. In respect to day-to-day operations, teams would be largely autonomous. Team members would be provided with extensive information on team operations and would use that information to make most day-to-day operating decisions and to provide themselves with feedback on their performance. The atmosphere in the team, its structure, and its operation would be designed to stimulate team members to share ideas, cooperate, engage in group problem solving, and reinforce each other for individual contribution and team accomplishments. Ketchum's 1984 description of the new paradigm is almost an exact description of *Workplace 2000*. Hiring, training, expectations concerning acceptable and unacceptable workplace behavior, the role of managers and supervisors, the role of unions, and many other facets of employment will be fundamentally altered as we move to this new workplace. Here is what Americans should expect.

The Two Types of *Workplace 2000* Teams

In an earlier chapter, we summarized a variety of workplace experiments conducted throughout the 1970s and 1980s. Some of these experiments, such as those at Tarrytown, Polysar Gulf Coast, the New York Department of Sanitation, and the Beaumont *Enterprise* retained most elements of the traditional American organizational structure and culture while increasing the flow of information to employees and providing opportunities for voluntary employee involvement in decision making and problem solving. Some of the other experiments we discussed were much more radical. At Kemper Life Insurance, Delco-Remy Fitzgerald, TRW Lawrence, GM Livonia, Digital Equipment Enfield, AT&T HOBIS, NUMMI, and Aid Association of Lutherans, supervisors and managers were largely eliminated and employees truly took charge. At TRW Ramsey and Hanes Sparta, supervisors were retained, but their role was drastically altered and employees were given much expanded responsibilities for day-to-day operations. Kemper Life Insurance, Delco Remy, and the others were experiments with what are called self-managed teams. TRW Ramsey and Hanes Sparta were experiments with what are called work-unit teams. Work unit teams and self-managed teams will be the two most prominent forms of team systems in *Workplace 2000*. In addition, we are likely to see a number of hybrid forms of team systems that do not quite go to the extreme of self-managed teams in turning over operational and other responsibilities to employees, but go beyond work-unit teams in terms of employee assumption of traditional managerial/ supervisory responsibilities. Our experience in working with major U.S. companies to implement both work-unit teams and self-managed teams suggests to us that—with the exception of new start-up sites—U.S. companies will first adopt work-unit teams that gradually evolve to self-managed teams or something very close to self-management.

Work-unit teams and self-managed teams are alike in that they shift traditional managerial and supervisory responsibilities for controlling performance and solving performance problems to employees. They are also alike in that team membership and employee participation in problem solving and performance improvement efforts is nonvoluntary. Under work-unit teams and self-managed teams, all employees are expected and required to attend team meetings, work on performance improvement projects, and participate in other team activities by virtue of their employment. Where these two types of teams differ is in respect to the effect of the teams on organizational structure and the role, or even existence, of managers and supervisors.

Under work-unit teams, the basic and traditional organizational structure of a plant or division is retained. The organizational chart of a plant or division with work-unit teams looks very much like that of a traditional organization, with perhaps some flattening of the traditional pyramid into fewer levels. Additionally, there may be no radical restructuring of the work process flow, at least initially. There is a much sharper definition of the unit's responsibilities and objectives, however. Work-unit team members develop a small set of key performance measures for the team (perhaps five or ten) that are linked back to company objectives and participate with their manager or supervisor in establishing goals for performance on these measures. Also, team members meet on a regular basis with their manager or supervisor to review performance on these measures, identify performance problems or areas needing improvement, and develop action plans or "projects" to solve performance problems they identify. Team members may also participate in problem-solving task forces very nature, teams—especially self-managed teams—change such expectations. Superstar performance might not be expected of every team member in every area of team functioning, but at a minimum, all team members would be expected to be very good in a wide range of former specialties and perhaps excellent in at least some.

A final change in expectations that represented an obstacle to rapid movement to self-management was the shift that occurs in team systems from individual to group contribution. Marc Bassin, director of management and organizational development for General Foods Worldwide Coffee and International, describes the problem this way:

> Business team peak performance is a group phenomenon; however, most business organizations are structured around individual performance and competition. Reward systems, promotions and a sense of identity are individually geared and generated. The individual and his or her contribution is the fundamental unit in work cultures, not the group.
>
> This is a different basic assumption than what is required for a peak performing team. In such a team, the group vision must be stronger than individual agendas. The opportunities for group members to help one another must be unencumbered by competition among them.
>
> If personal competition interferes with group cooperation, the possibilities for peak performance diminish. As in a sports team, if one member values his or her personal performance (above the team's), team cohesion is lessened and team performance suffers.[3]

It isn't only employee resistance that prevents most companies from moving rapidly to self-management. Perhaps the biggest obstacle American companies have faced has been dealing with resistance from managers and supervisors. In traditional organizations where managers and supervisors have been required to switch to team systems, a natural resistance has emerged simply because of the well-founded fear that team systems will lead to a reduction of managerial and supervisory jobs. But it wasn't only a fear of loss of jobs that caused many managers and supervisors to resist teams. Even managers and

established to work on particularly difficult problems or those that cross team boundaries. Under work-unit teams, managers and supervisors may be reduced in number, but the position of manager or supervisor is not eliminated. Managers and supervisors continue to perform traditional functions such as planning, budgeting, hiring, disciplining, and firing, although they may be required to seek greater employee input into these decisions. The greatest change in the managerial/supervisory role that occurs under work-unit teams is in respect to performance decision making and problem solving. In traditional organizations, managers and supervisors make decisions and solve problems with little, if any, input from employees. Traditionally, managers and supervisors are held responsible for the work group's performance. In work-unit teams, the team itself is responsible for the work group's performance. The manager or supervisor's role is to provide the team with information and resources, facilitate team meetings, and coach employees in problem-solving efforts.

Self-managed teams operate in a similar fashion to work-unit teams, but with employees assuming greatly expanded responsibilities. Additionally, the traditional organizational structure is drastically altered. The traditional organizational chart with divisions, departments, and sections drawn along functional lines may cease to exist. In its place are teams of five to twenty or as many as thirty employees. Each team has the responsibility, equipment, and other resources necessary to produce an entire product, deliver a service, or produce/deliver a major part of a product or service. Self-managed teams are structured to operate almost as small, independent business units. Where the work-unit team has a clearly defined set of performance objectives, the self-managed team has a "mission" to serve a customer or group of customers either internally (such as another self-managed team) or externally (consumers). Perhaps the most striking difference between self-managed teams and work-unit teams is the absence of managers and supervisors in the self-managed unit. Instead of having a manager or supervisor, employees in self-managed teams elect a team leader who facilitates team meetings and performs administrative functions for the team. Frequently, team leadership responsibilities rotate among team members so that eventually most, if not all, team members serve a term as team leader. In the absence of a formal manager or supervisor, the team members themselves assume responsibility for most traditional managerial and supervisory responsibilities. These extend not only to monitoring performance and solving performance problems, but also to areas such as planning, scheduling, budgeting, hiring, and discipline of team members. The few remaining formal managers in an organization composed of self-managed teams coordinate activities of the various teams, ensure that teams have the resources they require, advise the teams on technical issues, and help resolve disputes that might occur within or between teams.

The Obstacles to Self-Management

Obviously, self-managed teams represent a radical departure from traditional American management. In fact, the movement to self-managed teams is so radical that a number of obstacles occur that most companies find difficult to overcome in the short term. It is because of these obstacles—and American business's normal aversion to sudden radical change—that we feel American companies will adopt work-unit teams or something between work-unit teams and self-managed teams as the first step. Self-managed teams may ultimately evolve from these early team structures, but the process will likely take at least ten years. The one exception to this evolutionary process will be in new plants or divisions—the so-called greenfield sites. When a new plant is built or a new office is opened, many of the "obstacles" to self-management we list next don't exist (for example, there are no managers/ supervisors to be displaced or taught new skills) or can be avoided (for example, newly hired employees can be carefully screened to ensure that skills and motivation fit with the new culture).

The obstacles faced by companies experimenting with self-managed teams are well documented. We alluded to some of these in Chapter 7. One of the best summaries of these obstacles can be found in a study prepared by Janice Klein of the Harvard Business School in 1988 for the U.S. Department of

Labor.[2] In respect to employee reaction to self-management Klein notes: "Although they may have an excellent grasp of their day-to-day tasks, teams often face technical difficulties outside their sphere of knowledge. In addition, many teams have found it unpleasant, if not impossible, to discipline their peers; disciplinary action and documentation of poor performance are tasks that most team members prefer to leave to management." And it isn't only the technically difficult or merely unpleasant tasks that employees resist. Some employees don't want any part of self-management. They want a traditional supervisor—or at least someone—to tell them what to do and when to do it. Klein tells the following story from one Alcoa plant that had self-managed teams: "In the roll shop . . . , where a semi-autonomous work group has operated for more than 3 years, most employees are comfortable working without direct supervision. One employee, however, refuses to be self-managed, because he feels that the workload isn't shared equitably. He insists that his buddy on the same shift determine work priorities and assign them to him."

In a large measure, many American workers have resisted a rapid shift to self-management simply because such team systems are so radically different from what most Americans have known before. By their very nature, self-managed teams push responsibility down in an organization and greatly increase expectations for performance. As team members become more interdependent, a few superstars aren't enough for team success. All team members must exhibit or at least aspire to personal excellence. Most Americans have never experienced such expectations. Most have never expected peak performance from themselves or from most of their friends or coworkers. "Okay," "acceptable," "average," the "Gentleman's C," or, at best, the "Gentleman's B" was the rule. We might begrudgingly admire, idolize, or be jealous of the "superstar," but didn't expect superstar status from ourselves or most others that we knew. Plus, superstar performance—even for those few who could aspire to it—was very much, we thought, individual and confined to a relatively narrow specialty. A few might become "experts" in a single or few functional specialties, but we assumed one could not be excellent or, for that matter, even very good in a wide range of jobs. By the

supervisors whose jobs would not be threatened by the establishment of team systems because, for example, they were guaranteed movement into technical support or team coordination roles, resisted teams anyway. Many of these simply did not believe that employees, or at least the typical employee, could be self-managing and self-controlling in spite of the considerable experimental evidence to the contrary. All of the training and personal experience of these managers and supervisors convinced them that employees in general avoided work and responsibility. Janice Klein quotes these managers and supervisors: "Employees are children, not adults. Employees will just take advantage of the program to get out of work."

To help managers and supervisors overcome their predisposition to reject employee self-management, most companies moving to team systems in the 1980s devoted considerable effort to educating their managers and supervisors to the value of teams and training them in group dynamics and leadership skills. Yet many managers and supervisors found it difficult to put their new skills training into practice. In her 1988 study, Klein described some of the typical problems managers and supervisors faced in translating classwork into day-to-day realities in this way:

In one facility, "supervisory depression" persisted for over 3 years. . . . Supervisors started saying, "That's not my job, it's the team's problem." In essence, they became deserters, and many used teams as an excuse not to be concerned with any problems. . . . Supervisors took a back seat and would let the teams try to handle the problems as they arose. When the problems got to the point where the teams couldn't handle them, supervisors would come in with a heavy hand. The situation got to the point where the supervisors hoped the teams would fail in solving problems so that a need for supervisors would be shown. . . . In another factory, . . . supervisors (initially called "team advisors") felt powerless. Team members would often ignore supervisors' directions, believing that it was only "advice" and that they were not under any obligation to follow it. After 10 years, the management team relabeled the role "team manager" to emphasize the control the supervisors must, at times, continue to exercise. Although many supervisors thought it merely semantics, a good number found the name change (team manager) important, because it helped them to understand their role better.

A related problem for managers and supervisors in making the transition to employee self-managed teams was the difficulty in switching from management "by the book" to "management by principle." Klein described the dilemma managers and supervisors faced this way: "Many of the new work systems are built on the premise that each situation must be evaluated on its merits and that actions are taken based on doing 'what's right' for the business and the people involved; in contrast, in traditional organizations many managers and supervisors tend to reach instinctively according to a set of written or, often, unwritten rules and past practices." Not only did managers and supervisors have to "manage by principle," constantly seeking to "do the right thing" for the company and employees, but these decisions on how to resolve inter- or intra-team disputes had to be made in the open for all team members to see. "Diplomacy" and "deal making," the "bending and adjustment" of the rules to accommodate "unique" situations could no longer be conducted in secrecy.

Making the Transition to Self-Management

The obstacles to making the transition to employee self-management are numerous and take time to overcome. It is for this reason that we feel most American companies will evolve to self-management rather than make a sudden, radical change, particularly in non-greenfield sites where there is a history of traditional management and employee expectations to overcome. This evolutionary process will be different for each company. Some will move faster and some slower. Most American companies will make the transition, however, and they are likely to do so over the next decade. As we said, the exact evolutionary process will differ from company to company, but it will center around a change in managerial and supervisory roles. Carl Bramlette, a professor of management at Georgia State University in Atlanta, has outlined a process of change centered around the revisions to the role of the first-line supervisor that is typical of what is likely to occur.[4]

Bramlette starts his scenario with the traditional one-on-one supervisor who was still found in most American businesses at the end of the 1980s. This supervisor is primarily responsible for the performance of his or her work group and spends his or her time closely monitoring the work performed by his or her employees on a day-to-day basis. If the work process is highly technical, the supervisor most likely must be technically proficient and spends much of his or her time troubleshooting technical problems or making technical modifications and adjustments. In nontechnical areas, supervisors may be fast-track management trainees who are being groomed for higher-level roles and serving temporary stints as supervisors in order to get firsthand knowledge of operations. Whether the supervisor is just passing through or preoccupied with technical troubleshooting, employees begin to act somewhat independent of direct day-to-day supervision and begin to form informal subgroups with their own goals, norms, and informal leaders. Workers start these subgroups for both social and work-related reasons. In traditional American organizations, it was not unusual for managers and supervisors either to ignore the emergence of such subgroups or to actively discourage this natural process for fear that such groups would constitute cliques whose informal leaders would represent a challenge to formal authority. In the new, transitional American workplace, the natural tendency of workers to form into groups won't be resisted or ignored. Instead, supervisors will be trained to recognize the inevitability of such groups and the desirability of mobilizing group dynamics for the good of the organization. Supervisors will be trained in group dynamics and group leadership will be encouraged, even required, to exercise a group leadership role. At this point, we will begin to see the emergence of what we have called work-unit teams, where supervisors lead and encourage the formation of teams.

The supervisor as a group (or team) leader behaves quite differently from the traditional supervisor. Bramlette explains the group leader role this way: "The leader is responsible for the activities and production of a group who share norms and goals. The group leader is the focal point for group dynamics, which he or she initiates and manages. While maintaining contact with each individual and promoting and facilitating high levels of interaction among group members, the group leader may also share control and problem-solving duties with group members. But he or she stays in the center of the circle and continues to exert influence on group activities and performance."

Gradually, team leaders in work-unit teams change to more of a coordination rather than leadership role as the team develops. Bramlette describes the "coordinator" role of the supervisor: "As a team coordinator, the supervisor shares a great many group leadership functions with other team members. Various team members may take on specific leadership roles— initiating, seeking information—or consensus-testing for example. The team coordinator manages the group primarily through coordination of their skills and activities, and uses their resources as fully as possible. In addition to responsibility for the activities and production of the team, he or she also maintains contact with other groups and becomes involved in activities and projects outside the immediate group."

As the supervisor changes from day-to-day leadership, he or she becomes what Bramlette calls a "team boundary manager," removed from the group and no longer having direct control or perhaps even knowledge of day-to-day group activities. The group becomes responsible for day-to-day decisions, which, as a result of experience during previous stages, it has demonstrated it can handle. As team boundary manager, the supervisor acts more as a chief executive officer for the group or perhaps a number of groups. He or she collects data and gives the group feedback on its performance based upon such measures as production, quality, cost, or customer satisfaction. The supervisor, at this stage, focuses on managing environmental demands on and acquiring resources for the group or groups reporting to him or her by mediating with other groups and clients/customers. As a boundary manager, the supervisor is expected to have strong interpersonal skills, as well as strong technical skills or the ability to acquire technical assistance for the team when needed. At this point, the supervisor intervenes in the group only when the group is experiencing a technical or interpersonal problem. Over time, as the team becomes truly self-managing and can resolve most technical and interpersonal problems on its own, the supervisor changes to the final stage—that of "team resource person."

Bramlette describes the final resource person stage:

The team resource person is available to a work group for consultation or help that the group identifies itself as needing. The resource person can either furnish the help (technical or social) or obtain it from outside.

As a functioning organizational unit, the team has accountability for its own work. In essence, the first-line supervisory role no longer exists. Various leadership patterns may emerge within the work team but they are the responsibility of the team and are not dependent on external power . . .

The team resource person may be available to help several work teams, and, in mature organizations that deal with technology of only moderate complexity, the resource person may be phased out as team members acquire total technical competence.

Bramlette's scenario focuses on the supervisor's transition from traditional supervision to becoming only a resource to the team. Simultaneous with this transition in the supervisor's role, the role of employees as team members is changing also. In the beginning, employees have a day-to-day supervisor who closely monitors, controls, and oversees day-to-day operations. Employees essentially just do what they are told and, when they encounter problems, technical or otherwise, bring them to the supervisor for resolution. At this stage, employees have little if any responsibility or accountability for the work product of the group. If the group succeeds or fails, the supervisor is held responsible.

As the supervisor becomes a group leader, however, the role of employees changes also. No longer does the supervisor make all the decisions and solve all the problems. He or she is still present day to day, but employees are expected to share some of the responsibility for the unit's success or failure. Duties formerly performed by the supervisor are delegated first to some and then to all employees in the group. Group members are asked, even required, to solve their own problems. The supervisor is there to coach employees in problem-solving techniques, but no longer can employees expect to go to the supervisor each and every time and get a resolution to problems.

As the supervisor moves into a coordination role, employees assume even more responsibility for problem resolution and daily operations. Employees are also now asked to take on leadership roles in the work group—to seek out information the group requires, to make decisions without the supervisor's input, and to initiate action to change policies, procedures, methods of performing day-to-day activities. By this stage, the supervisor isn't necessarily available on a day-to-day basis for consultation. He or she still maintains relatively frequent contact with the group and is held responsible for the group's overall performance but no longer is directly involved in group activities.

During the next stage, as the supervisor moves into the role of boundary manager, employees are largely self-managed on a day-to-day basis. The supervisor may no longer have direct knowledge of day-to-day problems or decisions the group makes about how to respond to problems. The group itself must get together and reach such decisions by consensus. In addition, the group is now held fully responsible for performance on key measures. The supervisor helps the team manage relations with other teams and with customers and suppliers—he assists the team in acquiring resources—but the team collectively must decide what resources are needed and how these resources will be distributed and used within the team. Days elapse during which the supervisor/manager has only fleeting, if any, interaction with the group.

Finally, as the supervisor becomes a true resource manager, the team becomes truly self-managed. The team members collectively are accountable for the work product and internal operation of their group. Also, to a large extent, administrative, financial, and personnel matters are handled primarily by employees who schedule their own work, assign team roles and responsibilities, and resolve their own technical and other problems with little outside intervention.

What It Is Like to Work in a Team

As the workplace makes the transition to team systems over the next decade, American workers will encounter significant changes in the work environment. Hiring, training, orientation, and other practices will be greatly altered. So will the day-to-day work experience. Many, if not most, of the rules enterprising Americans have followed for success will fundamentally change. The skills and abilities Americans need to be successful in a team-oriented workplace are quite different from those required for success in the traditional American business. Here are some of the more significant differences.

Getting Hired

In *Workplace 2000*, peers will hire peers. Managers, supervisors, and the company personnel department will have much less control over hiring decisions. In the traditional organization, managers or supervisors decided if and when a vacancy existed, established skills they would be looking for among job applicants, and turned over responsibility for initial recruitment and screening to a personnel department. While the ultimate decision concerning who was to be hired rested with one or a few managers or supervisors, most Americans recognized that they first had to survive screening by a company's personnel department before they could get to those with authority to make a final hiring decision. Most job-hunting manuals popular in the 1970s focused on how to avoid getting screened out by a low-level personnel clerk somewhere so that one's application could be considered by the only person (or few persons) that really mattered—those managing the area in which the job vacancy was located.

The good news for Americans in respect to future hiring practices is that personnel departments and employment agencies will have much less control over who gets hired. While personnel departments and other third parties involved in the hiring process will be able to screen out some applications, their discretion will be greatly restricted. More applications will consequently get through to the ultimate decision makers.

The bad news for future job applicants is that there will be more decision makers. Managers and supervisors will no longer make hiring decisions or, at a minimum, will share such decision-making responsibilities. Employee team members will be intimately involved in hiring in the future. Team members will establish job requirements, design application forms, screen applications, conduct interviews and background checks, and make hiring decisions based upon consensus. In the past, identifying and impressing one manager or supervisor was sufficient to be hired. In the future, job applicants will have to be concerned about impressing an entire group of people who, if they are hired, will become their peers. And to impress this hiring team, which may include all team members if the team is small or six to ten representatives if the team is large, job applicants will have to demonstrate not only technical but also social skills. Writing in 1987, James Kochanski, a personnel manager for the Quaker Oats Division of Gaines Pet Foods, Inc., described the interviewing and hiring process that will be typical of *Workplace 2000*.

The face-to-face meeting of applicants and team members takes several forms: one-on-one interviews, group interviews, and assessment centers. The purpose of these interviews is twofold: to evaluate the candidates and to communicate to the candidates the unique nature of their position as a member of a self-regulating work team.

Peer interviewing is a unique experience for most job applicants. So to help the applicants decide if being a member of a self-regulating team is right for them and prepare them for the interviews, information about the job and the organization is provided through written information, slide or video presentations, and question-and-answer periods, usually prior to the interviews.

Interviews between team members and job candidates are

sometimes one-on-one and sometimes include two or more team members for a single candidate . . .

Interview questions focus on the social and technical skills required for the job. Some teams use the behavioral consistency interviewing approach, looking for examples of applicants' past behavior which indicate that they have demonstrated the required skills. For example, if the technical skills required by the team include knowledge of basic mathematics, ability to carry large objects, and the use of hand tools, then interview questions are built to examine each of these areas.

Social or team membership skills that are looked for in the interview may include problem solving, idea generation and implementation, and giving and receiving feedback. Other factors evaluated by interviewers are the applicant's ability to work with little supervision and to develop multiple skills rather than specialize in one area . . .

A type of interviewing used in some team-based organizations is the assessment center . . .

In assessment centers, a group of five or six applicants is given a task, such as selecting one member of the group to go to a seminar, or is given a problem to solve, such as the cause of a production difficulty. Applicants are rated on criteria such as participation, leadership, and listening and verbal skills as they work through the task or problem.[5]

Once interviews and assessments are completed, the team members themselves work through a process of narrowing down the job candidates to a final selection. Team members vote on candidates and develop rankings—high to low. The ultimate decision concerning who to hire is made by consensus. Since team members themselves make the decision about whom to hire, obviously the potential exists for abuse of the hiring process. Team members might engage in discriminatory practices or hire only friends or relatives. To avoid these problems, most companies adopting team systems with hiring authority train team members in the legal ramifications of hiring decisions and place some restrictions on the ability of teams to hire relatives, and perhaps even friends, of current team members.

By its nature, the team hiring process is more lengthy and arduous for applicants. There are more decision makers to satisfy and the questioning and testing are frequently more rigorously extended not only into technical areas but also into the areas of social and interpersonal skills. Most applicants also find it much harder to exaggerate their qualifications when the persons interviewing them perform the work on a day-to-day basis and are intimately familiar with all of its technical details and subtleties. Yet experience with team hiring has generally been very successful. On the whole, team members pick better candidates and the process of training a new employee into the workplace is smoothed. Kochanski notes in his article on team hiring: "Where the team process excels is in ensuring the candidates' success through the entire work group entry process. Teams prepare themselves for the acceptance of new members by team involvement in or control of the process that determines both the need for new employees and the desired qualifications. . . . Issues such as job assignments and reduced overtime are worked out ahead of time. Then, the selection system itself prepares the candidate for successful entry into the work group. With peers . . . predicting the success of the candidate by making the selection, they make a commitment to helping the new employee succeed. Also, candidates know that they were selected by the people who will be working most closely with them, which eases the transition."

Being Trained

In the traditional American company, once a worker was hired into a clearly defined position with a unique title and lengthy written position description, he or she was then trained in a job specialty. The new employee might receive some initial orientation to the company and then be sent to attend formal training that might last days or even weeks. Alternatively, after a brief orientation by the personnel department, the new employee would be sent to the job site and placed with a more experienced worker to learn on the job. Whether the initial training was conducted in the classroom or on the job, the typical employee would receive little additional training throughout his or her career. He or she occasionally might attend a short course or two that would be more or less job related as a type of "reward" for good performance, or he or she might receive some instruction in the operation of a new technology from a vendor representative. On the whole, however, employees could expect the "learning" phase of their employment with a company to occur early on in their career, but there would be little requirement or opportunity for the average employee to engage in anything approaching "continuous learning." If an employee was promoted into a supervisory role, he or she might expect to be required to attend a few days of basic supervisory training within the first few months in the new position. However, the training in supervision would likely be limited to learning administrative and personnel rules such as "the proper steps to follow in firing an employee." There would be little in the way of training on topics such as "leadership," "motivation," or "problem solving."

Workplace 2000 training will differ drastically from what most Americans have experienced in the past in frequency, form, and content. The first and most obvious difference most Americans will notice will be the sheer volume of training and the continuous nature of learning in the new workplace. In *Workplace 2000*, training will not be a one-time or occasional event. It will be ongoing. American workers can expect to spend at least several days or even weeks each year learning new skills or enhancing existing skills. Continuous learning will not only be a minimum requirement for job retention, but one of the few ways employees will have to increase their base compensation because of the prevalence of pay-for-knowledge compensation systems that tie base pay increases to the acquisition of job skills.

A second thing Americans will notice about training in the new workplace will be the content of the training itself. A significant portion of the training experiences of American workers will be nontechnical and will focus on interpersonal, team, and problem-solving skills. What might this nontechnical training be like? In 1988, William Hampton, a reporter for *Business Week*, spent some time observing training of employees at Mazda Motor Manufacturing (USA) Corporation's assembly plant in Flat Rock, Michigan. Here is how Hampton described the courses he audited. His description is typical of the training most Americans will experience.

I stop at one Mazda training room where 20 newly hired employees are learning about interpersonal relations. One worker describes difficulty getting her 10-year-old daughter to clean her room. "I'm open to suggestions," she sighs. A lively debate breaks out about rewards and punishments . . .

Down the hall, another group learns about encouraging new ideas, no matter how ridiculous they seem. Workers get six minutes to come up with 25 ideas for improving a bathtub. They suggest such things as sunlamps and a soft-drink dispenser. Then they're asked to think of 30 more ideas—in two minutes. "We're trying to loosen people up and unblock them," explains Kenneth J. Kumiega, director of training and development . . .

Elsewhere at Mazda, employees learn to chart quality by building paper airplanes and checking their flight performance. They also pick up pointers on the plant's quality system. "If a part doesn't meet specifications, you reject it," instructor Alan E. Blosser tells them. "That's your job . . ."

I audit one session where workers view before-and-after video tapes that show how jobs can be rearranged to balance time and effort. In one, a worker who once stood idle while another rushed to complete his job now shares the work. "Is he working harder?" asks the instructor. Heads shake, and one man murmurs: "Smoother."

Later on, I watch a . . . team that assembled 25 flashlights in just over three minutes. Now it's trying to do the same work with three workers instead of four. Using techniques learned in class, the team calculates that its new system is 90% "balanced" in terms of time per task.[6]

Hampton's description of training experiences of Mazda workers is typical of what we will see in most American companies in *Workplace 2000*. The average American worker, in addition to receiving more and better technical training, will receive extensive training in interpersonal relations, group problem solving, quality improvement, work methods improvement, and numerous other non-technical but critical team and self-management skills. A decade before only managers, supervisors, and selected support personnel received such training, if such training was offered at all.

The Work Environment in Teams

Having completed initial training and orientation, a new employee in *Workplace 2000* will arrive at his or her team's work site, which will be different from the traditional American workplace. The first thing that will likely strike our new employee is that his or her team is physically and psychologically separated from the rest of the organization. There will be clear physical and task boundaries and measurement of the team's input and output. Both physically and emotionally the team will be like a small business unto itself; teams will be analogous to small shops or boutiques in a shopping mall—each shop is part of a larger whole, but separate and distinct.

Observing the team in operation, our new employee will notice that there appear to be no clear job distinctions. Team members move from job to job as the need arises. No one is ever standing idle waiting for something to do. Also, team members are constantly helping each other perform tasks. If someone gets behind, someone else comes over to help out. Everyone seems to know how to perform every job and is willing to do so. There is also subtle, and on occasion not so subtle, peer pressure for everyone to perform to his or her potential. For example, a team member is late returning from a break. Other team members notice and send a worker to remind the tardy employee that the break is over and "the team needs help." Team members take this action themselves. No supervisor or manager is consulted.

Shortly after joining his or her team, our new employee will experience the first of many team meetings. Regular team meetings, he or she will learn, are the centerpiece of team coordination, planning, scheduling, performance monitoring, and problem-solving efforts. Led by the team supervisor (if a work-unit team) or by a team leader (if the team is self-managed), these meetings will be short (one to one and a half hours), but effective.

The agenda of the team meeting will vary from team to team. But regardless of specifics, *every* team meeting will cover a review of team performance on critical measures ("How are we doing?"); identification of performance problems ("In what areas do we need to improve?"); and problem solving ("What specifically should we do to improve?"). A typical meeting might proceed this way:

At 9:00 A.M., the meeting is brought to order by Vickie, the team leader. All team members are present and have been bantering and joking with each other. Prior to the call to order, the assembly has been rowdy and chaotic. Now everyone falls silent. It is time for business.

Vickie starts the meeting by briefly reviewing the agenda. Since the agenda is standard—every meeting covers the same basic items—everyone knows what to expect. Vickie is just reminding them of the sequence to be followed.

Quickly, Vickie moves on to the first order of business—a review of the minutes of the last meeting. Mary, who is taking her turn as "recorder," reads the minutes of the previous meeting she had recorded on a form team members designed as an easy way to keep track of meeting decisions. Mary pays special attention to any decisions and assignments that were made. When Mary finishes, Vickie asks if there are any additions or corrections. There are none.

Having completed the reading of the minutes, Vickie moves on to the next order of business—reports on team member assignments. Bill is asked to report on the results of a meeting he agreed to hold with members of another team concerning the quality and sequencing of incoming work from that team. Bill notes that the "just-in-time" system is significantly reducing the in-process buffer inventories (partially assembled parts coming from the other team) and that the previous team has agreed to take several steps to improve the quality of partially assembled parts they are providing if Bill's team can provide the previous team with some specific data on incoming quality they require. Vickie makes a note for the team to discuss the quality issue during a later section of the meeting. Once Bill finishes his report, several other team members are called upon to report on assignments they received at the last meeting.

Having reviewed all outstanding assignments, Vickie moves on to the feedback portion of the meeting. Angela, who maintains and updates charts the team keeps on key measures of performance, brings the team up-to-date. She pays particular attention to any emerging trends in the data on team quality, unit cost, customer satisfaction, and a variety of other measures as displayed on the large, colorful graphs she holds up for team members to see. Team members note several areas of improvement, which are greeted with a spontaneous round of applause, and a few disturbing trends, which Vickie lists on the agenda for further discussion.

Vickie thanks Angela for her presentation, then recognizes several team members individually for efforts they have made to help the team since the last meeting. She then opens the floor to any team members who would like to recognize someone. Ted says he has something. He wants to tell Bill how much he appreciates the help in troubleshooting the problem with the press, particularly Ted's willingness to work through his break and lunch hour to get the press back up and running. The team gives Ted a round of applause.

Since there are no more acknowledgements, Vickie moves on to problem solving. The first item of business is the quality issue Bill raised earlier in the meeting. The team brainstorms ways of providing the other team with the quality data they need. After discussing several alternatives, the team reaches consensus on a plan of action. Bill agrees to take the decision back to the other team to get their opinion and to report back at the next team meeting on their reaction. Mary records the action plan and Bill's assignment in the minutes of the meeting.

After discussing several other problems, including the disappointing trend in performance Angela noted in her feedback presentation, Vickie opens the meeting for questions and concerns from team members—any issues they would like him to raise with management. Several team members want to know if something can be done about the condition of the bathrooms—they are dirty and short on soap and hand towels. Vickie makes a note to raise the issue when she attends the management meeting. Other team members ask Vickie to find out if any decision has been made on the change in the company benefits package. At a previous meeting Vickie had passed along information about a significant increase in insurance premiums and that insurance benefits were under review. Vickie agrees to check on the status and report back at the next meeting. Mary records the bathroom and benefits issues in the minutes and assigns them as Vickie's responsibility.

Since there are no more questions or concerns from team members, Vickie makes a few announcements (the company picnic will be at 10:00 A.M. on Saturday; representatives of XYZ Company will be touring the plant on Friday). She then asks Mary to summarize decisions made in the meeting and review assignments given to team members. Vickie concludes the meeting by reminding team members of the date and time of the next meeting. The meeting ends at 10:38, a little over an hour and a half after it started.

Unions in the New Workplace

America's transition to team systems presents some troubling questions for the future of a long-standing workplace institution—the American labor union. Team systems are intentionally designed to promote partnership, cooperation, common interest between employees and management, and, in effect, turn over many traditional management and workplace rule-making functions to workers. In such a new environment, what possible role can a union play when the earlier foundation of the union movement and premise of American labor laws such as the National Labor Relations Act (NLRA) was that employers and employees are adversaries with inherently conflicting interests? This question concerning the future of the American labor movement was stated well at the 1989 State-of-the-Art Symposium on Labor-Management Cooperation sponsored by the Bureau of Labor-Management Relations and Cooperative Programs of the U.S. Department of Labor. The Bureau's "synthesis of the discussions" at this conference opens this way: "Labor must recognize that its traditional adversarial role is changing. . . . The need for traditional union activities, such as processing grievances, diminishes considerably in new work systems built on openness, trust, and shared responsibility. . . . [U]nless organized labor develops a new vision of itself, it risks becoming stuck in a defensive, reactive position. . . . The practical question, then, is: What is the role of labor unions in new work systems?"[7]

As the 1980s ended, there was no clear answer to this question. In fact, it was unclear whether labor had a role. More and more companies were making a strategic decision to operate without a union and were aggressively seeking to have their existing unions decertified or were relocating their plants to states without a history of support for unions. Where unions didn't exist, labor was finding it difficult, if not impossible, to win union representation particularly in plants with high employee involvement. For example, the UAW lost a major battle for representation at Nissan's assembly plant near Nashville in 1989 in what was billed as a "critical test for autoworkers." Finally, a substantial portion of the American public had switched its allegiance. Labor's approval rating among the working public had dropped from 75 percent in 1957 to about 55 percent by the late 1980s. Likewise, union membership had shown a slow, steady decline from over a third of the American work force in the 1950s to less than 17 percent in the late 1980s.[8]

There was very little doubt as the 1980s came to a close that labor unions as we had known them in the United States were in trouble. Yet some union leadership engaged in a kind of reality denial. They wanted no part of team systems. Unions, they argued, should stay aloof or actively oppose the creation of team systems. At a minimum, they said, team systems should be treated as something distinct from the labor contract. Management could go ahead with creating teams if it wanted to, but officially the union would have no part in the endeavor. Employee involvement and team systems could exist. But if they did, they would exist as a kind of parallel and unofficial system of labor relations. Officially, these labor leaders argued, the collective bargaining process worked just fine as the sole mechanism for ensuring employees due process and input into decisions.

Another group of labor leaders recognized the inevitability of teams. They felt it was dangerous for the union to remain uninvolved and allow parallel structures for employee involvement to be developed without union input. Bob Willis, president of the American Federation of Grain Millers, voiced the fear of many union leaders for such parallel systems when he said, "In situations where the company creates structures parallel to the union for shared decision making at all levels, the employees . . . eventually . . . wonder why they need a union at all. That's the one that scares me . . . because if someone asked me, 'Why do you need a union in that kind of relationship?,' I don't have the answer."[9] To make sure there was a role for the union, a number of union leaders were prepared to abandon the union's traditional adversarial role and cooperate with management to ease the transition to teams. Unions, they insisted, should become part of the solution for management and employees. Instead of standing idly by or opposing change, the union should become actively involved in making change happen. Once the transition to teams was accomplished, the union could then serve as the guardian of the spirit of the team system, ensuring that management lived up to its promises and did not use the new systems to exploit workers.

Some labor leaders argued that management and workers could design and install team systems without a union, but workers shouldn't assume that such a system would give them any real power, since without a union there was no guarantee management wouldn't suddenly renege on its promises if conditions changed and team systems no longer appeared so attractive to the company. Howard Samuel, president of the Industrial Union Department of the AFL-CIO, argued at the State-of-the-Art Symposium: "Workers can be treated with due process and equity and can be provided reciprocity (without a union). . . . The process could be one with some integrity, and management could assure a consensus before it moves ahead. But fundamentally the workers are not empowered, because all these things can be denied at any time. It's a benign dictatorship." Samuel goes on to add: "The best workers in a non-union situation could hope for is a 'sense' or 'perception' of empowerment that could disappear overnight. . . . 'It's a bit like free speech, which is easy when we're all singing the same song in the same key. It gets tough when we sing in a different key. As long as the issues that are raised seem to promote the company's efficiency and fortune, it's easy to give people power. But when workers raise things which make (managers) uncomfortable or (managers) think will affect the bottom line disadvantageously, then suddenly (employee) power is going to disappear. In a collective bargaining relationship, that can't happen."

A second role for unions in a high-involvement workplace, said these union leaders, was to provide a mechanism for employee representation company-wide. Companies could, of course, provide a vehicle for employees to express their opinions on major issues through "town hall meetings" or employee surveys. But both appeared inefficient and inadequate. Something else would be needed. And for these labor leaders, that something else was a union. At the company-wide level, a union or something very much like a union might be the only vehicle for giving workers a meaningful voice in high-level decision making. Instead of directly polling workers through meetings or surveys, unions could provide workers with knowledgeable, effective, and efficient representation. John Stepp, deputy under secretary of the U.S. Department of Labor, put it this way at the symposium:

> Direct polling of workers . . . presumes that those participating in the survey or those involved in the town hall meeting have the necessary of the prerequisite knowledge and expertise to make a meaningful input. . . . It strikes me that those means of direct participation are terribly inadequate, that if workers are going to have any opportunity to participate in higher-level decisions, it has to be through representative participation. And that representative form of participation has to give them access to the decision-making process, it has to provide them with a meaningful voice, it has to equip them with the necessary knowledge and expertise, and it has to assure that they have the kind

of strength and independence that they need so that they can say what they really believe without fear of reprisal or punitive action. Now, if you provide a representative form of participation that has those attributes, it strikes me that you've created a union, pure and simple.

Finally, proactive labor leaders of the late 1980s felt unions could play a critical role in educating workers in high-involvement workplaces so they could make informed decisions. Without adequate information from an impartial source, particularly with respect to technical issues, union leaders argued that management could manipulate worker decisions so that the process of employee involvement became nothing more than pseudo-participation. For example, at the 1989 symposium on labor-management cooperation, Bob Willis cited an instance where a company "empowered" its workers as their first team decision to select a sweeper to buy to sweep the warehouse area. "The company furnished them all kinds of information," said Willis, "and finally they selected the type of sweeper to buy. It wasn't three days later that they found out the company had had it on order for three weeks. The company maneuvered that thing down to where these people made exactly the decision they (management) wanted them to make."

As the 1980s came to an end, it was becoming more and more obvious that unions in the new workplace would look and act quite different from traditional American unions. It was clear they could no longer view themselves or allow the general public to view them as "specialized vehicles for opposing management."[10] Unions had to become a positive "value adding" force working with management as an independent ally rather than adversary. And unions had to become more of a representative body with a broad constituency that crossed jurisdictional lines (union to union) and even the traditional boundaries between labor and management.

As we have said, the exact form of union activity in *Workplace 2000* is unclear. In all likelihood, many if not most *Workplace 2000* organizations will have no union and many if not most *Workplace 2000* employees will see no need for a union. The few unions that remain, almost certainly, will be quite different from what we have known before. One possible form of union representation we might see in the future is that advocated by Charles Heckscher, an assistant professor of business administration at Harvard and author of *The New Unionism: Employee Involvement in the Changing Corporation*. Heckscher foresees a kind of "associational unionism" that encompasses a greater number of employees, not just traditional "workers," and is more decentralized and flexible. He notes that the American tradition and labor law recognizes—even insists upon—a clear distinction between workers (labor) and management. Unions, as we have known them, are worker organizations and managers by tradition and law are excluded from membership. Yet, Heckscher argues, in the new organization "the lines between management and workers are blurred, . . . upsetting the framework of the Wagner Act, which classifies people as 'workers' or 'managers.' This premise has been central to our labor relations system, yet it makes no sense to continue these classifications."[11]

In Heckscher's view, by giving up the traditional distinction between managers and workers, unions, or whatever the new representative groups called themselves, would gain a broader constituency and could truly add value to the workplace since they would represent everyone, or nearly everyone. Heckscher says: "I believe we must begin by embracing the notion that all employees deserve representation in the management of their work environment and working conditions as workers. . . . If we give up the notion of only two categories of represented bodies—workers and managers—then we realize that people need to be allowed to group together and be represented according to sensible groups within a workplace and around common interests. Presumably, under associational unionism, there would be a number of large associations—blue-collar employees, crafts employees, technical employees, or managers, for instance—all represented at the same time within a workplace."

What might these "new unions" look like? Heckscher sees the new union and various other interest groups speaking for a variety of factions in the work force. Workers would not be required to choose between exclusive representation or no representation. Instead, they would have a variety of options. Additionally, workplace problems addressed by these groups in multi-lateral negotiations would go far beyond those covered in the traditional union contract to address the interpretation of basic employee rights. Heckscher elaborates:

> The Shell-Sarnia plant in Canada is a fine example of a plant that is run by teams of workers for the most part and coordinated by a kind of works council. There they go beyond traditional union boundaries to functional groupings. They have a labor-management committee as well as problem-solving task forces in the plant. These groupings may seem complex, but they are flexible enough to permit employees to bring issues or problems to the forefront and get them solved . . .
>
> Unions based on the industrial model now in use require a rule-bound and centralized structure. What we are looking for, however, is a form of representation that can handle this new work environment, that is flexible, can handle functional groups, can form a common vision around a set of principles rather than rigid rules . . .
>
> What we need now is a national consensus on what are legitimate employee rights and responsibilities. There are certain employer rights which are seen as unfair: firing people without reason, interfering with free speech which does not directly harm the company, invading privacy. These kinds of actions have been partially limited by law. What we need to do is to clarify and consolidate those rights . . .
>
> When we combine rights with representation, we have a strong form of representation that is flexible, inclusive, and decentralized. Rights are fairly general and the representative body, or associational union, is there to interpret those rights in the workplace and establish agreements about how they are going to be implemented. It is not the court nor the government telling business what to do. It is the representative bodies within each business that will work out how to interpret the consensus on employee rights. A framework of this kind gives people at all levels representation and leverage to exert their interests."

Heckscher's idea for the "new unionism" represents a radical departure from what we have traditionally known. Certainly, such an approach to protecting basic worker rights would be preferable and more flexible than an expansion of laws, regulations, and litigation to accomplish the same goal. The question remains, however, whether either workers or management would see the need for the creation of such third-party intervention just at the time when unions were in a state of rapid decline, anti-union sentiment among management had peaked, and workers were experiencing both financial and social benefits from the new labor/management partnership.

Surviving in the New Workplace

Throughout this chapter we have suggested a transition that began in the 1980s and will be completed in the 1990s. A new American workplace is being created. In the not-so-distant future, most Americans will find that they have few or no direct supervisors. Instead, employees working in teams will be asked to take on more and more responsibility for traditional managerial and supervisory functions. Unions will disappear entirely or undergo drastic change. Management "by the book or union contract" will give way to management "by principle," with the clear advantage of greater flexibility and the clear potential for abuse and favoritism.

The transition we are likely to see to the new workplace will not come overnight. This change will be subtle rather than drastic for most Americans. Instead, we will see a gradual decline of direct supervision as teams mature.

Getting hired and surviving in the new workplace will require more and different skills from employees than ever before. No longer will it be sufficient to be good in a narrowly defined technical specialty. No longer will the path to advancement be assured by currying favor with a few influential bosses. The workplace will be more democratic. Key to success will be acceptance by one's peers. And to gain such acceptance, an American will have to demonstrate social, leadership, and problem-solving skills; a willingness to be flexible; and technical competence in a wide range of jobs. Above all, perhaps the most important things a *Workplace 2000* employee can bring to his or her job are a solid basic education and the willingness and ability to keep learning new skills.

CHAPTER 9

Education and the New Workplace

The new American workplace will require the most educated work force of any economic system in history. That prospect is frightening for a number of reasons. First, most Americans, and certainly most young Americans, lack the education to succeed (and perhaps even survive) in such a workplace. Second, American educational institutions, from primary schools to secondary schools to colleges and universities with few exceptions offer Americans almost no help in bridging their educational gap. Third, everyone who will enter the work force in the year 2000 has already been born and most have already completed or will soon complete their primary education. It is almost certain that most of these young Americans have received, at best, a mediocre educational foundation. Even worse, their immediate seniors in the work force, the generation before them is, if anything, more poorly educated and prepared for *Workplace 2000* responsibilities than they are. Within the next decade, America faces not only the challenge of revolutionizing its educational system—top to bottom— but reeducating a substantial portion of the current adult work force. The prospect of this being accomplished by public institutions alone are slim. The educational problem we are facing has been known for nearly a decade. Yet the problem persists and as the 1980s ended, we had neither a coordinated national effort nor clear national strategy to fix the problem. Instead, we were mired in a bewildering range of local experiments and a decade-long national debate. Any American wishing to retain the slimmest hope of financial security or even a decent standard of living for himself or his children must recognize the gravity of America's and his own personal educational crisis and take action to remedy the problem for at least himself and his family now. Even then, it may be too late.

The Crisis in American Education

In 1983, the National Commission on Excellence in Education published *A Nation at Risk*, the first national study to call attention to the problems with America's educational system.

The commission's report said, in part: "If an unfriendly power had attempted to impose on America the mediocre educational performance that exists today, we might have viewed it as an act of war."[1] America listened to what the commission had to say, then did nothing or next to nothing to rectify the problem. Nearly a decade later, our educational system was no better off than it had been when the commission issued its report. If anything, the crisis had worsened. By the late 1980s, 64 percent of America's largest companies listed education as their number one community-relations concern. David Kearns, chairman and CEO of Xerox, bluntly stated that the American work force was running out of qualified people. "If current demographic and economic trends continue," Kearns said, "American business will have to hire a million new workers a year who can't read, write, or count. Teaching them how, and absorbing the lost productivity while they're learning, will cost industry $25 billion a year for as long as it takes."[2] America's educational failure was, said Kearns, "the making of a national disaster." Brad M. Butler, former chairman of the Procter & Gamble Company, and James E. Burke, chief executive officer of Johnson & Johnson, agreed. Butler feared that because of our failures in educating our young, we were creating "a third world within our own country." Burke said it was "the American dream turned nightmare." David Halberstam, author of *The Best and the Brightest, The Powers That Be,* and *The Reckoning,* wrote: "The greatest threat to our national security is our educational system."[3] A *New York Times* article echoed that: "Corporate America has seen what the nation's schools are producing and it is alarmed."[4]

Corporate America certainly was alarmed. It had every reason to be. Kearns, Butler, Burke, Halberstam, and many others were merely reacting to the results of a wide variety of surveys and research reports that documented just how bad our educational system had become. Here are just a few of the frightening statistics they were seeing almost daily:

Overall, 25 percent of all American high school students dropped out of school before graduation.[5]

Among the poor, minority, and non-English speaking students in inner-city schools, the drop-out rate was nearly 60 percent. There were half as many black men in prison as there were in college.[6]

Even students who stayed in school didn't learn very much. For example, less than a third of high school seniors knew

- In which half-century the Civil War occurred
- What the Magna Carta or the Reformation was
- What the Declaration of Independence was
- Who wrote the Emancipation Proclamation

A third of the seniors didn't know

- That Columbus discovered America
- what *Brown* v. *Board of Education* was

A third couldn't recognize the best-known passages of the Constitution or the Declaration of Independence.

Given four possible answers of which "I don't know" wasn't

one, fewer than one student in five could match Dostoevski, Conrad, James Joyce, Hemingway or D. H. Lawrence with the books they wrote. The students scored *worse* than would have been expected from random guessing, which, in the words of a *Fortune* magazine article by Myron Magnet, suggested "an almost militant ignorance."

Less than one-fifth of two thousand eleventh-graders in a congressionally mandated study could write an intelligible note applying for a summer job at a swimming pool.

As the decade came to a close, only 39.2 percent of seventeen-year-olds could read well enough to understand and explain complicated information and only 4.9 percent could synthesize and learn from such materials.

Only 51.1 percent of the seventeen-year-olds could correctly perform moderately complex mathematical procedures and only 6.4 percent could perform multi-step problem solving and algebra.

In science, only 41.4 percent could analyze scientific data and only 7.5 percent could integrate specialized scientific information.[7]

At the college level, the survey results were equally bad.

Of college seniors surveyed in a Gallup poll, 25 percent didn't know that Columbus landed in the New World before 1500.

Only 58 percent knew that the Civil War was fought between 1850 and 1900.

Of the seniors, 23 percent thought Karl Marx's phrase "from each according to his ability to each according to his need" appeared in the U.S. Constitution.

60 percent of the seniors couldn't recognize the definition of the Reconstruction, the period that followed the Civil War.

58 percent couldn't identify Plato as the author of *The Republic*.

54 percent didn't know that *The Federalist Papers* were written to promote ratification of the U.S. Constitution.

44 percent didn't know that Herman Melville wrote *Moby Dick*.

42 percent couldn't identify the Koran as the sacred text of Islam.

Perhaps the ignorance of college seniors shouldn't have been surprising. Many never took classes in subjects that would have exposed them to such information.

Seventy-seven percent of the students could graduate from a college or university without taking a foreign language; 41 percent without taking a math course; and 38 percent without taking a history course. One wonders what they were required to take—if anything.[8]

It wasn't only kids. Adults also had their problems with simple facts, figures, reading, and locating things on a map.

In spite of frequent news stories about the area, 75 percent of U.S. adults couldn't locate the Persian Gulf on a map.

In a year during which the Democratic candidate for the presidency was the sitting governor of Massachusetts, 61 percent of the American public didn't know where that state was.[9]

In 1988, 44 percent of the job applicants at Prudential Insurance Company's Newark, New Jersey, office were unemployable because they couldn't even read at the ninth-grade level.[10]

Eighty percent of applicants screened by Motorola failed an entry-level test that required nothing more than seventh-grade English and fifth-grade math.[11]

Of twenty-three thousand young adults taking a simple qualifying exam for an entry-level position at New York Telephone, 84 percent *flunked the exam*.

Only 37 percent of twenty-one- to twenty-five-year-olds tested in one government-sponsored study could comprehend material in a simple *New York Times* article about an airline disaster.

Only 38 percent of young adults could use a chart to pick the right grade of sandpaper.

Only 38 percent could figure the amount of change they should receive from $3.00 if they order a 60¢ cup of soup and a $1.95 sandwich.

Only one in five young adults could read a bus schedule well enough to tell when a particular bus should reach the terminal.[12]

One third of the entire U.S. adult population was functionally illiterate. *Fortune* magazine published an article by Nancy Perry in 1988 that said: "It's like Pearl Harbor. The Japanese have invaded, and the U.S. has been caught short. Not on guns and tanks and battleships—those are yesterday's weapons—but on mental might. In a high tech age where nations increasingly compete on brainpower, American schools are producing an army of illiterates."

The cost of America's failure to educate its people adequately was staggering:

- $210 billion annually for formal and informal training
- $41 billion annually for welfare programs dominated by school drop-outs
- $16 billion each year in additional welfare costs because of teenage pregnancies (again dominated by school drop-outs)
- $25 billion each year in lost productivity
- $240 billion each year in lost earnings and taxes over the lifetime of each year's drop-outs because they couldn't get jobs at all or those they did get were marginal at best

It wasn't only the financial cost that was disturbing. America's failure to educate its people had an enormous social cost. Those most severely affected by the failure of America's educational system were the poor and disadvantaged who were most dependent on education as the primary vehicle for securing a better life for themselves and their families short of robbery or selling drugs (which, of course, many turned to, thus creating another social disaster). By failing to educate its general population, America was creating an ever widening gap between a few affluent "haves" and a multitude of angry, disenfranchised, and miserable "have nots." For those who hadn't passed through it already, the door to the American Dream was being slammed tightly shut and locked. Writing in 1985, Fred Hechinger, education columnist for *The New York Times*, described the social consequences of a failure to remedy our education problem this way in the *Harvard Business Review*. He wrote: "In the end, more is at stake than temporary dips in certain test scores. Those trends can, and must be corrected. . . . But what would be difficult, if not impossible, to correct are the consequences of abandoning the principle we have always entrusted to the public schools. It is the principle Thomas Jefferson had in mind when he talked about creating an aristocracy of talent rather than one of inherited wealth and privilege, the principle Horace Mann envisioned when he called universal education the 'balance wheel' of society, the principle that time and again has made it possible for the poor and disenfranchised from every part of the globe to seek and find success in the United States." Hechinger went on to note that affluent parents can always find a way to educate their young by, if necessary, hiring their own teachers and building their own schools. Thus, abandoning the public schools to mediocrity or worse will not significantly impair the ability of the rich to educate their offspring. It would, however, have disastrous consequences for the poor and in the long term for society as a whole. In the long run, said Hechinger, the failure of public schools would be "the road to national self-destruction. An open, upwardly mobile, optimistic society is not just the plaything of do-gooders; it is, in addition to being decent, a thriving, expanding, profitable society as well. The business community has a stake, perhaps the biggest stake, in such a society. And, thus it has a stake, too, in ensuring that public schools dedicated to quality and equality are once again America's balance wheel."[13]

As the 1980s came to an end, it was clear that something drastic had to be done immediately to correct the educational deficiencies of not only the young, but a large segment of the entire U.S. population. In 1988 then Secretary of Labor Ann McLaughlin put it this way: "Without immediate action . . .

large segments of our community will end up uneducated, untrained and unemployed and, in the workplace of today and tomorrow, perhaps even unemployable."[14] It was equally obvious that little was being done to correct the problem. We couldn't agree on the cause of the problem, much less on its solution.

Why and How America's Educational System Failed

As we entered the 1990s, it was clear that the American system of education had failed. But why had it failed? No one was entirely sure. Perhaps our system for educating the vast majority of Americans never had been very good. That's what Albert Shanker, president of the American Federation of Teachers (AFT), thought. He said: "It's not that our schools are worse than in the past. . . . We've NEVER really educated more than 15% to 20% of the kids in the country . . . up to the level of writing a simple letter."[15]

Others weren't prepared to condemn American education from its inception. There wasn't anything wrong with our educational tradition, they maintained. What was wrong was that we changed—we got away from the educational practices that served us well in the past. For example, E. D. Hirsch, Jr., author of *Cultural Literacy*, blamed our current failures on changes in educational practices going back decades. He said: "You can be darn sure that whatever's causing the decline started back in the 40s and 50s . . . that's when teaching styles changed to an emphasis on skills—the nuts and bolts of reading or math, for instance—rather than the knowledge needed to make those subjects meaningful . . . education for everybody became a national goal . . . (and) to keep kids in longer, to make them more comfortable, we've softened up the curriculum. It used to be a lot more difficult to graduate high school."

Others saw at least part of our tradition as being at fault. It wasn't that we had gotten away from tradition, they said; the problem was our stubborn maintenance of a traditional structure and culture for education that no longer worked very well. In September 1988, *Fortune* magazine convened a two-day summit on business and education at the Willard Hotel in Washington, D.C. It was attended by over one hundred leaders from American business, government, and academia. The consensus of the attendees? What America needed was a complete restructuring of its school system—in the words of William Bennett, former Secretary of Education who attended the conference, "something approaching a revolution." Conferees agreed that the culture and structure of schools as they operated in the late 1980s was all wrong, much as a nineteenth-century manufacturing plant would be all wrong for the competitive business climate of the 1980s and '90s. "Batches of boys and girls," they said, "still roll like widgets from room to room where . . . each teacher puts a part on the kid. Classes are large and impersonal, lectures predominate, and every 40 minutes, just when the children settle down—GONG!—the bell sends them off to their next station. The result: gaggles of graduates with the forbearance needed for unskilled manual labor, but devoid of the problem-solving skills necessary for today's globally competitive workplace."[16]

Still others, such as Joel Conarro, president of the Guggenheim Foundation, blamed our educational problems on the nation's leadership. He said: "The man who led our nation for eight years [Reagan] didn't know anything about anything . . . and I'm not sure Bush is any better. And Quayle is an absolute dunderhead. It indicates something troubling about our standards. If those at the top aren't interested in the life of the mind or education, that is part of the problem. There's not much to trickle down from those minds."[17]

Others argued that the cause of the failure of American education could be traced to the length of the school year. The academic year in U.S. schools was forty to sixty days shorter than in Japan or Europe, and American students entering college were therefore as much as two years behind their counterparts in other countries in educational accomplishment. American students spent much of the first years of college playing catch-up. Lengthen the school year, they said, and you just might get some results.

Still others laid the blame for our poor performance to the quality and availability of teachers and/or our failure to involve teachers in finding a solution to educational problems.

Certainly, there was research evidence to support such arguments. For example, a Carnegie Foundation survey of twenty-two thousand teachers found that one third had almost no say in shaping the curriculum they taught and two thirds were never asked their opinion about a school's policy concerning when and whether to hold a student back from advancing to the next grade. SAT scores of high school students planning to enter the teaching profession were 23 to 40 points below those of students pursuing different professions. In some states (for example, Massachusetts) as few as one in five elementary school teachers had any training in math or science.

Finally, it was projected by the leaders at the Washington "summit" that by 1995, given trends of the 1980s, American schools would be short seven hundred thousand qualified teachers. Apparently, few Americans wanted to go into the teaching profession. And those who did found they weren't allowed to change the system.[18]

The American educational establishment's continued inability to agree upon a cause, much less a remedy to our educational problems, was strange in a sense. As we have noted throughout this book, American business had learned some genuine lessons throughout the '70s and '80s: that employees were any organization's most important asset; that employee involvement was critical for solving quality and other problems; that the only way to attract, retain, and motivate good employees, regardless of the business, was to give them more control over their work environment; and that rigid, bureaucratic, slow-to-change structures were the least effective of organizational forms. We knew these things and we understood the universality of their application. Yet few, if any, of these concepts were understood or appreciated by the educational establishment. It was as if those in charge of education were entirely oblivious to the revolution occurring all around them.

The Demand for Education in the New Workplace

Our educational crisis would not have been as serious if the changes we alluded to above and have documented throughout this book weren't occurring. In the traditional American workplace, education was valued, but the illiterate could still find a place. The uneducated or undereducated could find a job. It might not be a good job, but at least it would be one. That will not be true in *Workplace 2000*. There will be no place for the functionally illiterate. In fact, there may be no place for anyone without at least some level of college education. The U.S. Department of Labor estimates that one year of college will be required for most jobs by the year 2000—less than a decade from now. Others place two years of college as the point of "minimum workplace literacy." The consequences of such a change in minimum job requirements are enormous, both in human and economic terms. Some—perhaps a large core of Americans—will be effectively unemployable at a time when large numbers of jobs go unfilled. To call such an occurrence a national disaster begs the point. It is nothing less than national economic and social suicide.

What got us to this point? Why is education so important now? Obviously, one of the reasons is the change in workplace practices that we have documented throughout this book, particularly the move to turn over more operational and problem-solving responsibilities to American workers. Such changes are not driven by desire—in fact, as we have noted, there has been a lot of opposition from managers and supervisors. These changes have been driven by competitive necessity. It isn't something American business necessarily wants to do. It's something American business has to do to compete. The alternative to changing is an economic disaster as bad or worse than that possible as a result of a failure of education. Given that we have no choice but to ask workers to take on more responsibility, we must—and we emphasize the word *must*—have workers with the education to exercise that responsibility. If workers in the new workplace do not come to their jobs with the necessary education to perform them, then business will have to educate its own work force or do without. "Going without" is unthinkable. In the new workplace, all those with minimum workplace literacy will be quickly hired, possibly at exaggerated salaries. To fill the remaining need for workers, U.S. businesses will have to dip into the remaining, largely illiterate, pool. The cost of educating this group of workers will be enormous. Earlier, we cited David Kearns's estimate that to educate the illiterate work force to the minimum level needed by American business would cost industry up to $25 *billion* per year "for as long as it takes." Adding a $25 billion annual cost to our already high operating cost may be (and probably is) more than the U.S. can take and still compete in a global economy. Perhaps another way to understand the problem we face is to take a simple example. Throughout the 1980s, the United States was being clobbered by Japan. One of the reasons we couldn't compete successfully with the Japanese was their reputation for producing high-quality products and our reputation for shoddy work. America has fought back. One of the weapons we used was a quality-improvement technique called statistical process control (SPC), wherein employees are trained to maintain statistical graphs and charts to keep track of variations in product quality. (SPC helps, but is probably not the best technique and we misused it often.) The quality of American products is better as a result of SPC and other steps we have taken. But we paid a high price for achieving parity in quality (and we may not be there yet). The price we paid is directly related to the education level of the American worker versus the Japanese worker. William Wiggenhorn, director of training at Motorola, has estimated that it costs two hundred dollars to train a worker in the U.S. in statistical process control versus forty-seven cents in Japan. What is the difference? Japanese workers are given a book to read. American workers must first be taught to read.[19] America pays a high price for remedial education. But that's not the only problem.

Something else is happening in the world. It goes beyond adapting to team systems, organizational changes, and introducing new techniques like SPC. The world itself is changing in respect to how and what type of human effort is valued. We are moving from a world in which human value was derived from physical prowess to one in which value is a function of mental acuity. We are moving from a world in which the strong not only survived, but prospered, into one in which quick wits are valued above brute strength. In the new world, the "philosopher," "thinker," "innovator," "creator," and "problem solver" is king. Perhaps George Gilder, author of *Microcosm: The Quantum Revolution in Economics and Technology*, said it best when he wrote: "The central event of the 20th century is the overthrow of matter. In technology, economics, and the politics of nations, wealth in the form of physical resources is steadily declining in value and significance. The powers of mind are everywhere ascendant over the brute force of things. . . . Today, the ascendant nations and corporations are masters not of land and material resources, but of ideas and technologies. . . . Wealth comes not to the rulers of slave labor but to the liberators of human creativity, not to conquerors of land but to the emancipators of mind."

In *Workplace 2000*, the most valuable commodity will be knowledge and the pulsating flow of ideas exchanging, interacting, and expanding. To participate in the game, Americans will have to possess the requisite skills.

The Skills Required for *Workplace 2000*

In the late 1980s, the U.S. Department of Labor and the American Society for Training and Development (ASTD) launched a joint research project to identify the "basic" skills employers wanted their workers to possess.[20] Researchers assumed that most employers would list primarily technical skills, such as computer literacy. They were wrong. What employers wanted and said they needed most desperately were workers with a solid basic education plus relationship skills and skills in self-management. Reviewing the results, ASTD lumped the most desired skills for workers of the future into seven categories: learning to learn; competence (reading, writing, and computation); communication; personal management; adaptability; group effectiveness; and influence. Each of these had a specific meaning for prospective employers.

Learning to Learn

"Learning to learn" was considered the most basic of all skills. Essentially, it meant that each person should acquire the self-knowledge concerning when and how he or she learned best. In our earlier book, *Maximum Performance Management*, we pointed out that most training (and we could have made the same statement about education) failed because the method of instruction, instructional aides, and learning conditions were usually geared to the "average" person and consequently were usually wrong for most people. We noted: "All of us learn under different conditions. Some of us learn best primarily through words, others need pictures, sounds, and symbols. Some of us can adjust to the pace of learning in a group, others need to proceed at their own pace—faster or slower than the group. Some of us learn best by listening to a knowledgeable lecturer, others have to be involved in and experience what is being taught." Learning to learn means that each person must have enough "learning experiences" and pay close enough attention to the methods and conditions of learning that work best for him or her (and we will all be somewhat different) so that he or she can seek out the best learning environment. The key is for each person to find the best method for him or her to master new skills. Why? Because the future American workplace will be one of constant change, and to retain their competency, American workers must continuously learn new skills. In fact, the need for continuous learning already exists in the workplace of today. For example, Thomas Lindem, vice president for technology at Ingersall Milling Machine Company, estimated in 1988 that as many as four to six out of every forty hours employees work in the future might have to be devoted to classroom training and retraining. He noted that as much as eighty percent of Ingersall's technical people were obsolete. "If they've been out of school two to three years, they are obsolete. It's not through any fault of their own; technologies change. . . . We've got to face the fact that re-education must be part of the day-to-day job." Reeducation and retraining will be even more critical in the future. James Anderson, a principal with Arthur Young's Manufacturing Consulting Group, has estimated that twenty-first-century knowledge workers would probably have to spend one year out of every seven in formal training, going back to school to update their skills.[21]

Competence

"Competence" refers to the basic skills of reading, writing, and math. But there is a difference. Not only must the worker of tomorrow know how to read a simple book, article, or set of instructions, he or she must also know how to read and interpret graphs, charts, and diagrams. He or she must be able to scan information quickly and pick out relevant information. So much information will be available that it will not be enough for a worker just to be able to struggle through written information a word or phrase at a time. Reading speed and comprehension, particularly the latter, will be critical. Employers want workers who can quickly digest complex material and then be able to use the information they acquire to solve problems. In writing, it will not be enough for a worker simply to be able to put together a grammatically correct sentence. Workers will need a level of writing skill that will enable them to communicate quickly and effectively. Workers will need the skill to prepare business documents that are clear, concise, accurate, specific, logical, and easy for readers to understand and use. Finally, the required math skills will be more conceptual than computational. It will be less important that workers know how to add a long series of complex numbers manually than to be able to scan computer-generated results and understand the computational routines used to arrive at these results. Since these computational routines are likely to be highly sophisticated, workers will require more than just the ability to add, subtract, multiply, and divide. At least some knowledge of higher-order mathematics, including a knowledge of business statistics, will be essential.

Communication

"Communication" refers to verbal and listening skills. Workers in the future will be members of teams. Much of the value of teams stems from the increased communication between team members sharing information and ideas. Workers of the future must be good communicators. They must have the skill to express their ideas and convey information to others quickly and effectively. They must also be good, active listeners, since much of the information they require to perform their jobs, solve problems, and work effectively with others will come from verbal interaction rather than written sources, which will be deemed too slow.

Personal Management

"Personal management" refers to an individual's self-esteem and self-motivation. More than any other time in the past, workers in the future will be relied upon to "get the job done" with minimum supervision. Employers will look for workers who take pride in what they do, feel good about themselves, understand their strengths, but at the same time understand their limitations. No longer will workers have someone to tell them what to do, solve their problems, or remind them to seek technical or other assistance when they need it. Workers will have to be able to make these decisions themselves. Since "intrinsic motivation" or internal drive to succeed on a job has much to do with how successful a person is in finding the right match between what he or she enjoys doing and what he or she does for a living, future workers will need skills in setting personal and career goals, and planning and managing their career in concert with these goals.

Adaptability

"Adaptability" refers primarily to creative-thinking and problem-solving skills. As we have emphasized throughout this book, *Workplace 2000* will place increased responsibility on employees for decision making and problem solving. Workers of tomorrow need the skills to "break mental sets," "think creatively," analyze problems, and find innovative approaches to problem resolution. Since much of this problem-solving activity will occur in team or group settings, employees need skills and experience in group-problem-solving activities.

Group Effectiveness

"Group effectiveness" refers to interpersonal and team skills. Employees of the future need the skills to work effectively in groups. They need to understand how their individual behavior impacts others. They need skills to negotiate, resolve conflict, handle stress, deal with undesirable behavior in others, share in task accomplishment, and build positive working relationships with others in a group setting.

Influence

"Influence" refers to skills in organizational effectiveness and leadership. The future worker needs an understanding of what organizations are, how they work, why they exist, what makes organizations effective or ineffective, and how external and internal forces affect organizational accomplishment. On the leadership side, employees need an understanding of what makes leaders effective and ineffective, how the leader influences members of the group, the role of formal and informal leaders, the importance of a "vision," ethical standards for judging leaders, and so on.

Achieving *Workplace 2000* Literacy

Acquiring the skills for *Workplace 2000* literacy will not be easy for many Americans, particularly those who are poor and consequently have few financial resources to pay for acquiring the skills on their own. Also, adults who are deficient in basic skills (reading, writing, math) because they dropped out of school or received a poor basic education will find themselves playing a game of catch-up where in a short period (less than a decade) they must not only acquire the basics but also go on to higher order skills. It would be nice if we could say that Americans could depend upon public and private institutions to help. But we can't. As we said previously, the nation's educational problems have been debated for nearly a decade with no signs of progress. The best we can offer is a set of dos and don'ts based upon research that has been conducted and some valuable educational experiments underway. Solving America's educational problems will be up to individual Americans. Here, then, is some advice.

Americans Must Take Personal Responsibility for Their Own and Their Children's Education—The Key Is Involvement of the Immediate Family

Some research, including an exhaustive study completed in 1966, suggests that spending per pupil, teacher salaries, class size, and a host of other factors including the size and location of the school all pale in comparison to one thing in determining the quality of education a student receives. What is that one thing that appears more important than all the others? Family—how effectively parents instill a love for learning and respect for the importance of education in their own children. The influence of the parents appears to be of overriding importance in determining how seriously children will take their education, how well they will do, and how far they will go.[22] Jerome Rosow, president of the Work in America Institute, has said: "The single biggest influence on a kid's ability to learn is parental involvement. . . . Research shows that the home outweighs everything, including intelligence."[23]

What specifically should parents due to ensure that their children receive the education they will require to survive in the workplace of the future? C. Jackson Grayson and Carla O'Dell, in their 1988 book *American Business: A Two Minute Warning*, made the following recommendations. They said, "It's not just setting students down to do homework and occasionally unplugging the TV, but, more importantly, setting the climate for learning and personally engaging in their education:

- Reading to them and encouraging them to read on their own
- Asking questions, expressing interest, concern, and excitement about the children's education
- Taking educational trips with children, providing study facilities and supplies

- Pressing school officials and legislators for changes in education
- Attending school events"

Grayson and O'Dell go on to note that Americans have to stop placing all of the responsibility on public institutions. "Too many U.S. parents," they say, "want the schools to raise their children, to educate them, to discipline them, and to babysit. Yet they are the first to deplore it when 'Johnny can't read.' "

Americans Should Ensure That Their Children Are Enrolled in a Quality Preschool By the Age of Three

In 1962, researchers began tracking the progress of one hundred children enrolled in the Perry Preschool Program in Ypsilanti, Michigan. The findings? By the age of nineteen, 67 percent of the preschool students had completed high school versus 49 percent of the non-preschoolers. Thirty-eight percent of the preschool children had gone on to college or job training versus only 21 percent of the non-preschool children. Thirty-one percent of the former preschoolers had been arrested versus 51 percent of those without preschool experience. Preschool students had the same advantages when it came to avoiding going on public assistance or having babies by age nineteen.[24] Owen Butler, chairman of Procter & Gamble and vice chairman of the Committee for Economic Development, a business research group, said about the importance of preschool education particularly for the poor: "We were frankly startled to find that the single most profitable investment our society could make in education was not in the kindergarten-through-high-school years, but rather in at least a year of very high-quality and expensive preschool for disadvantaged children beginning at the age of three."[25] Preschool education is so important that every parent should seek out early childhood, preschool education for his or her children. But that won't be easy. In spite of the significant advantages of preschool, it will likely be difficult to find. Such programs were available to only 20 percent of those poor enough to qualify in the 1980s. One problem was money to fund such programs. Another was the lack of teachers. Head Start, for example, had a 30 percent turnover rate in teachers. There are options, however, at least in some parts of the country. Lower-income families should look for business-, university-, and public-school-sponsored programs in their communities such as Project Help (Hartford Early Learning Partnership) in Hartford, Connecticut; the Beethoven Project in Chicago; and Success by Six in Minneapolis.[26] Many of these programs use innovative techniques to help children develop language, problem solving, and other basic skills and a sense of accomplishment early on plus offer family counseling and healthcare assistance.

Preschool education is expensive, but it doesn't have to be. Everything does not have to be done with a large bureaucracy or by hiring full-time specialists. For example, Arkansas launched a project called the Home Instruction Program for Preschool Youngsters (HIPPY). Based upon a program developed by the Israelis in the 1960s to prepare immigrant children for Israeli schools, the program provided storybooks, worksheets, and other assistance to parents willing to devote as little as fifteen minutes a day to providing preschool instruction to their three- and four-year-olds. Not only did the program result in a significant gain in the educational level for the children, but in two counties half of the mothers participating in the program—all on welfare—went back to high school, got a job, or enrolled in job-training courses.[27] Americans should encourage their own communities to study what Arkansas has done and start their own local self-help programs.

Americans Shouldn't Count on Educational Technology to Close the Knowledge Gap

In education, as in business, Americans in the 1980s became fascinated with technology and looked to it to solve all of our problems. Technology wasn't the ultimate solution in business and it wasn't, and won't be, in education. Take our experience with computers in schools. From nearly none in the early 1980s, the number of computers in America's public schools shot up to over 2 million by the end of the decade. Yet there was considerable question whether computers had had any impact on student performance. A 1989 *Business Week* article noted that "after a decade of enthusiasm, there's still no clear consensus about the role, value, or effectiveness of computers in schools. Well-thought-out goals are still lacking. Gains in achievement have proved modest at best. And, in many schools, initial fervor has given way to 'benign neglect.' "

The problem was that most schools were using their computers for nothing more than word processing, simple math drills, and the rudiments of computer literacy. Most teachers had received, at most, only a minimum introduction to the computer (basically "how to turn it on") and what software was available wasn't very good. Available software was a significant problem, since most programs did nothing more than replicate what could have been accomplished with flash cards.

While computers generally have not helped us very much, that's not to say they couldn't. They could if we used them the right way. In particular, we need more sophisticated and innovative educational software. An example of the type of educational software we need is that developed by the Bank Street College of Education and a group of textbook publishers in the 1980s. Called "The Voyage of the Mimi," this multimedia program received high acclaim. The Bank Street program simulated environmental and archaeological research expeditions and allowed students to direct the expeditions making use of their knowledge of map reading, navigation, and math. Yet such programs were expensive to develop and slow to provide a return on investment, thus shunned by most educational software developers.

Another way we could effectively use computers and other technology is in on-the-job training. Consider a factory of the future that builds many different things. There is very little repetition. The company needs to move quickly as customer and market demands change. It deals with a tremendous volume of products—some old and some new. Many new products and/or modifications to existing products are being added all of the time. Workers constantly have to learn new skills and/or refresh their skills when they are asked to perform a job they haven't performed before or haven't performed in some time. The demands for training and retraining in such an environment are enormous. Now suppose that at each workstation specific, visual instruction on how to perform any step in hundreds or thousands of operations to build the wide variety of products is available to every operator at the touch of a screen. Text, engineering drawings, still pictures, and full motion video instruction are available to every operator on demand. The operator asks a question: "How do I perform this task?" The operator gets an immediate answer or rather, an immediate demonstration on video. Sound farfetched? Not really. By the late 1980s, Apple Computer Company had already installed a primitive version of such a system at its Macintosh Assembly Plant in Fremont, California. While not truly interactive—the operator could only start and stop the video on command—the system could show each operator a fifteen-second video about a particular operation.[28] We need to encourage companies to develop more such applications.

Americans Shouldn't Count on Their State Legislatures to Solve the Educational Problem

The worse thing Americans could do would be to leave educational reform up to politicians and special interest groups. In 1985, Fred Hechinger pointed out what can occur when Americans depend upon politicians. He said:

> Virtually every state legislature . . . is enacting new educational requirements . . . minimum standards, competency tests, required units of instruction proliferate. Yet a host of existing legislative mandates has done little to bring about educational utopias and many have actually impeded real educational progress.
>
> Who but the dairy industry gains from a state requirement that every Wisconsin public school give instruction in the "true and comparative vitamin content and food and health values of dairy products?" What educational problems are solved by Maine's mandate that the public schools teach virtue and morality for not less than one-half hour per week?

Or by California's edict that "each teacher shall endeavor to impress upon the minds of the pupils the principles of morality, truth, justice, and patriotism" and that this includes "kindness toward domestic pets." Such legislative homilies do no great harm perhaps; they do suggest, however, that politicians tend to regard the schools as less than mature, adult, independent institutions."[29]

Obviously, legislation will be needed to solve our problems. But Americans shouldn't be lulled into some kind of educational complacency just because a politician says education will be his number one priority or a state legislature passes a new educational reform bill. The President, Congress, governors, and state legislatures can help by funding programs and requiring educational institutions to be accountable for their student's performance. But public officials can't be counted on to do the job alone. In fact, they can't necessarily be counted on even to do the right thing.

Americans Shouldn't Count on Business Alone to Solve the Problem

If Americans can't count on politicians to solve the problem, they also can't count on business. Many efforts by business have been a dismal failure so far. For example, in 1989 there were 140,000 private sector/school "partnerships" according to a White House survey. Sixty percent of these involved businesses. In fact, there were more such "partnerships" than there were schools. Unfortunately, many were "adopt-a-school" or similar efforts, and what research that was available suggested that such efforts had little, if any, measurable impact on student performance. Worse, there were notable failures where "partnerships" started with great fanfare but eventually fizzled out or were cancelled outright by their sponsors due to changes in company management, changes in school officials, or both. Notable failures were a Primerica Corporation-sponsored program for Martin Luther King, Jr., High School in New York; a Time Inc./CBS Inc. "High School of Writing" project for the New York City School System; and a job "guarantee" program launched by four New York area banks.[30] Too many adopt-a-school programs became nothing more than feel-good programs. Schools got uniforms for the band, pictures in the corporate newsletter, maybe a frozen-dessert machine for the school lunchroom, but nothing much changed.

Effective business-sponsored programs go beyond these limited efforts. One way businesses can help is by offering kids incentives to stay in school. For example, Merrill Lynch, working with the Urban League, established a program where the Merrill Lynch Foundation would contribute two thousand dollars per year to an investment fund for each of twenty-five six-year-olds. When the students graduated from high school, they would receive a college scholarship or tuition to pay for other advanced training from the fund. Cleveland has had a scholarship program for twenty-two years backed by the city's business community and designed to ensure that every Cleveland high school graduate who wanted to go to college got there. Since its inception, Cleveland's program has helped over sixty thousand students go to college. Eighty percent of these have earned their degrees. Other cities such as New York, Boston, Miami, and Baltimore started similar programs.[31]

Even individual businessmen can help. For example, Eugene Lang, a New York businessman, offered two thousand dollars toward the college tuition of children in his former elementary school as an inducement for them to stay in school. Business leaders in Dallas, Texas, started a similar program called the "I Have a Dream Foundation."

Another way businesses can help is by starting innovative programs to help improve the quality of instruction, particularly in math and science. For example, in the 1980s, Polaroid launched a program called Project Bridge to enable up to ten of its employees each year to switch careers and become math or science teachers. Polaroid would pay the participant's cost of a one-year teacher certification program and would pay their full base salary while they worked on obtaining their certification. At the same time, the company made it possible for teachers to take a one year sabbatical to work at Polaroid so they could learn more about the practical applications of math and science. In a similar effort, General Electric, through the GE Foundation, committed $1 million to fund SAT-preparation courses, teacher-enrichment programs, special math and science courses, and college scholarships for students in one rural county in Alabama where it had built a $700 million plastics plant.

A third way business can help is by promoting educational reform on a state-by-state basis. For example, South Carolina corporations donated one hundred thousand dollars to sponsor TV commercials and other activities in support of passage of that state's Education Improvement Act in 1984. Its passage was credited in large part to the effectiveness of corporate pressure and support.[32]

Finally, businesses can help by starting their own basic skills training program for their employees. Such training will be essential for adults already in the work force and young adults entering the work force between now and the year 2000. Since such training can be enormously expensive, it should be professionally designed and targeted to meet specific and systematically identified workplace needs. One such approach is that recommended by the American Society for Training and Development and described in *Workplace Basics: The Skills Employers Want*, by Anthony P. Carnevale, Leila J. Gainer and Ann S. Meltzer.

When Americans Have a Choice They Should Take It . . . If They Don't Have a Choice They Should Demand It

As the 1980s came to an end, a number of states were beginning to give parents a choice of the schools their children would attend. For example, Minnesota passed a law that allowed parents to send their children to any public school in the state. Thirty-six hundred dollars in state tuition would follow the child. In theory, "choice" programs would force schools to upgrade their quality in order to compete for students. Those schools unable to attract sufficient students risked being closed.

Many of these programs are new, and while there is no clear evidence that choice programs will necessarily boost student performance, some of the older programs show promising results. For example, a New York City school district in a largely black and Hispanic neighborhood adopted a choice plan in

1974. At that time, only 40 percent of the district's students attended school on a regular basis. By 1989, 90 percent of the students were graduating. In Cambridge, Massachusetts, SAT scores of public school students rose 89 points over a period of seven years after a choice plan was implemented. Successful choice plans provide some extra money to help the schools get going, give schools the right to reject students who may not thrive in the school's environment, grant teachers more say in selecting where they work and what they do in the classroom, and provide vigorous support to parents to help them make informed decisions concerning which schools are best for their child.[33]

Americans Should Seek Out and Enroll Their Children in the Educational Experiments

Americans should look for innovative practices and teaching techniques to give children practical, if simulated, real world experience early on. One such program, called Mini-Society, was created by Marilyn Kourilsky, dean of teacher education at the UCLA Graduate School of Education. Here is how a 1989 *Inc.* magazine article described the children's experience:

Welcome to "Starville"—known for most of the week as Mrs. Doris Stevenson's second-grade class at Brandywood School, in Wilmington, Delaware—proof that children can be taught how business and the economy work. Here, in a program called Mini-Society, children learn by creating a self-directed economic world that mirrors our own. Three times a week for 45 minutes, they become proprietors of small businesses, buying and selling refrigerator magnets or decorated cards, pencil holders or snacks. They create their own currency—the "moonbean" in Starville—and make up their own rules of commerce. They rent desk space, keep a P&L, and set and pay taxes. Over the semester they see firsthand why people work, what happens in a store, and the difference between an owner and an employee. They learn what happens if you make a customer mad, how competition lowers prices and raises quality, and what makes you go bankrupt—and how persistence and determination can help you start again. The children make the decisions, not the teacher, whose role is principally to "debrief" them on their experience; it is the students, after all, who live with the consequences, learning about cost-benefit analysis along the way.

How does a Mini-Society type of program help? It builds self-esteem, helps children to become more creative and self-reliant, and perhaps makes learning relevant and fun. And it works. Elementary school students experiencing Mini-Society score as well on tests as college sophomores enrolled in an introductory economics course on economic terms and concepts. The Mini-Society program creates a simulation of the real world. Other innovative programs go further. For example, the REAL programs (Rural Entrepreneurship through Action Learning) in North Carolina, South Carolina, and Georgia actually help students start their own businesses. Students conduct the needs analysis, write a business plan, raise capital, run and operate the business, and, if all goes well, share the profits.[34]

Experiments worth investigating aren't just reserved to general education. Some vocational schools have integrated academics with hands-on learning and are tying training closer to real world requirements. For example, in Montgomery County, Ohio, instructors in auto body work integrate communications into their courses. Students must give oral presentations on their job skills—for example, explaining how to put on a fender. Why the emphasis on communication? Says Rosalie Bernard, an English teacher at the school, "Our advisory committee of shop owners and foremen told us the kids they are getting today are skilled, but they can't communicate. They don't know how to diffuse customer anger. And that's the one thing the business community wants." To provide even more real life experiences for the students, once each semester "the class simulates a typical day in an auto body shop, with customers calling, vendors complaining, and employees whining."[35]

Another experiment in restructuring the school experience was conducted in Philadelphia. Volunteers from the city's largest companies joined with local universities to form the

Committee to Support Philadelphia Public Schools. The committee's goal was to increase employability of students, reduce dropout rates, and boost college attendance. The committee raised funds to sponsor projects such as a network of eleven high school "academies" offering specialized training in business, electrical and automotive repair, health service, and environmental studies in addition to academics. *The Wall Street Journal*, in a 1989 special supplement on education, describes one of these academies:

> The 160 students enrolled in the Business Academy at Strawberry Mansion High School go to class an extra hour each day. Besides reading, writing and math, they study data-processing, bookkeeping and office machine operation, and are soon to begin training on Apple computers. The academy's dropout rate is near zero, compared with 40% for the high school as a whole.
>
> Classes are small. Students are assigned the same math, English, and science teachers year after year. "We really get to know the students," says Diane Holliday, who teaches English . . . "We know areas that give them the most difficulty. We even get to know their problems at home." . . .
>
> Teachers insist on developing students' verbal skills to prepare for the corporate world. Ms. Holiday, for example, often requires her students to deliver short speeches to their classmates . . . A class in job interviewing includes video-taped dry runs at school, followed by field trips downtown for mock interviews with real employers.[36]

Americans interested in securing a better education for their children should search out and enroll their children in this kind of experiment. Some of the experiments may not work. But at least they offer hope. It's clear that traditionally structured learning environments too often don't work.

Americans Should Insist That Educators Provide Social and Financial Incentives to Improve

In 1984, the Florida legislature passed a bill to form what was called the District Meritorious School Program, designed to provide financial rewards to "quality schools" in the state that could demonstrate improvements in student academic and physical achievement. After passage of the state program, the Dade County public schools and United Teachers of Dade (teachers' union) agreed to a labor/management cooperative program called the Quality Instruction Incentives Program (QUIIP). Under QUIIP, schools in the district could apply for participation in the program by developing and submitting a plan for instructional improvement. At the end of the year, participating schools that have achieved the most improvement on annual standardized student achievement tests share in a pool of money set aside by the state legislature. Teachers, administrators, secretaries, cafeteria workers, and custodians in the winning schools all share the financial rewards. In the 1987–88 school year, sixty-nine schools participated and $3.2 million in incentive awards were distributed. Between 1984 and 1989, Dade County public school employees shared in more than $16.9 million in QUIIP awards.[37]

Throughout this book, we have emphasized the importance of providing incentives for employees to perform. That's a major reason U.S. businesses are adopting more and more pay-for-performance systems, as we described in Chapter 5. It is time educators received the same kind of financial incentives and variable pay systems. We must send a message that we will pay well for performance, but only for performance.

Acquiring the Skills for *Workplace 2000* Leadership

Americans who wish to acquire the skills necessary for them to play leadership roles in the workplace of the future face almost as great a problem as do those who simply aspire to decent employment. The reason for this is that the American institution that should be preparing our future leaders—the American graduate school of business—is almost a total failure. We only need to look at what graduates of business schools (our M.B.A.'s) have accomplished or, more to the point, failed to accomplish. For example, Thomas Nourse, a San Diego investment adviser, compared the performance of industrial companies run by M.B.A.'s, by founders or CEOs with technical or industry-specific degrees, and by the Japanese. Not surprisingly, on cash flow, the Japanese companies came out far superior to companies run by M.B.A.'s or technical CEOs. Companies run by M.B.A.'s came out the worst of the lot.[38]

Harvard Business School Professor Robert Hayes said of M.B.A. performance in the real world of business: "There is no evidence that the money spent on business schools in the past 25 years has served the country well." Hayes couldn't find any clear return on the roughly $3 billion a year spent on business-school education. Graduates of American business schools, including some of the "best," are equally critical of the training they received. For example, a Wharton graduate said: "At no time in two years did any of my classes discuss organized labor, the role of the government and business in society, the causes and possible solutions of the trade deficit, America's industrial decline, or any other issue that can't be solved in 80 minutes." A Duke graduate said: "My lasting regret is that I spent $40,000 to learn useless tools from academicians who never worked for a real business. I can crunch numbers to death, but I didn't learn anything about managing, motivating, and leading people." A Columbia graduate said: "I and most of my classmates graduated with virtually no knowledge of manufacturing or operations. But we all learned a hell of a lot about portfolio hedging strategies that have nothing to do with management." American business schools have been particularly weak in training their students to lead and manage people. Andrew Grove, chairman of Intel Corporation, has said that as far as American business schools are concerned, "The art and practice of managing people is a nonsubject." Worse, Grove goes on to report that when he pointed that out to a business school dean, the dean responded, "We tend to think that trying to teach students that [how to manage people] in the classroom is like trying to teach animal trainers with stuffed animals." Grove goes on to remark that that kind of attitude is like the CEO of an airline saying, "Why use a pilot simulator to teach people to fly? Why not have them go out and crash planes? It's inane." A Wharton graduate said, according to *Business Week*, that "he was taught that 'every human being is only a factor of production' and 'every business a nugget of value to be bought, sold, or closed down based on return on investment alone.' "[39] In our own consulting practice which specializes in leadership, human performance, motivation, management, and compensation practices, we screen as many as 250 candidates with graduate degrees to fill a single consulting position. Rarely are we able to find an M.B.A. with the requisite skills, including M.B.A.'s from the supposedly "best" American business schools.

The failure of American business schools to prepare their students for leadership roles is so bad that a number of major companies such as Westinghouse, USX, and Marriott Corporation had abandoned or were no longer actively recruiting M.B.A.'s. And 858 of *Business Week's* Top 1000 did no significant recruiting at business schools at all. Responding to the American business rejection of their graduates, some business schools are attempting to change. For example, Stanford had added fourteen elective courses in international business, the Sloan School was engaged in a joint program with MIT to provide its students access to courses on manufacturing and operations, Duke was adding courses in information technology, and Wharton was adding courses in government relations, organizational behavior, and communications.[40] Some business schools were adding what they called the "soft-side" or "people" courses. However, these tended to specialize in the outmoded "touchy-feely." Students signed up for courses where they would practice conversing only with the word "Oh" (to learn something about nonverbal communication), or participate in role-playing games, or practice résumé writing, or participate in survival trips. One business school even installed a mandatory six-week "finishing school" course in wine-tasting and entertaining.[41]

If the aspiring business leader of tomorrow can't look to American business schools to provide the training he or she needs to succeed, then what should he or she look for? Perhaps a place to start is for him or her to understand the skills he or she will require. *Fortune* magazine spelled out some of these in a 1989 article. It said the leader of the future will "speak a foreign language fluently and be intimate with a foreign culture, Japanese preferred in both cases. He (or she, in the case of one-third of the graduates) should have a strong grasp of ethics, be sensitive to others' feelings, know how to negotiate, have polished business manners, speak and write well, and understand the uses of technology. The new [leader] should also be familiar with the political, economic and regulatory situations in the U.S. and Europe, and have vision, an entrepreneurial spirit, leadership qualities, and a capacity to innovate."[42]

We think that's a good place to start. But getting such an education might require that the future leader pursue a significantly different type of higher education. Maybe we can take instruction from Colin Balydon of Dartmouth College's Amos Tuck School of Business. He had the following advice for parents wishing to prepare their child to take over the family business or any business: "After high school," said Balydon, "steer the youngster into a broad college liberal arts program—a bachelor of arts degree in the major he chooses." Blaydon recommended psychology, economics, political science, or the humanities. What about basic business courses such as accounting, finance, management science, or marketing? Have the student take them as electives, said Balydon. Once the kid graduates, said Balydon, he or she should spend a few years working as an apprentice in the real world of business. Then, and only then, does he or she go back for a M.B.A., which should focus on specific business skills.[43]

We would agree with Balydon, but go one step further. Balydon recommends a liberal arts undergraduate degree and then a graduate degree in business. We would stick with the liberal arts undergraduate degree, but we are not sure that we would recommend a graduate degree in business. At least until there are significant changes in graduate business schools, we would recommend that the future leader explore alternatives. In addition to a few elective courses in business, the future leader might be better advised to look for his or her leadership training in the humanities. The skills required of the *Workplace 2000* leader, in our opinion, may be found among the historians, philosophers, and political scientists, and perhaps even the psychologists, sociologists, and English majors with an extensive grounding in the great literature. We would look for any discipline that can provide our future leader with a thorough awareness of the sweep of humanity—its history, culture, longings, beliefs, failures and foibles, hopes and dreams—from ancient to modern times. In our opinion, it is only by developing a great understanding for and appreciation of the "human condition" that anyone can hope to lead.

Leading—even working—in the workplace of tomorrow will require much skill from all of us. We can't look to others for our salvation to provide us with the skills we require. We must, in the final analysis, do it ourselves—each of us individually.

CHAPTER 10

The Demands and Expectations of the New Workplace

The traditional American workplace was, for most Americans, one of limited demands. Employees were expected to come to work on time and do what they were told. The work might be physically demanding and even stressful at times, particularly if there were a flood of orders or customers. Yet there were minimum demands and minimum expectations. And it was the minimum that employees had to meet. Perform at the minimum and you were assured of keeping your job. The company couldn't ask for more than that—"a fair day's work for a fair day's pay." That was it. Sure, managers and supervisors occasionally railed about quality, or service to customers, or getting things done fast and on time. But those things weren't employee responsibilities. Not really. The "quality assurance" people took care of quality. Managers, supervisors, engineers, or planners set the work schedule and "pace" at which work was performed. Getting things done fast and on time was their job, not the workers. "Customer service" was usually handled by "customer service representatives." They took customer complaints and tried to fix what was wrong. Of course, there were standards for all of these things. But they were somebody else's standards, and anyway, they were usually pretty low. In general, everybody's expectations were pretty low. We did "the best we could." Not anymore. In *Workplace 2000*, expectations for speed, quality, serving customers, and generally doing a whole lot more with a whole lot less will increase a hundredfold—perhaps a thousandfold. And these increased expectations will fall directly on American workers. There will be new techniques and tools to help American workers meet these expectations. But the responsibility will be theirs.

The Increased Demand for Speed

One of the first and foremost expectations of *Workplace 2000* will be "get the job done—now!" Speed in designing products, manufacturing, and delivering services will be critical for three reasons. First, consumers demand it. Barbra Feogom of Grey Advertising's Strategic Services has said: "Time will be the currency of the Nineties."[1] No longer will consumers wait for weeks or months for product orders to be filled or wait in line for services to be delivered. Instead, they will search out those manufacturers and service deliverers who can meet their needs fastest. By the close of the 1980s, we had already conditioned the consumer to expect speed. For example, "pizzas should be delivered in thirty minutes"—preferably less. A second reason speed will be critical is that being fast has significant strategic advantages for most companies. For example, in new product development, the company with the ability to get to the market first with a new or redesigned product reaps enormous benefits. Companies with the newest product or newest technological innovation can often charge more and leave their competitors having to reduce prices on what is now "outdated" technology. Also, when development time is shortened, the final product is more likely to reflect consumer preferences (the marketing forecast is more accurate since the projection is not years into the future, but only a few months). And companies that can develop new products quickly can capture a market niche since they get there with a product to fill a genuine need sooner than anyone else. Internally, rapid product development helps because the developers get more experience (go through the product development cycle more often than their counterparts in a competing firm). Also, when the product is developed and brought to the market fast, fewer changes have to be made in the product design during the development process. Long development cycles, in contrast, often mean that significant revisions are necessary as the product is under development because the original product concept (or idea) has changed. Making these changes to stay in tune with the constantly changing market further complicates and lengthens the development process.[2]

The third reason speed will be critical in *Workplace 2000* is that the stakes have changed. Recognizing that speed does have strategic advantages and that fast response is something customers not only want but demand, in the 1980s many companies—foreign and domestic—placed great emphasis on shortening the time it took for them to design products, manufacture products, and deliver services. Their success increases the "time competition" for everyone. We have already mentioned the conditioning of the consumer to expect quick pizza delivery. Once one company provides such fast response and the consumer begins to expect it as a minimum acceptable standard, all other manufacturers or service providers in competition with the "time leader" have to at least match (and preferably better) the leader's performance. That is, they do if they want to remain competitive. In the 1980s, the time stakes were being raised enormously. As the 1980s came to an end, many companies were significantly shortening the time it took for them to develop new products and bring them to the marketplace. For example:

AT&T had cut development time for phones from 2 years to 1 year.

Navistar had cut development time for trucks from 5 years to 2.5 years.

Hewlett-Packard had cut development time for computer printers from 4.5 years to 22 months.

IBM had cut development time for its mainframes from 3 years to 18 months, partially as a result of using new simulation techniques that allowed it to cut the number of prototypes for new integrated circuits from three to two, thereby saving 70 percent in development time.

Honda and Toyota were taking new cars from concept to market in 3 years compared to 4 years for Ford and 5 for General Motors. Most automakers were working on finding ways to reduce the time to 1 year in the 1990s.[3]

In manufacturing and service delivery, companies were also drastically shortening the time it took to make products and process orders. For example:

The Limited could get new fashions from design into its thirty-two hundred stores in as little as 60 days compared to months for other retailers. From point of sales computers, The Limited collected data on sales daily and issued reorders to its plants worldwide that could fill those orders within 48 hours. Leslie Wexner, chairman of The Limited, warned: "That's not fast enough for the Nineties."

GE could deliver circuit breaker boxes in 3 days compared to 3 weeks for other suppliers.

Motorola could deliver pagers in 2 hours compared to 3 weeks.

Hewlett-Packard could deliver electronic testing equipment in 5 days compared to 4 weeks.

Brunswick could deliver fishing reels in 1 week compared to 3 weeks.[4]

Efforts by Brunswick, IBM, The Limited, AT&T, and all the others have raised consumer expectations. One consequence of this will be increased demands on all American workers to "move quick" and meet or beat ever shortening deadlines for work performance. Americans will find that they will have little time to relax or just coast through the day in the new workplace. Unavoidably, there will be increased pressure, stress, and tension. Americans will simply have to become accustomed to an even faster-paced work lifestyle. But it won't be just doing the same old things faster. New technology, methods, and work processes will help. Here are some of the more promising "time savers" being used in various American businesses as the '80s came to an end. We will see a greatly expanded use of these techniques in *Workplace 2000*.

Employee Problem-solving Teams Will Focus on Identifying and Eliminating "Time Wasters"

At Federal Express, Union Carbide, Grumman's Aircraft Systems Division, and a number of other companies, employee teams have been specifically assigned to find ways to speed service to customers. For example, a Federal Express team trimmed fifteen minutes off the time it took to load delivery vans in the morning by finding and eliminating downtime during the loading process. At Union Carbide, an employee team streamlined the manufacturing process at the company's Tonawanda, New York, plant and cut a month off the time it took to deliver a finished product while improving quality. At Grumman, a cross-functional team found a way to cut two months off the cycle time for developing a new business proposal for government contracts.[5] In the future, we will see more and more of these employee team efforts focused on cutting out wasted motion, revising work methods and procedures, and streamlining processes, all in an effort to save time. As these efforts succeed, even more pressure will be placed on employee teams to find additional time savings. It will be a never ending process of continuous improvement. What took months will have to be cut to weeks—weeks to days—days to hours—hours to minutes.

Products Will Be Designed for Quick Manufacture and Assembly

The search for ways to save time will be a key component of the design process. New products will, of course, have to be designed to meet or exceed customers' needs and desires. But they will also have to be designed for ease of manufacture and assembly.

As the decade came to an end, a number of companies were already finding ways to reduce manufacture and assembly time significantly. For example, NCR Corporation's 2760 electronic cash register was designed with 85 percent fewer parts than older models. Additionally, the entire cash register was designed so that it required no screws or bolts in assembly. As a result of these changes, the 2760 could be assembled in 25 percent of the time it took to assemble the company's previous low-end model, the 2160. Simplified designs were also helping IBM. It analyzed dot-matrix printers being produced for it in Japan and discovered that the printers could be produced with 65 percent fewer parts and a 90 percent reduction in assembly time.[6]

The concept being used by NCR and IBM to obtain this kind of time saving is called Design for Manufacturability and Assembly (DFMA). In addition to NCR and IBM, companies such as Ford, General Motors, Motorola, Whirlpool, and many others were also using DFMA as the 1980s came to an end. A key element of DFMA is computerized design analysis, which allows designers to identify opportunities to reduce the part count in new products and design products so that they are easy to assemble.

Credit for the concepts behind DFMA goes to Geoffrey Boothroyd who, as a professor of manufacturing engineering at the University of Salford in Britain in the 1970s, first started developing guidelines for creating products that would be easy to assemble. Boothroyd argued that not only would such simplified designs save time in assembly, but they would also reduce product manufacturing costs since it was known that 75 percent to 95 percent of the total cost of making a product was fixed once the design was completed. In spite of his arguments, British manufacturers in the '70s showed little or no interest in Boothroyd's ideas. Consequently, Boothroyd turned to the United States and in 1977 won a National Science Foundation research grant to develop his ideas further. Later, a number of major U.S. corporations such as Digital Equipment, GE, Westinghouse, Xerox and, in particular, Ford provided Boothroyd with additional funding. The result of

Boothroyd's efforts was the development of inexpensive software (some costing as little as fifteen hundred dollars) product designers could use to look at their designs and simplify the manufacturing and assembly process. The impact of using DFMA software has been impressive. For example, Texas Instruments used such software to examine a gun-sight component. As a result, it was able to identify ways to reduce the number of parts in the component by 75 percent, the number of assembly steps by 78 percent, the time for metal fabrication by 71 percent, and the time for assembly by 85 percent. In assembly time alone, what took over two hours before DFMA analysis was reduced to twenty minutes as a result of DFMA-suggested design changes. As we said, DFMA software is already being used by a number of U.S. corporations. We can expect greatly expanded use of such software in *Workplace 2000,* and we are likely to see a marriage of DFMA software with artificial intelligence resulting in a new software that will act as a kind of "real time" advisor monitoring the design process and making suggestions for improvements. The result of wider use of DFMA in its present and newer versions will be products that are much easier to assemble, which, of course, translates into significant time savings.[7]

New Technology Will Make the Design Process Faster and Easier

Instead of building clay models, in the 1980s engineers were beginning to use computer-generated math models in the design of new products, thus eliminating the need for time-consuming construction of various prototypes. In addition to saving time, the computer-generated models also simultaneously produce detailed specifications that allow manufacturing engineers to get a head start on developing tooling for production. We can expect a greatly expanded use of such technology in the future.

The Sequential Method of Product Design Will Be Replaced with a Method Using Design Teams with Representatives from Marketing, Engineering, Design, Manufacturing

In order to reduce development times, American companies in the late 1980s were totally revamping their approach to product development. Instead of the old sequential method where marketing handed off an idea to designers who fleshed out the concept and passed it on to engineers who built expensive prototypes that were then passed to manufacturing, companies were setting up task forces or "tiger teams" to get all the departments working together from the start to come up with a product that met the customers' needs but still could be manufactured efficiently.

The common practices being followed by companies to achieve rapid new product development in the late 1980s were:

1. Each new product was developed by a small, focused team with authority to take action and make decisions. The team was made up of representatives from all relevant functions, such as marketing, engineering, manufacturing.
2. The team was responsible for all phases of the development efforts: definition, design, manufacturing startup, and improvement.
3. Team members worked together throughout the development cycle in the same location and often in the same room during critical steps in the process so that there was ample opportunity for communication.
4. The team had access to the latest resources (market research, design tools, cost-estimating tools).
5. Senior management layers were kept to a minimum and devoted to providing the design team members with the resources, incentives, and work environment where they could be fast.[8]

Companies Will Seek Strategic Alliances with Their Suppliers to Shorten the Total Cycle Time for Manufacturing

In 1989, apparel makers, textile, and fiber firms began to co-operate in a Quick Response Program designed to reduce the fiber-to-retail cycle from sixty-six weeks to twenty-one weeks. Such coordinated efforts will help companies dependent on each other to cut out unnecessary delays, reduce inventories, and speed products into distribution channels. American workers will be spending less time waiting for raw material or component part deliveries because of the kind of partnership arrangements that are developed between manufacturers at different steps in the production chain.

The Demand for Perfection

In the 1970s and '80s, in many U.S. companies, 95 percent good quality was considered to be good enough or, at least, American plant managers, workers, and engineers argued that it was the "best they could be expected to do." There were numerous excuses for the 5 percent bad quality that got through to the customer—"antiquated equipment," "the natural variability in raw materials," "the impossibility of perfection when humans were involved." As a country, we expected at least a certain number of mistakes, errors, things made poorly, and things that didn't work. "Ninety-five percent good quality was really pretty good," we said, "all things considered. What more could we expect from people? After all, this wasn't a perfect world." In *Workplace 2000*, not only will 95 percent quality be considered *not good enough*, it will be considered a *disgrace* bordering on a criminal offense. In fact, 96 percent, 97 percent, 98 percent, and even 99 percent won't be considered good enough. What will be good enough? Try what Motorola calls Six Sigma Quality—99.9997 percent perfection—just 3.4 defects per million products or services. And even Six Sigma Quality may not be good enough. One hundred percent good products—perfection—may be necessary for a company to compete. And note we said compete, not be the leader. Also, we aren't just talking about what gets to the customer (certainly that had better be 100 percent good quality). We are talking about perfection or near perfection in every step of the production process. *Workplace 2000* will tolerate no mistakes, no errors, no waste anywhere in the production chain—zero, none period. That will be the expectation.

Why does the quality have to be that good? Why will workers of the future be expected to do absolutely everything right the first time and every time? Again, it is the consumer who sets the standard. And the consumer of the future will be the most demanding consumer in history—the adult baby-boomer. In the year 2000, baby-boomers will be thirty-six to fifty-four years old. They will head 43.5 percent of households and will account for 56 percent to 58 percent of purchases in most consumer categories. These consumers will be extremely experienced and demanding buyers seeking the best possible quality and total reliability. Laurel Cutler, vice chairman of FCB/Leber Katz, a New York advertising agency, and vice president for consumer affairs of Chrysler, says: "The consumer of the Nineties will be the smartest consumer we have ever dealt with. Despite the figures about our educational system, one thing we are training people to be is very smart consumers. And respecting the smarts of the consumer is going to create major changes. . . . The consumer is going to insist on making her own trade-offs, and what she's going to reject are manufacturers' compromises. The middle is going to be threatened—the mass, compromised, blended-down, offending-nobody brands. The consumer will want either the best, if it's in a category important to that consumer, or the cheapest of the good-enoughs. Pure value."[9]

Quality, really perfection, will be so important in the American workplace of the future that it will be drummed into employees' heads constantly. Companies will continuously run orientation and training (really indoctrination) programs designed to emphasize and reemphasize the necessity for world-class quality. Bonuses and incentive awards will all have a quality component. In fact, it will be hard to make gains under gain sharing, retain pay-for-knowledge supplements, or participate in profit sharing without demonstrating excellent quality and quality improvement. We are already seeing this emphasis. For example, 40 to 60 percent of Ford managers' bonuses are tied to contribution to quality improvement. And McDonald's regularly evaluates stores on quality, service, cleanliness, and value. Results determine a large portion of a store manager's compensation and a failing score can result in the manager being fired or losing the franchise.[10]

To ensure that employees have the necessary skills to produce excellent quality, *Workplace 2000* will require substantial investment in training programs. Most companies will greatly expand the training they offer their employees on the most popular quality-improvement technique of the 1980s, statistical process control (SPC). Those few American workers who have not been exposed to SPC, particularly in manufacturing, will almost certainly be trained in it during the next few years. However, many U.S. companies will go beyond SPC to train their employees in much more advanced quality improvement techniques. Chief among these will be something called design of experiments (DOE). There is very little doubt but that DOE will become one of the primary tools for quality improvement in American companies. This movement from SPC to DOE represents a further evolution of America's approach to quality.

To understand the evolution of America's quality crusade, we have to go back to the early 1980s. Until that time, most U.S. manufacturers used inspection and testing almost exclusively to improve quality. The entire focus of the effort was to detect and sort out defective products before they could be shipped to the customer. That approach to quality improvement (it was really quality control because there was little, if any, effort made to improve) was soundly rejected by most American companies in the 1980s. (Sadly, even by the late 1980s some companies still hadn't changed their approach.) The primary reason for the rejection of inspection and testing, aside from the point that it did nothing to improve quality, was that it drove up costs enormously. A number of "quality gurus" demonstrated in the '80s that inspection and testing (that is, sorting out bad quality) was extremely expensive. There were costs associated not only with inspection itself (salaries, test equipment), but also cost of rework, scrap, paying warranty claims, and so on. When bad quality was just inspected out and good quality wasn't built in, the cost of nonconformance (cost of doing things wrong in the first place) just went up and up.

By the late 1980s, U.S. manufacturers were moving rapidly away from inspection and testing and moving to adopt statistical process control as their primary approach. Under SPC, instead of inspecting and testing to detect problems, firms focused on training operators to monitor quality constantly, using what were called quality control charts to detect trends toward poor quality early on. Basically, quality control charts provided the operator with a graph showing the range of variation allowable in design characteristics (width, height, strength, weight) of a product or component of a product being produced at the operator's workstation. Periodically, samples of what was being produced were taken as the operator plotted these results on the chart. In some cases, sampling and plotting of results was fully automated. If the product got out of control (that is, the variation in product specifications exceeded the allowable limits on the chart) that signalled that something needed to be done. Assuming the operator couldn't identify the cause and correct it immediately the problem was turned over to an employee problem-solving group. Cause-and-effect diagrams and brainstorming were the primary methods most team members were taught to use to identify potential causes of out-of-control situations and develop plans of action to correct them. Brainstorming was an effective but primitive technique basically used to "loosen up" the group and generate as many creative ideas as possible about causes of a quality problem. Employees were encouraged by a trained facilitator to "freewheel," "build upon each other's ideas," and generate as many ideas as possible, some good and some very much off the wall. The hope was that given the volume of ideas generated (and brainstorming often produced hundreds of ideas), some good ideas for solving a particular problem would emerge. Cause-and-effect diagrams (also called fishbone charts) were similar to brainstorming, but provided more structure. Instead of just freewheeling, participants generated ideas about possible causes grouped into major categories

—usually "material," "machine," "method," and "man." Causes were plotted on a chart that resembled the skeletal remains of a fish, thus the name *fishbone chart*. Participants then tried to determine which of the various causes under the main categories might have the most impact on the desired result—the quality product. Action plans were then developed to correct deficiencies the group identified. Sometimes data were collected on check sheets or presented on Pareto diagrams (special bar charts designed to graphically show the major cause[s] of problems), but most of the time employees, supervisors, and managers barely analyzed the problem before jumping to brainstorming solutions.

While an improvement over inspection and testing, SPC was still relatively unsophisticated. In fact, by the late 1980s, Japanese firms that had used SPC since the 1950s had moved beyond SPC to the much more sophisticated design of experiments. Under DOE, the objective was not just to detect out-of-control situations and eliminate individual causes one at a time, but to use highly sophisticated statistical methods to isolate all the specific causes of variations in product specifications and simultaneously eliminate as much variation as possible.[11]

Design of experiments was practically unheard of in manufacturing in the United States before the 1980s. That fact in itself astounding. First of all, much of the food Americans put on their table was available as a direct result of design experiments. Agronomists in the U.S. had used the technique for years. In fact, the origin of the technique could be traced back to agricultural research by British scientists in the 1920s and '30s. Shortly afterward, American scientists began applying the technique in the United States. It was the "amber waves of grain." Basically, agricultural scientists used DOE to discover the right amounts of fertilizer, crop rotation, planting methods, and so on to produce the best yield. We then ignored the power of these same techniques in manufacturing for product quality. Although DOE was applied in the U.S. chemical industry, the first company to apply it, like too many other American

not in the U.S., but in Japan. Again, as we did so many times, we taught the Japanese how to beat us.

The Japanese engineer who learned how to use DOE to improve product quality in manufacturing was Genichi Taguchi. Taguchi taught Japanese manufacturers a relatively quick way to test a large number of possible causes of defects or variation in product quality and to statistically isolate those few that had the most impact on the quality of the end product. Instead of guessing and tinkering with a production process, changing this and that in the hope of finding something that would improve a process, with Taguchi's method engineers conducted systematic "experiments" designed to locate those few variables (for example, temperature, pressure, raw materials, cycle time) that had the most impact on the quality of the finished product. The Japanese enthusiastically embraced design of experiments, particularly after 1970.

As we noted, DOE was basically ignored in the United States until 1980. Even as the decade came to an end, it was being used only on a limited basis in contrast to its widespread use in Japan. Perhaps one of the reasons DOE didn't catch on in the United States until later is that the technique is rigorous and sophisticated. Practitioners of DOE use terms such as "fraction factorials," "orthogonal arrays," "analysis of variance," "evolutionary optimization," and others that the average American (and even the average American engineer) finds mystifying. Yet there is no reason why Americans can't learn to use DOE. In fact, given the power of DOE versus other methods of quality improvement such as statistical process control (as we will explain later), Americans will have to learn to use this more powerful technique to achieve the levels of quality (that is, "perfection") demanded for *Workplace 2000*. An American, Dorian Shainin, has developed a version of DOE that Keki Bhote, a senior corporate consultant on quality for Motorola and associate professor at the Illinois Institute of Technology, has called simpler, more logical, easier to implement, and more accurate than Taguchi's method. Because it is simpler, Shainin's method of DOE may, in fact, be the version Americans adopt in the future. In any case, most American companies will adopt some form of DOE (classical,

Taguchi, or Shainin), and American workers will have to become accustomed to thinking about quality improvement in a totally new way.

What is DOE? How does it differ from what Americans have learned about quality improvement in the past? How does DOE differ from SPC, the most popular quality technique of the '80s? A full technical explanation of DOE is beyond the scope of this book. We can say, however, that DOE differs from SPC in two key ways. Both are important in terms of the future direction of American efforts to improve product quality.

The first difference between SPC and DOE is philosophical. SPC tolerates a certain amount of variation in product characteristics. DOE doesn't. Traditionally, design specifications for a product specify a "target value" and a certain amount of allowable variation. For example, specifications a machine shop might receive for a bushing could be that the bushing is to be made to a length of 0.500 inches plus or minus 0.002 inches. In other words, a perfect bushing would be exactly 0.500 inches long, but bushings as short as 0.498 inches or as long as 0.502 inches would be acceptable. In the past in the U.S. and with SPC, we have assumed that the customer would be happy as long as the product was produced within the design specifications regardless of how narrowly it met the specifications. Thus, the customer, we assumed, didn't really care if all the bushings were 0.499 inches, 0.500 inches, or 0.501 inches. Here is where DOE differs sharply from SPC. Under DOE, any variation from the target—any bushing not measuring exactly 0.500 inches—is considered bad. In fact, Taguchi has developed a mathematical formula to calculate the cost of customer dissatisfaction that occurs as a result of any variation from the target value and has demonstrated that costs increase exponentially as a product's characteristics move away from the target even when they stay within design specifications. Under DOE, the objective is to eliminate all or as much variation as possible so that all products cluster very closely around the target value. DOE assumes that "customers want uniformity of product, consistency—not units that vary all over the map, even if they fall within specification."[12]

Beyond philosophical differences about the importance of eliminating variation, SPC and DOE differ in their approach to variance reduction and the correction of quality problems. Earlier we noted that under SPC, out-of-control situations (quality problems) were turned over to employee problem-solving groups for resolution. These groups used a variety of techniques such as brainstorming and cause-and-effect diagrams to identify potential causes of quality problems. Once various possible causes were identified, the group would make adjustments in the manufacturing process hoping to correct the problem. Essentially, these adjustments involved a lot of trial-and-error tinkering with the process. DOE differs from SPC in that its approach to identifying and correcting quality problems is much more systematic and sophisticated. The actual diagnostic and problem-solving tools used in DOE are highly technical, and it would take too long to explain them here. However, Thomas Charette, a manufacturing consultant, has proposed a simplified explanation of DOE—called the Popcorn Example—that illustrates the key features of the technique. Charette begins with the assumption that a family dispute has broken out over the best method for popping corn. He says: "Imagine you come home one evening to find your teenage son making popcorn with a hot air popcorn maker. . . . He's holding it at a backward angle because he's discovered that more kernels pop if it's held in that position. You say that's unlikely because the company had a highly trained, highly paid engineer design the machine and it's doubtful he'd overlook something like that. Your wife, who has heard the conversation, says there are more popped kernels because she recently switched from a generic brand of popcorn to gourmet. Besides, her mother taught her that more kernels pop when the popcorn is kept in the refrigerator."

Charette notes that the kitchen scenario concerning the best method for popping corn has many similarities to industrial problems. First, a process isn't working at optimum levels (some kernels aren't popping). Second, people have different opinions about how to improve the process (tilt the popper at an angle, use gourmet popping corn, or keep the corn at a certain temperature). Third, some possible solutions to the problem are being rejected outright without any effort to test their validity (the teenager's idea about tilting the popper is immediately dismissed as ridiculous). Fourth, the most plausible ideas are immediately accepted without any testing (it's probably the gourmet corn or keeping the corn in the refrigerator that makes the difference since those options appear most reasonable—they just make sense). Charette argues that this is what normally happens with SPC and other quality-improvement techniques. Instead of experimenting, managers, engineers, and workers jump to the most plausible conclusion and start tinkering. Often, several things are tried at once. As a result, even if the problem is corrected, no one knows exactly what worked or why. Consider, says Charette, how the popcorn problem might be addressed under a design of experiments approach.

"To solve the problem of the unpopped kernels, you have to design an experiment to determine the influence of the three variables on the yield. We have three variables (Angle, Brand, and Temperature) and two proposed levels or choices for each (i.e., "At Angle" vs. "Level"; "No Name" vs. "Premium" popping corn; "Cold" or "Warm"). This means that we have eight different ways to make popcorn: Angle-No Name-Cold; Angle-No Name-Warm; Angle-Premium-Cold; Angle-Premium-Warm; Level-No Name-Cold; Level-No Name-Warm; Level-Premium-Cold; and Level-Premium-Warm."

Essentially, DOE involves experimenting with these various ways of making popcorn to determine not only which method produces the greatest yield, but which of the variables (Angle, Brand, or Temperature) has the greatest impact on the desired result—increased yield. Charette points out that one method of conducting the experiments is to try all eight different methods. But, he says, that isn't necessary. DOE provides a technique for selecting which methods to try and thus minimizes the number of experiments that have to be conducted. (The actual selection techniques are technical and require some training to use properly; however, they can be taught.)

In Charette's popcorn experiment, he illustrates just four experiments that lead to a solution of the problem of increasing yield. The results of the experiments were as follows:

Run	Angle	Brand	Temperature	% Popped
1	At Angle	No Name	Cold	98%
2	At Angle	Premium	Warm	94%
3	Level	No name	Warm	78%
4	Level	Premium	Cold	74%

The results of the experiments (which Charette maintains were actually conducted by a variety of training classes) clearly show that the best yield was obtained with the popper set at an angle using cold, No Name popping corn. But there is more to DOE than just identifying the best method. DOE can help identify the contribution of each variable. For example, how much difference did it make to tilt the popper at an angle versus keeping the corn cold? Here are the results as reported by Charette:

Choice	Yield First Run	Yield Second Run	Total Yield	Average Yield	Difference
At Angle	98	94	192	96	
Level	78	74	152	76	20%
No Name	98	78	176	88	
Premium	94	74	172	84	4%
Cold	98	74	172	86	
Warm	94	78	172	86	0%

Obviously, the biggest difference occurs with changes in the tilt of the popper. There is only a 4 percent gain in yield when the brand of popping corn is changed and no gain from keeping the corn cold. Charette notes: "This experiment shows the strength of experimental designs. It took just four runs to learn how to improve a product quality characteristic—how to improve the number of popped kernels. There also is a cost and investment benefit. You don't have to spend money for a premium brand or on refrigeration."[13]

DOE represents a significant advance over SPC and other quality-improvement techniques. By using DOE, American companies can quickly (often, with just a few experiments) identify the major variables contributing to product quality. Not only that, but companies can distinguish between variables that are of major importance versus those that make only a minor (or perhaps no) contribution to the quality of the end product. In the past, we have assumed that the only way to improve overall product quality was to tighten all specifications for materials, temperature, cycle time, and so on. We treated all of these variables as equally important. With DOE, however, we can sort out the important from the less important. Often, as a result of DOE experiments, some specifications must be tightened. For example, we might determine that in a pressing operation the pressure setting is critical and we need more precise pressure gauges and control devices. Yet at the same time, we might determine that there is little, if any, difference between the performance characteristics of two alternative materials used during the pressing operation. Cheaper material might work equally well provided the pressing setting is held to a tight tolerance. Obviously, the possibilities for cost savings in such a situation are enormous. We not only produce a better-quality product, but we significantly reduce unit cost for the product by being able to use less-expensive materials.

DOE, as we have said, is a tremendous step forward. It will help us come closer to producing products that very closely (if not exactly) match their design—batch after batch. But how do we know that the design is what the customer wants? In the 1980s, we learned that the customer defined quality. It didn't make any difference how good we thought the product was; if the customer didn't think it was good (that is, represented true value to him or her), the product wasn't, by definition, acceptable. Therefore, in the future, expectations for quality will not be just to produce products that "meet specs," but rather products that meet or exceed customer needs and expectations. To help us do that, another quality improvement tool will gain prominence in *Workplace 2000*. It is called quality function development.

Quality function deployment (QFD) was used by Ford in its Taurus/Sable program in the mid-1980s. It has also been used at Digital Equipment, Black & Decker, and others. Toyota and other Japanese manufacturers use the process. Many that use QFD won't discuss it because they consider it an important competitive weapon. Those who do discuss the technique say it reduces engineering changes by 30 to 50 percent; shortens design cycles by 30 to 50 percent; reduces start-up costs by 20 to 60 percent; and reduces warranty claims by 20 to 50 percent. Perhaps most importantly, QFD ensures that a product's design matches customer requirements. The main tool of QFD is what is called a house of quality—a planning matrix that provides a record of customer requirements, competitive analysis, and technical specifications for meeting customer requirements. The QFD process is iterative and dynamic and carried out by a six- to eight-member multi-functional team consisting of representatives from areas such as marketing, design, engineering, manufacturing engineering, quality, purchasing, and accounting. The team starts by compiling a list of what the customer wants in the product in the customer's own words. The "wants" are then translated into technical language—what the "wants" mean in terms of technical requirements. Also, "wants" are weighted according to customer preference (how important is it to the customer?). Then technical people must evaluate the competition in terms of how successful it is in meeting the customer's requirements. Once this first step (product planning) is completed, those elements that are new, different, and difficult become key elements in the second step—design planning. The results of design planning become input to process planning. And the results from process planning become input to process control planning. Primarily, QFD is a planning, communication, and documentation system that seeks to ensure that customer requirements are translated into technical specifications and that there is a record of what is being done, why, and the trade-offs.[14]

The New Expectations for Serving Customers

The way we treated customers in the 1970s and '80s was awful, bordering on criminal. Delivery and salespeople didn't show up when they said they would. Americans waited hours in check-out lines while other registers were closed and clerks who could have opened those registers talked on the phone to their friends. Our requests for help were met with a blank stare and "It's not my department" or "I don't know." American companies didn't listen to their customers and acted as if they didn't care what their customers thought, felt, or experienced. The attitude of too many employees was, "This would be a great business if it weren't for all the damned customers."

Michael and Timothy Mescon, business professors at Georgia State University and Salisbury State University respectively, provided a perfect story of 1980s "customer service." The story involved a customer's first call for assistance to her emergency road service organization after fifteen years of paying annual dues for herself and her family. One day, her two-year old Ford Escort wouldn't start. "No problem," she thinks, "I'll just call my service." In summary, here is how the Mescons described her experience:

12:30 P.M. First call for emergency assistance.

WOMAN: "My 1987 Ford Escort won't start. I believe the battery is dead."

CLERK: "How do you spell Escort?"

WOMAN: "E.S.C.O.R.T."

CLERK: "What kind of vehicle do you have?"

WOMAN: "It's a 1987 Ford Escort."

CLERK: "What year?"

After a few more such questions, the clerk finally promises that help is on its way.

2:20 P.M. No help has arrived. The woman calls the service again, identifies herself, describes the problem, and informs the clerk (a different one from the one before) that she had called at 12:30.

CLERK: "We've received eight hundred calls in the last hour since the thunderstorms started."

WOMAN: "I called an hour before the rains began."

CLERK: "Oh well, then we had eighty calls that hour."

The woman provides all the information—her name, make of car, problem, service number—again, just as she had done at 12:30.

CLERK: "I can't find you in the computer. Did you use the same member number when you called before?"

WOMAN: "Look, I'm using my real name and my real number. Send help!"

CLERK: "What kind of car do you own?"

WOMAN: "It's a 1987 Ford Escort with a tired battery!"

CLERK: "You need towing, right?"

WOMAN: "Wrong, all I need is the battery charged."

CLERK: "Okay, that sounds easy enough. What year is your car?"

After a few more questions, the woman is assured by the clerk that she will get "priority" service.

Fifty minutes later a tow truck arrives.

DRIVER: "Lady, where do you want the car towed?"

WOMAN: "I don't need a tow. I just need a jump start."

The driver reluctantly jump starts the car. The woman drives to a service station, buys a battery, has it installed, and returns home. Then the phone rings: "Hello," the caller says, "this is Shirley with the emergency service. I understand you need a tow truck."[15]

The Mescon story is funny. But it is also tragic because it is all too real.

As the '80s came to an end, it was clear that American consumers were fed up with the way they had been treated. They were voting with their wallets and sending a clear message concerning what they wanted (no, correct that, demanded). "Give me the service I demand," said the American consumer, "or, I'll go elsewhere." What did American consumers want? Their desires fell into four distinct categories:

Reliability/dependability. "Do what you say you're going to do," our customers told us. "If you say the package will be there overnight, get it there overnight." "If you say the service man will be there at 10:00, don't have him show up at 11:00 or 12:00."

Responsiveness/fast delivery. "I want what I want when I want it," said our customers. "I don't want to have to wait. I don't want to have to stand in lines. I don't want to have to come back next week or next month because 'you think it might be in by then.' Give me what I want *now* or I'll go elsewhere."

Quality/accuracy. "If you are going to do something for me," said our customers, "the least you can do is do it right." "Don't make me have to complain or come back for you to do something over because you didn't do it right the first time. I don't have time for that."

Commitment/caring. "Show me you care. Don't treat me like a number. Don't treat me like you hate to see me coming. Appreciate me and empathize with my needs, my cares and my concerns," customers told us. "Accommodate me. Don't make me feel like a number or make me adjust my life (or even my mood) to accommodate your company or your employees."[16]

In the 1980s, American companies began to respond to customer concerns about poor service by implementing a variety of "service improvement" programs and making promises to consumers to improve. For example:

- Harris/3M implemented what it called Customer Vision to encourage every level of business to see the company through the customer's eyes. It also made the Harris/3M Promise—98 percent up-time on copiers or refund of money while a copier was down, free loaner if a copier was out of service for more than eight hours, and a toll-free after-hours help line to assist customers in minor emergencies.

- Hertz provided an expanded range of services for its customers such as a computer profile of customers to speed rentals and "business centers" at the busiest airports. These business centers provided Hertz customers with access to telephones, facsimile machines, overnight courier service, information on hotels and restaurants, direct lines to ticket offices for sporting and cultural events, flight monitors, computerized driving directions, and instant return (hand-held computers that calculate rental bills, print receipts and let renters check in at the car without having to go to a Hertz counter).

- Budget Rent-a-Car implemented its "Blueprint for Quality" program. Under this program, teams were sent from one location to another to evaluate service quality using a "blueprint for quality" form. The visiting team conducted a two-day assessment of all aspects of service including facility appearance, employee appearance, telephone techniques, service at the time of rental or return, and complaint handling.[17]

- In the late 1980s, IBM discovered that its customers wanted a lot more than just newer, faster, and more reliable equipment; they wanted to help in solving their specific business problems. John F. Akers, chairman of IBM, described the realization IBM came to in this way: "When we began regularly sitting down with our customers on a large scale, we learned that they expected us to be not simply a supplier but a genuine partner in their businesses. . . . It became clear that our competitors were sharing their product plans and future directions much more aggressively and eagerly than we were. . . . [W]e weren't communicating with our customers as much as we should. They didn't have a clear idea of what was going to be coming from IBM, and we didn't use their perspective as well as we should in bending and shaping our development efforts." In response to that realization, IBM moved 21,500 employees out of areas like manufacturing, development, and administration and into marketing and programming. An additional 11,800 IBM employees were reassigned as field sales people and systems engineers to act primarily as technical consultants to customers.[18]

- Merck, rated the number one drug company for service by pharmacists and doctors, kept that rating by emphasizing training. It put new salespeople through intensive training, including ten weeks of basic medical training, three weeks training on Merck products, six months on trial making field presentations along with district managers, and finally, three weeks at company headquarters refining their presentation skills. Before going out on their own, new salespeople have eleven months of training. Then they must continue to attend regular medical classes conducted at Harvard, Johns Hopkins, and other universities.
- American Express implemented over 100 programs to recognize and reward employees for customer service.[19]
- Holiday Inn authorized its hotel staff to take a range of actions to satisfy an unhappy customer, including handing out gift certificates and eliminating the charge for a service. If the customer was still unhappy, hotel managers were given the authority to waive charges for the customer's night stay.
- Federal Express implemented a Golden Falcon award, which included a formal award program, official plaque, and ten shares of Federal Express common stock to recognize good service. Under the company's "Bravo Zulu" award, any manager in the company could give an employee up to $100 in cash or the equivalent for a free dinner or ticket to theater or sporting event immediately upon observing an instance of good service and file the cost on his or her expense report.
- American Express implemented a "Great Performers" award to recognize 30 to 35 employees nominated each month by other employees, bosses, or card members for their contribution to good service. Winners received $200 to $800. At the end of each year, grand-prize winners were chosen and received $4,000 in travelers' checks, round trip tickets to New York for wining and dining and to meet with the American Express president.[20]
- Procter & Gamble sent its new customer service repre-

sentatives to four or five weeks of classroom training to teach them how to solve customers' problems and diffuse anger.

- Motorola changed the compensation system of its communications section so that customer satisfaction as shown on mail and phone surveys was a factor in calculating every salesperson's bonus.
- Federal Express became obsessed with serving customers and went to extraordinary lengths to fix anything that went wrong. For example, when a Federal Express employee made a mistake and a Europe-bound package missed its plane, Federal Express dispatched a courier with the package on a commercial flight. Charles Hartness, managing director of human resource analysis and employee relations at Federal Express said: "In the end, the deal cost us a couple of thousand dollars rather than earning us a couple of hundred. . . . But what is important is that the customer will probably come back to us."[18]
- Domino's regional offices rated the corporate staff on the quality of service they provided. Bonuses for corporate staff members were based, in part, on these ratings. Domino's stores also rated distribution company employees on service and product quality. Monthly bonuses for distribution employees were made contingent on the results of these ratings. Domino's also paid ten thousand "mystery customers" to buy twelve pizzas throughout the year and evaluate quality and service. Store managers' compensation was based partly on these scores.[21]

All of these programs and promises were designed to improve service to customers. But we soon began to realize that service to customers required something much more than just a program and a promise. It required a certain kind of attitude. Customer service, we came to understand, was intimate—the direct customer/employee relationship. It also involved feelings and perceptions on the part of the customer. Unlike speed and quality, superior customer service was difficult to quantify and often even difficult to describe. In the final analysis, it was the way each employee viewed and related to each customer. Perhaps the best way to explain what we mean by a superior customer attitude is to relate two stories told by Stew Leonard, owner and operator of Stew Leonard's, a grocery store in Connecticut nationally recognized for superior service to customers. Leonard tells the following story of what happened one day when one of his customers complained. He says:

Tom Leonard is in charge of what will someday be our second store: a farmer's market in a circus tent in Danbury, Connecticut. He has a customer suggestion box which he often opens two or three times a day. In so doing, he's taking our customers' pulse.

At about 6:00 p.m. one evening, Tom found a note that had been written only half an hour earlier: "I'm upset. I made a special stop on my way home from work to buy chicken breasts for dinner, but you're sold out and now I'll have to eat a TV dinner instead." As Tom was reading the note, Les Slater, our Norwalk front end manager who lives in Danbury, stopped by on his way home to say hello. Just then, the big white Perdue chicken truck backed into the loading dock to make a delivery. Tom and Les got an idea. Five minutes later, Les was in his car taking a little detour.

You can imagine the smile on the customer's face when he answered the door at 6:20 p.m. and found Les Slater with a complimentary two-pound package of fresh Perdue chicken breasts—just in time for supper!

Leonard's second story involves an incident that occurs frequently in American business. In this case, an "unreasonable" customer was refusing to follow store rules and procedures. Here, in Leonard's words, is what happened:

Marion Murphy works at our customer service desk. A very unreasonable customer came up to her and slammed two cases of empty soda cans on the counter and said, "Look, lady, I'm not going to put these 24 cans in those automatic can-refund machines of yours, one at a time. I want my money back . . . now!"

Marion replied, "Sir, this is not the can return department, and we don't take cans here. But I can see that you're in a hurry, so let me give you your refund out of my pocketbook. I'll put the cans in the machine on my lunch hour and get reimbursed."

The customer's expression changed and he said, "You'd do that?" Marion answered, "It's no problem, that's my job—to create happy customers." The man blushed and said, "I can't let you do that for me. If you've got the time, I've got the time."[22]

Tom Leonard, Les Slater, and Marion Murphy were extraordinary employees for an American company in the 1980s. They responded to customers with a superior customer attitude. Leonard, Slater, and Murphy won't be extraordinary in *Workplace 2000*. All American workers will be expected to exhibit such a attitude. The expectation will be "treat customers well or don't work here."

Making Do With Less of Everything

Writing in 1990, Reed M. Powell, a professor at California State Polytechnic University, said that a key concept for competitiveness in the 1990s would be "doing more with less." He noted that when he broached that idea to managers and workers in the U.S., he had found that it was "one way to become unpopular quickly."[23] Well, at the risk of becoming unpopular quickly, we must say that we agree with Powell. "Doing more with less" will most likely be a key to the survival of American businesses in the decades ahead.

In truth, we have been lucky in the United States for a very long time. With few, relatively short-lived exceptions, we haven't had to live with scarcity. We have enjoyed an abundance of natural resources, an abundance of time, an abundance of customers for our products and services, and often, an abundance of profits that, if we were honest about it, weren't that hard to make. We could, as a nation, afford to waste a lot of things—time, resources, money, space. If we made bad quality, we could just scrap the bad or rework it. If we overproduced, we could just throw the excess away or stack it in inventory. If we lost a customer, we weren't too concerned. We could always get another one. For employees, there wasn't too much need to be personally concerned about fixing things or solving problems. They would either go away or someone else would fix them—the manager, supervisor, engineer, or support staff.

The 1980s changed all of that for America. We woke up to discover that our abundant resources were being exhausted. The situation won't change in the years ahead. In fact, it will get worse. There will be even fewer resources than there are now—less time, less money, fewer managers and supervisors to make the decisions, less opportunity to make mistakes, less job security. Powell put it this way: "Our future lies in the adoption of a continuing-survival-mode philosophy." Such a prospect, when one first faces it, appears extremely negative. But it doesn't necessarily have to be viewed as negative. It can be viewed as an exciting challenge.

CHAPTER 11

Achieving World-Class Performance in Quality, Service, and Innovation

In our opening chapter, we noted that the changes in management and compensation practices that will lead to *Workplace 2000* weren't planned. American management did not set out in the 1970s or '80s to create a new workplace. All of the changes we have documented in this book—the flattening of the organization, the increased information sharing with employees, the new motivation and leadership practices, the new pay systems and the new team systems—were a response to a compelling need. American business had to change to survive. We had to fix our quality, customer service, and innovation problems. Luckily, the changes we implemented worked. We say "luckily" because they weren't implemented in a coordinated fashion. No one group or person sat down, thought through, and planned the kinds of changes necessary to impact quality, service, and innovation. We learned piecemeal through an experiment on improving quality here, an effort to improve service there, a desperate effort to speed up research and development somewhere else. Yet in spite of the fact that these efforts weren't coordinated, they worked together. As the 1980s came to an end, we were learning that there was a kind of synergy to these changes. Team systems not only helped us improve quality, but they could also help us to improve customer service and speed up new product development. Changes in pay systems helped teams to function better and provided powerful incentives for employees to be concerned about matters such as product quality, service to customers, and bringing new products and services on line faster and cheaper. At the beginning of the 1980s, Americans weren't sure it was possible for us to compete in a global marketplace. By the end of the decade, we had learned our lessons and were beginning to think perhaps we could compete, provided we were willing to make some fundamental changes. And we were beginning to make these changes. No longer were these just "experiments." We were creating a new workplace. Comprehensive—total—change was taking place. We had our success stories and our stories of companies— large and small—making a fundamental commitment to a new future. Harley-Davidson, Motorola, Sara Lee, and little-known Spencer Industries are good examples.

The Harley-Davidson Story

In 1973, Harley-Davidson had 75 percent of the super-heavy-weight motorcycle market in the United States. By 1983, it was barely hanging on to 25 percent or less of the market. Harley had fallen from grace and few people gave it a chance to survive. But it did. By the late 1980s, Harley had recovered. It had recaptured most of the market it had lost (primarily to the Japanese) in the late 1970s and early '80s. How did Harley save itself? By implementing many of the changes we will see in *Workplace 2000*.[1]

Poor quality was a major reason Harley was losing market share in the mid-1970s. At that time, half the motorcycles Harley produced had missing parts when they came off the production line. Dealers had to fix up the bikes just to sell them. Old-time Harley loyalists were willing to buy the bikes even if they had to modify them themselves. New buyers weren't. They bought the better-made, if less nostalgic, Japanese models. Harley's first step in the mid-'70s to fix its quality problems involved significantly increased quality control and inspection. That helped. Quality did improve. But costs shot up dramatically. With an emphasis on control and inspection, Harley could get a decent bike out of its production facility. But it was spending $1,000 extra per bike to get a $4,000 bike in good enough shape for its dealers to sell.

Harley also had a problem with its engines. The outdated engine design Harley was using resulted in bikes that leaked oil, vibrated, and couldn't compete with the high-performance, smooth-running Japanese bikes.

Initially, Harley saved itself by making cosmetic changes to its existing bikes. William G. Davidson, Harley's styling vice president and grandson of one of the company's founders, was able, as a result of his understanding of Harley's customers, to create a number of new models that had the look and feel of bikes Harley's customers were assembling themselves. Until Harley could come up with some really new designs and reengineer its engines, the company survived by creating new models from old components, decals, and paint. Since Harley couldn't make a new bike, it survived by redesigning what it had. At least the "new" Harley's "looked right" to the customer.

Harley was still having problems with manufacturing, however. Its quality still couldn't match the Japanese and its costs were too high. Finally, in the early 1980s, the company decided to scrap its old-time production system at its York, Pennsylvania, assembly plant in favor of a "just-in-time" system like the kind the Japanese used that would eliminate long production runs and mountains of spare parts that ran up inventory carrying cost. To implement its new system, Harley took the then unusual step of involving its employees in deciding how the changeover to the new system would be handled. Instead of having managers and engineers make all the decisions and announce them to workers, Harley managers spent several months discussing the desired changes with everyone. The company didn't move ahead until there was consensus among employees about what to do and how to do it. When the company did move ahead, instead of complaining about the inevitable changeover problems, employees cooperated with management to get the problems fixed.

Since employee involvement worked so well in helping the company make the transition to just-in-time, the company decided to involve employees in finding ways to fix its quality problems. Employees were taught statistical tools for monitoring and controlling their own quality, and plant managers and supervisors were trained to become team leaders. The result? Not only did quality improve (for example, reworks were cut 70 percent), but employee morale improved. Eventually, employee involvement, just-in-time, and statistical operator control became three components of what Harley began to call its productivity triad.

Harley's adoption of its productivity triad helped the company improve its quality and reduce its costs. As a result, Harley was able to eliminate much of the advantage the Japanese had in manufacturing. Then the company went further. It began to listen closely to its customers and it found a market niche in which neither the Japanese nor other manufacturers could compete. Peter Reid, author of *Well Made in America: Lessons from Harley-Davidson on Being the Best*, explained Harley's market niche strategy this way: "Since Japanese motorcycles are priced 25% under Harleys, the company stressed advantages that Japanese bikes didn't have—custom styling, American origin, and the mystique of a powerful American road machine. Japanese makers responded by developing virtual Harley clones, but Harley touted its mystique heavily in advertising. . . . Harley convinced the market that only it offered the real thing . . . that anything else was a cheap substitute. Ironically, Honda's lower prices were almost proof of this."[2]

To get close to its customers, Harley formed HOG (the Harley Owners Group). By 1989, HOG had one hundred thousand members and a bi-monthly newsletter. It also began to sponsor motorcycle events throughout the country, and Harley managers and their spouses participated in these events. Harley put its top managers in personal touch with its customers. Reid notes: "Harley-Davidson became an expert at this. Almost all executives ride motorcycles and mingle with customers at motorcycle events." As a result, says Reid, Harley was quick to get the reaction of customers to things it was doing and, since the feedback was direct, there was little distortion in the information. Consequently, Harley-Davidson managers learned "to separate unrealistic comments ("I want an engine twice as big at half the price") from feedback that can be translated into actual product changes ("I want traditional styling . . . and easier access to spark-plugs . . . and higher overall quality to keep the machine out of the repair shop").

Harley became an American success story because it was forced to undertake fundamental and lasting changes. Harley created for itself a "new workplace" and a new method of doing business. So did Motorola.

The Motorola Story

In the early to mid-1980s, Motorola was in trouble. The Japanese had begun dumping better-quality pagers and cellular phones on the U.S. market and, as a result, Motorola was rapidly losing market share in those product lines. Motorola's Semiconductor Products Sector was in similar, if not worse, trouble. In only a few years, Motorola had gone from being second in worldwide chip sales to being an also-ran behind NEC, Toshiba, Hitachi, and Texas Instruments.

Just five years later, Motorola was back. By 1989, Motorola was number one in semiconductor chip sales in the United States, the number three supplier in Southeast Asia (the fastest-growing chip market), and number four worldwide. The company was performing equally well in its cellular phone and communications businesses.

Much of Motorola's success came as a result of significant improvements in quality, cost containment, and efficiency. For example, production time (order to shipment) for two-way radios was cut from thirty to just three days. Cellular phone development (design to start of production) was cut from three years to fifteen months, and assembly time for portable cellular phones was cut from forty hours to as little as two hours. Product defects company-wide were cut from 3,000 per million units in 1983 to less than 200 per million in 1989. In 1988, because of such gains in performance, Motorola won America's Malcolm Baldridge National Quality Award.

How did Motorola make its comeback? The company fundamentally changed the way it did business. Here is just a partial list of some of the key changes:

1. Motorola spent billions of dollars for research and development, training, and capital improvements—19 percent of revenues in 1989 alone.

2. Once biased against products invented elsewhere, the company became heavily involved in R&D consortiums such as Sematech and developed strategic alliances with other chip makers in the U.S. and throughout the world. For example, in 1987, Motorola developed a close relationship with Toshiba, which enabled it to reenter the dynamic random-access memory (DRAM) chip market, the largest in the world, which Motorola had been forced out of in 1985.

3. To improve quality, the company set a goal of attaining "Six Sigma" quality—just 3.4 defects per million products. By 1989, it had reached that level of quality on simple products like calculators. By 1992, Motorola expects to be able to achieve "Six Sigma" on its other product lines.

4. To train its workers, Motorola launched an education drive to reach all of its 105,000 employees. Courses covered such topics as global competitiveness, risk taking, statistical process control, and techniques for reducing product cycle times. Motorola spent $60 million on education in 1989.

5. Bob Galvin, Motorola's chairman, began a series of visits to key customers in 1987 to gather information on customer reaction to Motorola products. He visited not with the top managers of these companies, but with their employees—the actual users of Motorola's products. These visits were so successful that Motorola adopted a policy that the CEO and all top executives would regularly make such visits, and a senior manager in each product group was appointed the "customer champion."

6. The function of quality-assurance employees throughout the company was changed from checking and con-

trolling the quality of work performed by Motorola employees to one of facilitating internal groups in interpreting customer needs.

7. As a service to its customers, Motorola began offering training to customer employees in advanced quality-improvement techniques and coaching its customers' employees in techniques for solving quality problems.

8. Internally, Motorola changed its definition of "customer" to "next operation as customer" (NOAC). Each work group became a "process owner" and each "process owner" had an internal "supplier" (the previous "process owner") and internal "customer" (the next "process owner"). "Process owners" were required to serve their "customers" to the fullest—timeliness, accuracy, completeness, and lowest cost.

9. Each support group and white-collar operation within Motorola was required to complete the following six steps as its own version of the Six Sigma process:

   a. Define the major functions and services it performed
   b. Identify its internal "customers" and "suppliers"
   c. Identify its customer's requirements and develop measures of its customers satisfaction
   d. Identify the requirements and measurement criteria its "supplier" must meet
   e. Flow chart its service delivery process
   f. Continuously improve the effectiveness, quality, cycle time, and cost of its service process

10. To ensure that employees were focused on quality and customer satisfaction, Motorola

    a. Reduced managerial and supervisory layers and increased spans of control
    b. Limited each organization's size to encourage teamwork and employee ownership
    c. Integrated departments to break down artificial functional barriers
    d. Changed the headquarters organization's traditional role from one of policing to one of coaching

    e. Made quality the first order of business in every meeting

    f. Made quality the key component of performance reviews, compensation, and reward programs

11. To encourage employee involvement, Motorola established teams throughout the company to strive for quality improvement and cycle time reduction. Teams set short-term improvement goals and received bonuses for reaching these goals. To ensure they had the necessary skills, team members were trained in problem solving and quality-improvement techniques. In 1990, Motorola's goal was for each of its employees worldwide to participate in a minimum of forty hours of education and training.

In the space of half a decade, Motorola fundamentally changed the way it did business. By 1989, at a time when some Japanese were having a good time "bashing" American companies for being too slow or incompetent to ever improve, Motorola had become, in the words of *Business Week*, "the rival Japan respects."[3]

The Sara Lee Story

Harley-Davidson and Motorola undertook fundamental change out of desperation. For them, finding a new way to manage their businesses was, in many respects, a survival issue. They had little choice and little to lose by undertaking major change. But what about an American company that wasn't faced with impending disaster? Would an American corporation undertake major change in how the business was run at a time when it was positing record per-share profits? It would if the company was Sara Lee Corporation.

In 1989, Sara Lee (formerly Consolidated Foods Corporation) celebrated its fiftieth anniversary with a second year of record per-share earnings, over $11 billion dollars in sales, and over 100,000 employees. It was a highly successful worldwide manufacturer, marketer, and distributor of food and consumer packaged products such as Sara Lee bakery products, Jimmy Dean sausage, Kahn's wieners, Hanes underwear, and L'eggs pantyhose. Given its success, would Sara Lee undertake fundamental change in its traditions of management and compensation? Yes it would.

As the 1980s came to a close, Sara Lee Corporation, under the leadership of John H. Bryan, chairman and CEO and Paul Fulton, president, was undertaking many of the changes we have described in this book. In particular, they were taking bold steps to change compensation practices for Sara Lee employees and to involve employees in every aspect of the business through adoption of work-unit teams like those we described in Chapter 8. A key objective of these changes was to involve every Sara Lee employee in a concerted effort to implement a primary corporate strategy—become the low cost producer in all of the company's product categories. What did Sara Lee mean by "low cost producer"? Fulton defined the term this way in a speech to the company's Corporate Affairs Conference in April of 1989: "What do we mean by low cost producer? We mean, very simply, understanding what real quality is to [the] customer or consumer . . . and then . . . beating the competition on the total cost . . . direct and indirect . . . of producing and bringing to market [the] particular product or service." Fulton went on to say, "I am absolutely convinced that the leading companies of the 1990s will be low cost producers, and that the people throughout the ranks of those companies will share the entrepreneurial spirit of determination to do everything in the best, most productive, and highest quality way possible." To implement its "low cost" strategy and ensure that people throughout the company shared the "entrepreneurial spirit" Fulton thought was so important, Sara Lee launched a number of initiatives in the late 1980s. For example, Sara Lee established an employee stock ownership plan (ESOP) that would eventually bring employee ownership to over 10 percent of the company's outstanding shares. It established a year-end profit-sharing plan in each of its operating companies so that employees would receive additional pay if their operating company met its profit goals. It implemented a quality productivity improvement program that placed responsibility for process improvement in the hands of office and factory employees serving on improvement teams. And it developed Sara Lee/vendor teams where employees of Sara Lee worked directly with employees of companies supplying Sara Lee to improve the procurement process Sara Lee followed and the quality of raw materials coming from suppliers. At the individual plant level, Sara Lee began implementing gain-sharing programs and work-unit teams. It also began eliminating individual incentive programs, started offering lump sum payments instead of annual percentage increases in hourly rates for workers, and began experimenting with pay-for-knowledge systems in some of its plants. (See Chapters 5 and 6 of this book for an explanation of these changes in management and compensation practices.) As the 1980s ended, Sara Lee was methodically changing the work environment for its 100,000-plus employees to create the conditions of *Workplace 2000*.

The Spencer Industries Story

Sara Lee was a large American company undertaking major change to position itself for the future. But it wasn't only large American companies that were betting their future on new forms of management and compensation. Small American companies were also actively pursuing fundamental change. One good example was Spencer Industries in Dale, Indiana.

Incorporated in 1981 as Spencer Plastic Products Corporation, Spencer Industries produced thermoform plastic parts such as back panels for large television sets. By the late 1980s, it had become one of the largest producers of polystyrene camcorder cases in the United States. In its first three years of operation, the company lost over $2 million. Then, in 1985, Spencer's sales and profits began to grow rapidly. From 1986 to 1987, sales and number of employees more than doubled while profits shot up over 540 percent. In the midst of the chaos and stress that normally accompany such rapid growth, Spencer, under the leadership of its president and CEO Jim Edwards, totally changed its management and compensation practices. Within a period of six months starting in January 1988, Spencer sent each of its managers and supervisors to forty hours of formal training in team-leadership skills and implemented work-unit teams throughout the company. In 1989, Spencer implemented a 401K profit-sharing plan and an employee stock ownership plan funded entirely from company profits and with a target of 30 percent employee ownership. In 1990, the company added a gain-sharing program and the first of several planned pay-for-knowledge systems. What made Spencer unique was the speed and dedication with which it embraced and accomplished fundamental change. In recognition of its efforts, the company won three awards in 1989 for competitiveness and innovation, including the State of Indiana's first ever Global Competitiveness Award.

The Wal-Mart Story

Of all of the American companies we have mentioned in this book, the one company that perhaps most epitomizes *Workplace 2000* is Wal-Mart. In information sharing, leadership, employee motivation, the effective use of technology, customer service, quality, innovation, and most importantly, the ability to build a genuine partnership with employees, Wal-Mart undeniably comes closest to the ideal. Wal-Mart is an American company that exemplifies the best of what the future holds for American workers and the American economy.

Wal-Mart was founded in 1962 by Sam Walton, who was at that time the owner of several Ben Franklin franchises in Arkansas. Walton, who prefers to be called just Sam or, if you insist, Mr. Sam, was a brilliant merchandiser who recognized early on the potential for discount retail in the United States. Even more importantly, and perhaps the key to Wal-Mart's enormous success, was "Mr. Sam's" recognition of the importance of employees (whom Walton called "associates") in making a company successful. Between its founding in the early 1960s and 1990, Wal-Mart grew to become a retailing giant. During the 1980s, its annual sales increased at a compound rate of 25 percent per year. It grew from being a $1.2 billion discount chain to a $26 billion a year retail sales giant operating over fifteen hundred full-line discount stores, wholesale clubs, "SuperCenters," and hypermarkets. Wal-Mart's average annual return to investors from 1977 through 1987 was 46 percent. It was a major American success story; a stockholder's dream. The kind of company where a thousand-dollar investment grows to be worth nearly a half a million dollars in less than two decades.[4] Because of its extraordinary success, in 1989 Wal-Mart was designated "Retailer of the Decade" by Discount Store News.[5] Wal-Mart had become the retailer to emulate.

But what made Wal-Mart stand out? Why was it so successful? After all, it sold the same merchandise as hundreds of other retailers. John Failla, publisher of *Discount Store News*, explained Wal-Mart's success this way: "The answer is simple—developing people and recognizing the achievement of associates. This is as important a priority at Wal-Mart as anything else. This unusual commitment to people by management has resulted in 250,000 employees genuinely trying to do their best and all working in the same direction. From headquarters to the back room, every Wal-Mart associate possesses an obsessive desire to succeed. When this type of energy and drive is forged with the belief that every day they must try to do their job just a little bit better and their ultimate responsibility is to take care of the customer, the results speak for themselves." We agree. Certainly Wal-Mart did a lot of things well. For example, it was an early and very effective user of technology such as bar code scanners and satellite transmission to move information rapidly from store to headquarters and on to suppliers. It operated an extremely efficient distribution system that could quickly and economically restock stores. It offered customers a high level of service and "Every Day Low Prices." And it developed and maintained a strong, demanding, but positive relationship with its suppliers. Wal-Mart did all of these things well and they all contributed to the company's success. But what Wal-Mart did best was build a partnership with its employees, or rather, in Wal-Mart's terms, its "associates," based upon three basic tenets laid down by Mr. Sam:

1. Treat employees as partners. Share with them both the good news and bad so they will strive to excel. And allow them to share in the rewards of their achievements.

2. Encourage employees to always challenge the obvious. The road to success includes failing, which is part of the learning process, not a personal or corporate defect or shortcoming.
3. Involve associates at all levels in the total decision-making process. Managers should share ideas with associates and solicit ideas from them. Wal-Mart employees aren't just asked or allowed to get involved. They are required to get involved.

Having such tenets is one thing. Many American companies proclaimed such beliefs. What made Wal-Mart different is that it actually lived its beliefs. The tenets weren't just words.

Wal-Mart executives didn't proclaim a partnership with employees and then hide in headquarters in plush executive suites behind locked doors. Wal-Mart's headquarters was in Bentonville, Arkansas. But there were no fancy trappings in Bentonville—no executive suites, no army of secretaries and assistants, no hushed and carpeted offices.[6] *Fortune* magazine described the "headquarters amenities" for Wal-Mart's executives this way: "Glass [Wal-Mart's CEO] . . . drives a Mercury station wagon and occupies a small, plain office equal in size to those of other senior officers. Sam's [Sam Walton's] office, with the same cheap paneling, is only slightly bigger, and all are about what you would expect to find at the regional depot of some truck line."[7]

There was nothing elaborate or special about Wal-Mart's executive offices. Of course that didn't matter very much. After all, the company's executives rarely spent an entire week there. Most days, they were out visiting Wal-Mart stores, talking to associates and customers, and checking out what their competition was doing. When they weren't talking directly with their associates during one of their visits to Wal-Mart stores, Wal-Mart executives, including Mr. Sam himself, were staying in close touch via satellite. *Fortune* described one of the satellite transmissions in a 1989 story:

In November [1988], with the Christmas season approaching, Wal-Mart associates across the country arrived at work to find Sam—wearing his ubiquitous mesh ball cap—waiting to "visit with" them by satellite on a subject he said he was "totally obsessed with": aggressive hospitality to the customers. This isn't just a sales pitch; it's a self-improvement video that Dale Carnegie would have envied.

Sam rambles on about the hunting he's been doing and demonstrates his bird dog whistle, then gets down to his idea. "I don't think any other retail company in the world could do what I'm going to propose to you," he says. "It's simple. It won't cost us anything. And I believe it would just work magic, absolute magic on our customers, and our sales would escalate, and I think we'd just shoot past our K-Mart friends in a year or two and probably Sears as well." He proposes that whenever customers approach, the associates should look them in the eye, greet them, and ask to help. Sam understands that some associates are shy, but if they do what he suggests, "it would, I'm sure, help you become a leader, it would help your personality develop, you would become more outgoing, and in time you might become manager of that store, you might become department manager, or whatever you choose to be in the company. . . . It will do wonders for you." He guarantees it.

Then, just to make sure, Sam asks the associates to raise their right hands and execute a pledge, keeping in mind that "a promise we make is a promise we keep." The pledge: "From this day forward, I solemnly promise and declare that every customer that comes within ten feet of me, I will smile, look them in the eye, and greet them, so help me Sam."[8]

Executives staying in close touch with their employees was one thing that made Wal-Mart exceptional. But perhaps the thing that made Wal-Mart unique was that executives and managers in the company really practiced what Mr. Sam preached.

Mr. Sam proclaimed that a mistake or failure by an associate was okay—that failing was just a learning process. Wal-Mart executives and managers lived up to that tenet. Associates weren't fired for a mistake. They were just encouraged to find a way to learn from it, correct it, and turn it around in the company's favor. For example, in 1985, John Love, an assistant store manager of a Wal-Mart discount store in Oneonta, Alabama, placed an order for Moon Pies (a marshmallow sandwich made by Chattanooga Bakeries). By accident, Love ordered four to five times more Moon Pies than the store needed. It was a stupid mistake that could have gotten Love fired if he had worked for any of a number of other companies. Not at Wal-Mart. Love's boss just told him: "Use your imagination, be creative and figure out a way to sell it." Love did. He created the first World Championship Moon Pie Eating Contest and held it in the Wal-Mart store's parking lot. The contest and the promotion were so successful for the company that it is now held on an annual basis and draws thousands of spectators (and customers) to the Oneonta store from throughout Alabama and several nearby states.

Mr. Sam proclaimed that he wanted employee ideas and total involvement from employees. Wal-Mart managers and executives live up to that promise. For example, if a salesclerk, checker, or stockman got an idea for selling and promoting a particular item of merchandise, he was allowed to order it, stock it, and feature it as long as he could sell it. From the top down, everyone in Wal-Mart was encouraged to think like and act like a merchant and to continually come up with ideas to make the company better.

When Sam Walton talked about sharing the rewards of achievement, Wal-Mart, the company, backed up that promise with real cash. For example, in 1988, Wal-Mart paid out $170 million to store managers and employees in the form of incentive bonuses.[9]

And Wal-Mart really did share the good and bad news with everyone in the company—just as Mr. Sam said it should. Wal-Mart's associates saw information on costs, freight charges, profit margins, and so on—more information in more depth than most American companies share with their general managers.[10]

The Wal-Mart culture was, of course, demanding. Associates, as true partners, were expected to make a strong personal commitment to the company and to sacrifice some of their personal lives to be successful in the company. For example, it was not unusual for a Wal-Mart employee to put in a twelve-hour day and then attend a company-sponsored activity such as an exercise class or participate in a company promotional event such as the Moon Pie eating contest.[11] But after all, isn't that what being a partner is all about? It certainly is what the future American workplace will be all about.

American Resurgence

The 1990s will be a decade of American resurgence. We have little doubt about that. Harley-Davidson, Motorola, Sara Lee, little Spencer Industries, Wal-Mart, and thousands of other American companies are, even as we write this in the spring of 1990, leading the way to a new American workplace—a new and, we believe, better future for all Americans. That future won't come without the agony of change. And all aspects of that future won't be good. But on the whole, we are enormously optimistic. The new American workplace will certainly be challenging. But it will also be enormously rewarding.

As we enter the 1990s, America is coming out of a malaise that has gripped us for nearly two decades. We've passed the point of questioning whether we have what it takes for us to compete in a global marketplace. Now we know we can compete with anyone. We've finished denying that we weren't as good as we thought we were. We accept now that we did get sloppy—and yes, also lazy. We'll admit now that our expectations for quality, and customer satisfaction, and rapid innovation weren't as high as they should have been. We'll admit that we did get beaten and that our bludgeoning wasn't just because our opponents took us off guard or had some minor advantages. But we've been beaten before. We've lost battles and come back. Those who have forgotten that should visit Harley-Davidson, or Motorola, or one of Sara Lee's team plants, or little Spencer Industries, or go shopping at Wal-Mart. The Japanese and others who doubt what we can do should go and visit all of the other American companies we have mentioned throughout this book who are creating the new American workplace . . . No, we take that back. We don't want them to go. Let them be surprised.

Notes

1. The Future American Workplace

1. David Kearns, "Xerox: Satisfying Customer Needs with a New Culture," *Management Review* (February 1989): 61–63.
2. *Fortune* and Forum Corporation Study of Customer Expectations (1989).
3. Robert L. Desatnick, "Service: A CEO's Perspective," *Management Review* (October 1987): 41.
4. Richard Whiteley, "Beyond Customer Satisfaction Through Quality Improvement," *Fortune* Fourth Annual Quality Improvement Section (1989).
5. Desatnick, "CEO's Perspective," 41.
6. Karl Albrecht and Ron Zemke, *Service America: Doing Business in the New Economy* (Homewood, Ill.: Dow Jones Irwin, 1985), 6.
7. *Fortune* and Forum Corporation Study.
8. Bro Uttal, "Companies That Serve You Best," *Fortune* (December 7, 1987): 98.

9. Joseph T. Gorman, "We Can't Survive 'Business as Usual,'" *Commitment Plus* (July 1987): 5.

2. Future Structure and Culture

1. Patricia Sellers, "Why Bigger Is Badder at Sears," *Fortune* (December 5, 1988): 79.
2. Jeremy Main, "At Last, Software CEO's Can Really Use," *Fortune* (March 13, 1989): 77–83.
3. Paul M. Noaker, "Develop Your Own Expert Help," *Production* (March 1989): 82–86.
4. Rosabeth Moss Kanter, "The Contingent Job and The Post-Entrepreneurial Career," *Management Review* (April 1989): 22–28.
5. Harriet C. Johnson, "More Execs Strike Out on Their Own," *USA Today* (May 10, 1988): 1B.
6. Walter Kiechel III, "The Microbusiness Alternative," *Fortune* (October 24, 1988): 219–20.
7. Joel Kotkin, "Natural Partners: A New Source of Start-Up Financing," *Inc.* (June 1989): 68.
8. "Consumer-Product Giants Relying on 'Intrepreneurs' in New Ventures," *The Wall Street Journal* (April 22, 1988): 35.
9. Stuart Gaines, "America's Fastest Growing Companies," *Fortune* (May 23, 1988): 31–32.
10. Peter F. Drucker, "Playing in the Information-Based 'Orchestra,'" *The Wall Street Journal* (June 4, 1985): 32.
11. Robert Howard, "High Technology and the Reenchantment of the Work Place," *National Productivity Review* (Summer 1984): 257.
12. David L. Kirp and Douglas S. Rice, "Fast Forward—Styles of California Management," *Harvard Business Review* (January–February 1988): 79.
13. Robert Levering, *A Great Place to Work* (New York: Random House, 1988), 231.
14. "Who Survives," *Inc.* (July 1988): 22.

3. Future Information Sharing

1. Richard E. Kopelman, "Improving Productivity Through Objective Feedback: A Review of the Evidence," *National Productivity Review* (Winter 1982–83): 43–55.
2. John Miller, "Productivity's New Math," *Brief 67*, American Productivity and Quality Center (October 1988). Also Callie Berliner and James A. Brimson, eds., *Cost Management for Today's Advanced Manufacturing, the CAM-I Conceptual Design* (Boston: Harvard Business School Press, 1988).
3. Joseph H. Boyett and Henry P. Conn, "Developing White-Collar Performance Measures," *National Productivity Review* (Summer 1988): 209–18.
4. Obviously, the determination of target costs is a much more complex issue than suggested in this brief discussion. For more complete information on target cost and other new cost management issues, please refer to Berliner and Brimson, *Cost Management*.
5. Edwin A. Locke, "Toward a Theory of Task Motivation and Incentives," *Organizational Behavior and Performance* (May 1968): 157–89.
6. W. A. Shewhart, *Economic Control of Quality Manufactured Product* (New York: Van Nostrand, 1931).

4. Motivating Workers in *Workplace 2000*

1. Peter F. Drucker, *Management: Task, Responsibilities, Practices* (New York: Harper and Row, 1974), 235.
2. Eugene Louis Cass and Frederick G. Zimmer, *Man and Work in Society* (New York: Van Nostrand Reinhold, 1975), 278–306.
3. Victor H. Vroom, *Work and Motivation* (New York: John Wiley and Sons, 1964). Also Lyman W. Porter and Edward E. Lawler III, *Managerial Attitudes and Performance* (Homewood, Ill.: Richard D. Irwin and Dorsey Press, 1968).
4. Robert D. Nye, *What Is B. F. Skinner Really Saying?* (Englewood Cliffs, N.J.: Prentice-Hall, 1979).
5. "At Emery Air Freight: Positive Reinforcement Boosts Performance," *Organizational Dynamics* (Winter 1973):

41–50. Also Fred Luthans and Robert Kreitner, *Organizational Behavior Modification* (Glenview, Ill.: Scott Foresman, 1975), 67–68. Also Philip J. Hilts, *Behavior Mod* (New York: Harpers Magazine Press/Harper and Row, 1974), 90–101.

6. Patti Watts, "Preston and the Teamsters Keep on Trucking," *Management Review* (March 1988): 22–24.
7. Douglas McGregor, *The Human Side of Enterprise* (New York: McGraw-Hill, 1960), 33–48.
8. Howard, "High Technology and Reenchantment," 261.
9. Richard E. Walton, "From Control to Commitment in the Workplace," *Harvard Business Review* (March–April 1985): 77–84.
10. *Ibid*, 81.
11. Robert Stauffer, *Manufacturing Engineering* (July 1989): 3–37.
12. Anne M. Hayner, "Apple Power," *Manufacturing Engineering* (July 1989): 38.
13. Anne M. Hayner, "Trust and Openness at Digital," *Manufacturing Engineering* (July 1989): 41.
14. Robin P. Bergstrom, "The HP Way," *Manufacturing Engineering* (July 1989): 45.
15. Howard, "High Technology and Reenchantment," 262.

5. A Different Type of Pay

1. *The Wall Street Journal* (October 6, 1988): A4.
2. Thomas R. Horton, "Compensation in Changing Times," *Management Review* (July 1987): 3.
3. *The Wall Street Journal* (August 30, 1988): 1.
4. Carla O'Dell and Jerry McAdams, "The Revolution in Employee Rewards," *Management Review* (March 1987): 31–33.
5. "The End of An Era?" *Compensation Quarterly*, Hay Management Consultants (Fall 1987): 1–2.
6. Horton, "Changing Times," 3.
7. Edward E. Lawler III, "What's Wrong with Point-Factor Job Evaluation?" *Personnel* (January 1987): 38–43.
8. Sheldon Friedman, "The Compelling Case of Cutting Ex-

ecutive Compensation," *Management Review* (March 1988): 62–63.

9. Carl C. Hoffman, "Are Multiple-Pay Systems Worth the Risk?" *Managment Review* (July 1987): 39.

10. American Productivity and Quality Center, "People, Performance and Pay: Major Findings" (1987): 18.

11. Peter F. Drucker, "Worker's Hands Bound by Tradition," *The Wall Street Journal* (August 2, 1988): 20.

12. Nina Gupta, Douglas Jenkins, and William P. Curington, "Paying for Knowledge: Myths and Realities," *National Productivity Review* (Spring 1986): 110.

13. Corey Rosen, "Using ESOPs to Boost Corporate Performance," *Management Review* (March 1988): 30.

14. Carla O'Dell and C. Jackson Grayson, Jr., "Flex Your Pay Muscle," *Across the Board* (July–August 1988): 48.

6. Leadership in the New American Workplace

1. Kenneth Labich, "The Seven Keys to Business Leadership," *Fortune* (October 24, 1988): 58–62.

2. Jay A. Conger, *The Charismatic Leader: Behind the Mystique of Exceptional Leadership* (San Francisco: Jossey-Bass, 1989), 38–61.

3. Richard E. Byrd, "Corporate Leadership Skills: A New Synthesis," *Organizational Dynamics*, vol. 16, no. 1 (Summer 1987): 38.

4. "Being the Boss," *Inc.* (October 1989): 50.

5. Walter Kiechel III, "A Hard Look at Executive Vision," *Fortune* (October 23, 1989): 207–11.

6. Conger, *Charismatic Leader*, 61–93.

7. "Leadership Expert Ronald Heifetz," *Inc.* (October 1988): 37–48.

8. Walter Kiechel III, "The Workaholic Generation," *Fortune* (April 10, 1989): 50–62.

9. Kiechel, "Executive Vision," 207.

10. John Gardner, *On Leadership* (New York: Free Press, 1990), 29–165.

11. Burt Namus, *The Leader's Edge: The Seven Keys to Leadership in a Turbulent World* (Chicago: Contemporary Books, 1989), 82–84.

12. Chris Lee, "Can Leadership Be Taught?" *Training* (July 1989): 21.

7. Experiments in *Workplace 2000*

1. American Productivity and Quality Center, "Employee Involvement Board But Not Deep, Study Finds," *Letter*, vol. 9, no. 2 (August 1989): 3.

2. Robert H. Guest, "Quality of Work Life—Learning from Tarrytown," *Harvard Business Review* (July–August 1979): 76–87.

3. "High Commitment Work Teams: Office Teams at Kemper," *Commitment-Plus* (August–September 1986): 2–3.

4. Gino T. Strippoli, "Is This Any Way to Run a Cable Business?" *The TRW Manager*, vol. 1, no. 1 (October 1982): 7.

5. Cynthia Raybourn, "Polysar Gulf Coast, Inc.: Participation in Total Quality Earns Payoff for Plant and Its Employees," *Case Study 58*, American Productivity and Quality Center (May 1987): 2–5.

6. "Reducing Costs and Improving Efficiency at New York City Department of Sanitation," *Commitment-Plus*, vol. 1, no. 6 (March 1986): 2–3.

7. Kevin C. Shyne, "Labor-Management Teamwork at General Motors: Two Success Stories," *Tapping the Network*, American Productivity Management Association (1984): 2–4.

8. Barcy H. Proctor, "A Sociotechnical Work-Design System at Digital Enfield: Utilizing Untapped Resources," *National Productivity Review* (Summer 1986): 262–70.

9. Thomas O. Taylor, Donald J. Friedman, and Dennis Coutre, "Operating Without Supervisors: An Experiment," *Organizational Dynamics* (Winter 1987): 26–38.

10. "TRW and the 80s," (1980). Also William A. Ruch and William B. Werther, Jr., "Productivity Strategies at TRW," *National Productivity Review* (Spring 1983): 109–25. Also Donald J. Schilling and Thomas F. Bremer, "Implementing Productivity Strategies: A Program Case Study at TRW Ramsey," *National Productivity Review* (Autumn 1985): 370–84.

11. Ruch and Werther, "Productivity Strategies," 115.
12. Schilling and Bremer, "Case Study at TRW Ramsey," 382–83.
13. Robert R. Rehder, Robert W. Hendry, and Marta Medaris Smith, "NUMMI: The Best of Both Worlds?" *Management Review* (December 1985): 36–41.
14. John Holusha, "No Utopia, But to Workers It's a Job," *The New York Times* (January 29, 1989): business section. Also "Detroit vs. the UAW: At Odds Over Teamwork," *Business Week* (August 24, 1987): 54–55. Also "The UAW Rebels: Teaming Up Against Teamwork, " *Business Week* (March 27, 1989): 110–14.
15. This discussion of change efforts at Hanes' Sparta plant is based upon extensive notes and documentation maintained by consultants during the course of the intervention. The "Sparta Story" is being published for the first time here with the permission of Sara Lee Corporation, particularly Paul Fulton, President and Jack Ward, Vice President, to whom we are very grateful. The reader should be aware that the story we tell focuses only upon one specific team-building effort undertaken at Sparta. It is presented in some detail in order to convey a sense of the process of change and implementation problems that must be overcome during change efforts. Yet this team building effort was just one of a number of steps taken over several years to build Sparta into a more competitive plant, particularly efforts by Tyler Cole, V.P. Manufacturing, and his staff. It would misleading for the reader to view what follows as more than a contributing factor to the significant improvement that occurred at the plant. Other efforts that contributed significantly to the turnaround were as follows:

- The introduction of Performance Clubs/President's Clubs to recognize outstanding performance by individual employees;
- Senior management making it clear to plant employees in a "survival speech" given in August 1986 by Tyler Cole (V.P. Manufacturing) that the company was committed

to undertake major change as an integral part of the survival of the plant;
- The introduction of a new conveyor material-handling system in the plant in June 1986 that significantly improved machine operator efficiency;
- Growth at the plant that enabled Hanes to hire a number of new employees who had not experienced the "old culture" and were more enthusiastic about the changes being made at the plant;
- The use of an external technical consultant to resolve several other issues standing in the way of plant performance; and
- Specific redirection given to the Sparta plant manager concerning corporate objectives concerning the plant.

Finally, we should note that Sparta was not the only Hanes plant that underwent major change during the mid-1980s. For example, Hanes's Galax plant, just fifteen miles away from Sparta, experienced many similar problems and, according to Sara Lee Knit Products management, actually had a faster and more significant turnaround as a plant than did Sparta.

16. Kathleen Myler Drummond, "Employee Participation Groups Are Big News at Beaumont Newspaper," *Case Study 69*, American Productivity and Quality Center (March 1989): 8.
17. "Work Teams Can Rev Up Paper-Pushers Too," *Business Week* (November 28, 1988): 64–72.
18. *Business Week* (July 10, 1989).

8. Employees Take Charge

1. Edward E. Lawler III, Gerald E. Ledford, Jr., and Susan Albers Mohrman, "Employee Involvement in America: A Study of Contemporary Practice," American Productivity and Quality Center (1989).
2. Janice A. Klein, "The Changing Role of First-Line Supervisors and Middle Managers," Bureau of Labor-Manage-

ment Relations and Cooperative Programs, U. S. Department of Labor, *BLMR 126* (1988): 7–17.

3. Marc Bassin, "Teamwork at General Foods: New & Improved," *Personnel Journal* (May 1988): 62–70.

4. Carl A. Bramlette, Jr., "Free to Change," *Training and Development Journal* (March 1984): 32–40.

5. James Kochanski, "Hiring in Self-Regulating Work Teams," *National Productivity Review* (Spring 1987): 153–59.

6. William J. Hampton, "How Does Japan Inc. Pick Its American Workers?" *Business Week* (October 3, 1988): 84–88.

7. U. S. Department of Labor Bureau of Labor-Management Relations and Cooperative Programs, "Labor-Management Cooperation: 1989 State-of-the-Art Symposium," *BLMR 124* (1989): 3–18.

8. "The UAW vs. Japan: It's Showdown Time in Tennessee," *Business Week* (July 24, 1989): 64–65. Also Rod Willis, "Can American Unions Transform Themselves?" *Management Review* (February 1988): 14.

9. U. S. Labor Bureau, "Labor-Management Cooperation," 10.

10. U. S. Labor Bureau, "Labor-Management Cooperation," 9.

11. "A Conversation with Charles C. Heckscher: Creating New Workplace Organizations," *Labor Relations Today*, vol. IV, no. 3, U. S. Department of Labor, Bureau of Labor-Management Relations and Cooperative Programs (May/ June 1989): 4–5.

9. Education and the New Workplace

1. Fred M. Hechinger, "Turnaround for the Public Schools?" *Harvard Business Review* (January–February 1985): 136–44.

2. William H. Miller, "Employees Wrestle With 'Dumb' Kids," *Industry Week* (July 4, 1988): 47–52.

3. David Halberstam, *Inc.* (April 1989): 72.

4. Edward B. Fiske, "U.S. Businesses Brace for a 'Disaster': A Work Force Unqualified to Work," *The New York Times* (September 25, 1989): A1.

5. Nancy J. Perry, "Saving the Schools: How Business Can Help," *Fortune* (November 7, 1988): 42–56.
6. Ellen Graham, "Retooling the Schools," *The Wall Street Journal Reports* (March 31, 1989): R1–36.
7. "The Nation's Report Card," *The Wall Street Journal Reports* (March 31, 1989): R15.
8. Kenneth H. Bacon, "College Seniors Fail to Make Grade," *The Wall Street Journal* (October 9, 1989): B1.
9. Anita Manning, "Are We a Nation of Nitwits?" *USA Today* (February 13, 1989): 1D–2D.
10. Graham, "Retooling the Schools," R3.
11. Julie Amparano Lopez, "System Failure," *The Wall Street Journal Reports* (March 31, 1989): R12.
12. Myron Magnet, "How to Smarten Up the Schools," *Fortune* (Special Report, February 1, 1988): 86–94.
13. Hechinger, "Turnaround for Schools," 143.
14. "Business and Education: The Demand for Partnership," *Business Week* (May 2, 1988): 123–35.
15. Miller, "Employers Wrestle," 50.
16. Perry, "Saving the Schools," 44.
17. Manning, "Nation of Nitwits," 2D.
18. Perry, "Saving the Schools," 50.
19. Nancy J. Perry, "The Education Crisis: What Business Can Do," *Fortune* (July 4, 1989): 71–81.
20. Anthony P. Carnevale, Leila J. Gainer, and Ann S. Meltzer, *Workplace Basics: The Skills Employers Want* (American Society for Training and Development: Alexandria, Va.: 1988). Also Virginia Hall and Joyce Wessel, "As Today's Work World Changes So Do the Skills Employers Seek," *Atlanta Journal & Constitution* (December 3, 1989): 53s.
21. *Production* (December 1988): 39–52.
22. Robert Ricklefs, "More Than Money," *The Wall Street Journal Reports* (March 31, 1989): R34.
23. Perry, "The Education Crisis," 81.
24. Perry, "The Education Crisis," 77.
25. Miller, "Employers Wrestle," 51.
26. Lisa I. Fried, "Corporations Commit to Catch 'Em Young and Start 'Em Right," *Management Review* (October 1989): 22–26.
27. Perry, "Saving the Schools," 54.

28. Lawrence Henry, High-Tech Training for the High-Tech Factory," *Training* (August 1989): 41–43.
29. Hechinger, "Turnaround for Schools," 142.
30. Gary Putka, "Learning Curve: Lacking Good Results Corporations Rethink Aid to Public Schools," *The Wall Street Journal* (June 27, 1989): A1.
31. Nancy J. Perry, "How to Help America's Schools," *Fortune* (December 4, 1989): 137–42.
32. Perry, "Saving the Schools," 44.
33. Jaclyn Fierman, "Giving Parents a Choice of Schools," *Fortune* (December 4, 1989): 147–60.
34. Curtis Hartman, "Business School," *Inc.* (September 1989): 52–60.
35. Nancy J. Perry, "The New, Improved Vocational School," *Fortune* (June 19, 1989): 127–38.
36. Julie Amparano Lopez, "System Failure," *The Wall Street Journal Reports* (March 31, 1989): R12.
37. Donna St. John, "A Unique Labor-Management Partnership Has Made Dade County Public Schools a Model in Education Reform," *Labor-Management Cooperation Brief*, U. S. Department of Labor, Bureau of Labor-Management Relations and Cooperative Programs, no. 16 (June 1989): 2.
38. "B-Schools Are Failing the U. S.," *Business Week* (November 28, 1988): 190.
39. "Where the Schools Aren't Doing Their Homework," *Business Week* (November 28, 1988): 84–87.
40. "Schools Aren't Doing Their Homework," 85.
41. "Chicago's B-School Goes Touchy-Feely," *Business Week* (November 27, 1989): 140.
42. Jeremy Main, "B-School's Get a Global Vision," *Fortune* (July 17, 1989): 78–86.
43. Colin Blaydon, "How to Educate Your Child to Take Over the Family Business . . . Or Any Business," *Boardroom Reports* (January 1, 1988): 13.

10. The Demands and Expectations of the New Workplace

1. Anne B. Fisher, "What Consumers Want in the 1990s," *Fortune* (January 29, 1990): 108–12.

2. Gary Reiner, "Cutting Your Competition to the Quick," *The Wall Street Journal* (February 21, 1988): A16.
3. Jeremy Main, "The Winning Organization," *Fortune* (September 26, 1988): 50–60.
4. "How Managers Can Succeed Through Speed," *Fortune* (February 13, 1989): 54–59.
5. "Speed on the Cycle Helps Companies Win the Race," *The Wall Street Journal* (October 30, 1989): A10.
6. "The Best-Engineered Part Is No Part at All," *Business Week* (May 8, 1989): 150.
7. "Psst! Want a Secret for Making Superproducts?" *Business Week* (October 2, 1989): 106–10.
8. Reiner, "Cutting Your Competition," A16.
9. "Stars of the 1980s Cast Their Light," *Fortune* (July 3, 1989): 66–76.
10. Y. K. Shetty, "The Human Side of Product Quality," *National Productivity Review*, vol. 8, no. 2 (Spring 1989): 175–82.
11. Keki R. Bhote, "DOE: The High Road to Quality," *Management Review* (January 1988): 27–33.
12. Keki R. Bhote, *World Class Quality* (New York: AMA Management Briefing, 1988), 50–51.
13. "Case Study: Taguchi's Design of Experiments," *Productivity*, vol. 10, no. 2 (February 1989): 5.
14. Gary S. Vasilash, "Hearing the Voice of the Customer," *Production* (February 1989): 66–68.
15. Timothy S. Mescon and Michael H. Mescon, "Loyalty Within, Loyalty Without," *SKY* (December 1989): 100–106.
16. Dr. Michael LeBoeuf, "The Secrets of Truly First-Class Customer Service," *Boardroom Reports* (July 15, 1988): 5–6. Also Dr. Jane Hiller Carpenter, "Super Customer Service Time," *Boardroom Reports* (December 15, 1987): 9–10.
17. *Fortune* magazine and Forum Corporation Study of Customer Expectations (1989)
18. "Beyond Customer Satisfaction Through Quality Improvement," *Fortune* (1989): Special Quality Improvement Section.

19. Bro Uttal, "Companies That Serve You Best," *Fortune* (December 7, 1987): 98–116.
20. Aaron Sugarman, "Can Your Employees Deliver?" *Incentive Marketing* (January 1988): 16–19.
21. Patricia Sellers, "Getting Your Customers to Love You," *Fortune* (March 13, 1989): 38–49.
22. Stew Leonard, "Love That Customer!" *Management Review* (October 1987): 36–39.
23. Reed M. Powell, "A Point of View: Doing More With Less—A Key Concept for the 90s," *National Productivity Review*, vol. 9, no. 1 (Winter 1989/90): 1–2.

11. Achieving World-Class Performance in Quality, Service, and Innovation

1. Peter C. Reid, *Well-Made in America: Lesson from Harley-Davidson on Being the Best* (New York: McGraw-Hill, 1990). Also "How Harley Beat Back the Japanese," *Fortune* (September 25, 1989): 155–62. Also Peter C. Reid, "How Harley-Davidson Beat Its Toughest Competitors," *Boardroom Reports* (January 1, 1990): 1–6.
2. Reid, "How Harley Beat Its Competitors," 6.
3. "The Rival Japan Respects," *Business Week* (November 13, 1989): 108–18.
4. John Huey, "Wal-Mart: Will It Take Over the World?" *Fortune* (January 30, 1989): 52–64.
5. *Discount Store News* (December 18, 1989): 1.
6. *Discount Store News* (December 18, 1989): 104.
7. Huey, "Will It Take Over the World?" 56.
8. Huey, "Will It Take Over the World?" 58.
9. *Discount Store News* (December 18, 1989): 83.
10. Huey, "Will It Take Over the World?" 52.
11. *Discount Store News* (December 18, 1989): 85.

Index